IDIOT'S GUIDES
AS EASY AS IT GETS!

Unlocking Your Creativity

by Doreen Marcial Poreba

ALPHA
A member of Penguin Random House LLC

This book is dedicated, with love, to my awesome sons, Steven and J. P., and my late friend, Sue, who continues to inspire me.

ALPHA BOOKS

Published by Penguin Random House LLC

Penguin Random House LLC, 375 Hudson Street, New York, New York 10014, USA • Penguin Random House LLC (Canada), 90 Eglinton Avenue East, Suite 700, Toronto, Ontario M4P 2Y3, Canada (a division of Pearson Penguin Canada Inc.) • Penguin Books Ltd., 80 Strand, London WC2R 0RL, England • Penguin Ireland, 25 St. Stephen's Green, Dublin 2, Ireland (a division of Penguin Books Ltd.) • Penguin Random House LLC (Australia), 250 Camberwell Road, Camberwell, Victoria 3124, Australia (a division of Pearson Australia Group Pty. Ltd.) • Penguin Books India Pvt. Ltd., 11 Community Centre, Panchsheel Park, New Delhi—110 017, India • Penguin Random House LLC (NZ), 67 Apollo Drive, Rosedale, North Shore, Auckland 1311, New Zealand (a division of Pearson New Zealand Ltd.) • Penguin Books (South Africa) (Pty.) Ltd., 24 Sturdee Avenue, Rosebank, Johannesburg 2196, South Africa • Penguin Books Ltd., Registered Offices: 80 Strand, London WC2R 0RL, England

International Standard Book Number: 978-1-61564-772-9
Library of Congress Catalog Card Number: 2014954039

17 16 15   8 7 6 5 4 3 2 1

Interpretation of the printing code: The rightmost number of the first series of numbers is the year of the book's printing; the rightmost number of the second series of numbers is the number of the book's printing. For example, a printing code of 15-1 shows that the first printing occurred in 2015.

Printed in the United States of America

Note: This publication contains the opinions and ideas of its author. It is intended to provide helpful and informative material on the subject matter covered. It is sold with the understanding that the author and publisher are not engaged in rendering professional services in the book. If the reader requires personal assistance or advice, a competent professional should be consulted. The author and publisher specifically disclaim any responsibility for any liability, loss, or risk, personal or otherwise, which is incurred as a consequence, directly or indirectly, of the use and application of any of the contents of this book.

Most Alpha books are available at special quantity discounts for bulk purchases for sales promotions, premiums, fundraising, or educational use. Special books, or book excerpts, can also be created to fit specific needs. For details, write: Special Markets, Alpha Books, 375 Hudson Street, New York, NY 10014.

Publisher: *Mike Sanders*
Associate Publisher: *Billy Fields*
Executive Acquisitions Editor: *Lori Cates Hand*
Development Editor: *Kayla Dugger*
Senior Production Editor: *Janette Lynn*

Cover Designer: *Laura Merriman*
Book Designer: *William Thomas*
Indexer: *Heather McNeil*
Layout: *Ayanna Lacey*
Proofreader: *Amy Borrelli*

Contents

Appendixes

Introduction

Congratulations! By choosing to read this book, you've already made an important investment in yourself. Learning how to "unlock your creativity" could be a game changer. I dare say that expressing your creative nature on a regular basis could literally change the direction of your life—for the better! I know this from my own experiences both personally and professionally. I've also witnessed amazing transformations on the part of creativity clients whom I have coached. But don't just take my word for it. If you do the work—and yes, exploring, understanding, examining, and executing your creativity will involve some work—you will see for yourself just how powerful this process can be.

Simply put, unlocking your creativity comes down to freedom of expression. Each of us is an exceptional individual like none other. You and I have a need to express ourselves, and by virtue of the fact we're different, the why, the how, and the results of our creative expression will be unlike anyone else's. The problem enters when you do not allow yourself to fully express your creativity—whether it's via spoken or written communication, painting, singing, or another vehicle. This book will address that problem head on and ask you to go through an illuminating self-discovery in the process.

Throughout the book, you will be asked to take an honest look at yourself and reflect, learn, and apply the principles that resonate with you. You'll also learn how to engage your playful, child-like spirit, combining both your right brain and left brain into whole-brain thinking. And to give you some extra motivation, I've provided real-life stories of people who have embraced their creativity.

Think of this as an enriching creative journey. While you may not become the next Picasso (or perhaps you will!), you can expect to undergo positive life shifts. It is my hope that each time you resume reading this book, you will do so with enthusiasm, actually looking forward to picking up where you left off.

When you finish reading this book, you will likely feel more confident about your creativity. You'll be more open to exploring new possibilities and you'll know yourself better—what drives you, your loves, and your dislikes. You will have moved beyond the blocks that kept you from being all you can be and you'll be more attuned to your creative abilities and ways in which to express them. Enjoy your creative journey!

What You Will Learn in This Book

This book is divided into five parts that will lead you on a path to uncovering, discovering, and recovering your creativity.

Part 1, Craving Creativity, explains just what creativity entails, which goes well beyond the arts. Creativity can be described in different ways, so I give you traditional and new working definitions for it, as well as information on whether this visionary process can be learned. This part also asks you to make a commitment to your own creativity as you discover its value and discusses how consciously creating can enhance your life (such as an increase in energy, motivation, productivity, and prosperity; a deeper connection with others; and a feeling of freedom, independence, and completion).

Part 2, What It Takes to Create, examines that undeniable urge to create that either sneaks into your psyche quietly or yells loudly, like a cheerleader with a megaphone. I cover the different types of motivation and what drives you to create. This part also walks you through the creativity process—which involves both sides of the brain—and how your thoughts can go from a flash of an idea to something that actually comes to fruition. I also discuss the traits and success strategies of famous people and how to further develop your own attributes. I close this part with potential blocks to your creativity, or what's keeping you stuck in the "creativity closet." One by one, I take you through some of the most common barriers and some ways you can get past them. (Don't worry—you'll get out of the creativity closet eventually!) This part can be challenging, yet it's a necessary piece to the puzzle that will require profound, authentic rumination on your part.

Part 3, Finding Your Keys to Creativity, starts to shift you from a feeling of doubt to more of a hopeful "I can do it!" feeling. I begin by giving you suggestions on how you can overcome your obstacles and how it all begins with your beliefs. This part also talks about how to move closer to your creative goals by laying the groundwork for an inviting creative space, including using all six of your senses. You then get to test some fun activities that are designed to jump-start your creativity, such as grading yourself with an A, making your technology vanish, and going on solo dates. This part also teaches you how to use different creative thinking techniques, as well as how to look through the lens of your passions. Finally, you learn how you can support and elevate your creativity through various partnerships.

Part 4, Creativity and Innovation in the Workplace, explores the demand for creativity and innovation, which is becoming more important today as employees and managers are realizing the benefits. This applies to corporations, small businesses, government institutions, school systems, nonprofit organizations, or self-employment. Perhaps you are the one who is constantly pushing for more creativity within your workplace but the higher-ups have not allowed the space for this to happen, or your manager or clients have expressed a need for you to be more creative. Whatever the case, you get ideas on how to develop a creative culture within your organization and how you can be more creative at work. I provide information on more innovative thinking techniques, how the rut of routines can hamper your creative efforts, the value of teamwork, and how to deal with burnout.

Part 5, Living Creatively Every Day, begins by talking about how you can support the creativity of those around you, such as children or loved ones as they age. In this part, I also delve into what can be a scary step—sharing your work with others. You learn how to prepare yourself, gain tips for dealing with positive and negative feedback, and discover how you can touch others' hearts by sharing your talents. I then get into the flow of creativity, how synchronicity occurs more when you're creative, and how handwriting can tap into a part of your brain that will assist your creative efforts. You also review your creative progress, reconnect with your creative spirit, and participate in some additional creativity techniques (including meditation). This part ends with considerations for your ongoing creative journey, addresses the question of whether you can force creativity, and provides pointers for remaining true to yourself. You can then celebrate and proclaim your creativity!

At the back of the book, you will find a glossary, a resource list of recommended books and websites, and bonus creative play exercises that are designed to keep your creativity in flow.

Extras

Throughout this book, you will find four types of sidebars that give you a greater understanding of the chapter's material, inspire you with a notable quote, or illustrate an inspirational real-life example. I also provide a special type of boxed text that allows you to apply what you've learned.

 **DEFINITION**

These sidebars clarify the meaning of words that may go beyond the traditional dictionary definition and how they apply to creativity.

 CREATIVITY KEY

These pieces of information provide you with hints or tips to help you unlock the door to your creativity.

 INSPIRATIONAL INSIGHT

Creativity is often stimulated by inspirational quotes and others' viewpoints, so these sidebars share words of wisdom spoken by some of the most well-known and not-so-known creators.

CREATIVITY COMPASS

These sidebars are intended to give you a sense of direction by relating real-life stories of creativity in action (some of the names have been changed). The examples reinforce the text's meaning, show you that you're not alone, illustrate how to apply key principles, and provide some role models for your journey. Allowing yourself to be vulnerable is a big part of creativity, so I even open myself up to you by sharing some of my own stories of what helped me grow creatively.

Creative Play

In every chapter, you are given the opportunity to participate in various exercises that will be set off in boxed text. These are designed to help you gain a better understanding of your own creativity through self-reflection and fun! Appendix C even contains additional creative plays for continued inspirational support.

Acknowledgments

This book would not have been possible without the love and support of my partner, David Crandall. He not only serves as an amazing creativity role model through his work as a full-time custom goldsmith and part-time flute maker, he also cheers me on with all of my creative pursuits—writing, photography, videography, singing, songwriting, playing various instruments, and recording my music. He was the first to share in my joy of writing this book and has been with me every step of the way!

A huge thank you also goes to my incredible parents for giving me the support and tools I needed to pursue my creative interests at a young age. They taught me the value of encouraging my own two sons, Steven and J. P., to pursue and act upon their dreams.

Thanks to my four sisters and two brothers, who have influenced and motivated me with their own styles and brands of creativity through the years.

I'd also like to thank Nancy Julian, my spiritual counselor and a great creativity mentor, for her inspiration and ongoing support.

Big thanks as well to Patty Jensen, my longtime friend and one of my biggest "fans," who supported me since the beginning of this book project.

Thanks to the Creativity Coaching Association for providing me with excellent training in becoming a certified creativity coach.

And finally, I wish to thank God, the Creator of all creators, and the Synchronous Universal Energy that helped bring this opportunity and book into being.

Trademarks

All terms mentioned in this book that are known to be or are suspected of being trademarks or service marks have been appropriately capitalized. Alpha Books and Penguin Random House LLC cannot attest to the accuracy of this information. Use of a term in this book should not be regarded as affecting the validity of any trademark or service mark.

PART 1

Craving Creativity

You have come here because you have already recognized you have a thirst … a hunger … perhaps a voracious desire to experience more creativity in your life. You might call it a craving. At the very least, you have a curiosity to learn more about creativity and how it can enrich your life. The fantastic news is that this book begins by opening you up to the idea that *everyone* is creative! Regardless of how you feel day to day about your own creativity, the fact is, everyone is born with the ability to create.

In addition to exploring these concepts, you also get to explore just what creativity involves and its various meanings and whether creativity can be learned. Sometimes you forget what you once knew and just need some gentle reminders. Other times, you need a giant wake-up call! Either way, before you even finish this book, I hope you'll be motivated to create what's in your heart's desire.

Moving on, I invite you to consider the value of creativity, the everyday invitation to create, and how you can benefit from tapping into your skills to fulfill your creative potential.

Everyone Is Creative

Picture yourself seated at a creativity workshop I'm hosting. I ask you what images, words, and phrases come to mind when I say the word *creativity*. I give you a few minutes to ponder this, and then I ask you to write down your feelings associated with creativity. It's probably a safe assumption that some of the images you pictured were arts related: painters, sculptors, actors, musicians, singers, songwriters, jewelers, photographers, writers, filmmakers, and the like. But artists and nonartists alike are creative in their everyday lives.

In this chapter, I take you through the different ways creativity can be defined, as well as how creativity infuses every aspect of your existence.

In This Chapter

- The tried, true, and new definitions of creativity
- How creativity is everywhere
- The origins of creativity
- Can you learn how to be more creative?

Defining Creativity

The Merriam-Webster dictionary's definition of *creativity* is "the ability to make new things or think of new ideas." Other phrases used to describe creativity include initiating useful ideas that are unique, innovative, novel, fresh, or original. So while the idea you come up with may not be brand new, the way in which you advance it may be different.

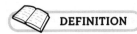 **DEFINITION**

> **Creativity** is initiating, activating, and implementing ideas that are original, unusual, useful, or innovative. The ideas may advance an existing concept or seemingly spring forth from nowhere.

In terms of defining creativity, psychologists and creativity experts will add that for an idea or product to be creative, it also must be useful and put into action. If you have an imagination with more ideas than the colors and patterns in a kaleidoscope and don't act on them, are you creative? This certainly demonstrates that you have the ability to drum up new things in your mind, but if they stay hidden in your personal chambers, the creative process stops there.

But what if your weakness is generating ideas, while your strength is taking other people's ideas and figuring out how to make them happen? This kind of connection, which happens during collaborative sessions, shows how creativity happens in stages as part of a process rather than as an idea you simply come up with and put into place. (We look at this more in later chapters.) This means we have to go beyond the standard Merriam-Webster definition of creativity.

One definition that works well with the overall philosophy of this book is one by Joseph V. Anderson, who states in "Weirder than Fiction: The Reality and Myths of Creativity." "Creativity is nothing more than seeing and acting on new relationships, thereby bringing them to life." When you read the word *relationships*, it's natural to think in terms of people. But a relationship also can be a link, association, or connection between ideas, too, which is why this definition is more apt than the Merriam-Webster one. It connotes an open, encouraging feeling, a sense of freedom, which helps creativity flourish.

 CREATIVITY COMPASS

> What we bring into being as our own creations can be influenced by our past and present surroundings. I wrote a song titled "Where Do We Find God?" and all I had to do to stir my muse was to look around me and notice the beauty of the trees, the birds chirping, and the sounds of a nearby brook. The way I specifically strung the words together was an original expression that was inspired by nature. See what connections or associations you can make with songs, drawings, paintings, sculptures, nature, and any other surroundings that inspire you.

Another way to think of creativity, according to psychotherapist and creativity coach Eric Maisel, is not necessarily as a special talent or ability, but rather as "the fruit of a person's decision to matter." This opens up creativity even more to encompass not only talented artists, but also the work done in the business world and beyond. So while you'll read about examples from the arts world in this book, as many hobbies and professional careers revolve around this field, the chapters will not be limited to the arts or any singular aspect of creativity.

How You Encounter Creativity Every Day

You can see examples of creativity everywhere you look. Some of what you see can be easily traced and credited to an individual or a group of people, while other things aren't as readily apparent. These everyday occurrences can be categorized three ways:

Creations from well-known people: These are the creations of people that others seem to know the world over. For example, you can't say J. K. Rowling without thinking of Harry Potter, the character in the wildly successful and amazingly imaginative universe she created.

Creations from people you know personally: There are plenty of folks you know personally whom you may consider to be highly creative. They may not be household names, but their creativity is apparent to all who see their work. Perhaps you know a seamstress who goes beyond doing basic alterations, combining her skills and imagination to make unusual purses, dazzling hats, baby headbands, and embroidered banners.

Creations from people you don't know: Do you actually think about who created the spoon and fork you pick up each day to eat your meals, or the ink pen with which you write? These crafters took an everyday, utilitarian item and used their creative ideas to make and offer a product that is used by everyone.

These categories cover a wide range of people and ideas, showing how there is no set formula for creative expression. You don't have to be a well-known inventor, a best-selling author, a noted composer, or an award-winning artist to creatively express yourself.

> **CREATIVITY COMPASS**
>
> I've worked with clients who keep getting stuck because their creativity doesn't relate to inventing or the arts. It's essential to understand and believe that creativity happens in the workplace and at home, with professionals and hobbyists, anytime and all the time. While most creations don't make headlines, they can provide far more meaningful benefits than making the news.

Creative Play: Seeking Another Purpose

This exercise challenges your creative thinking to look beyond the obvious.

Tools Needed: Your ingenuity!

To start, think of an item you are either looking to buy or have bought in the past. It can relate to a hobby or be an everyday item.

Next, generate at least one possibility (more is better) that can accomplish the same purpose as the item you brought to mind. For example, I was in the market for a new photo bag. Instead of buying an expensive case that was designed for that purpose, I purchased a soft-sided cooler bag instead and used bubble wrap inside to place in between my camera and accessories. Not only was it less expensive, it kept my equipment cooler and concealed itself so it wasn't obvious I was carrying costly equipment.

Use your imagination and have fun with this exercise! This is a technique you can use in everyday life and may even lead to you developing your very own new product.

The "Affiliations" of Creativity

There are some common affiliations you probably associate with creativity, beginning with children. If you've spent even a little bit of time around kids, you've witnessed how they use their imaginations. They make it look so easy as they visit the "Land of Make-Believe" so cheerfully. Most of them lack the inhibitions that show up later in life into adulthood, so they freely express themselves. They're not afraid to be silly, laugh heartily, pretend to be anything they can imagine, and explore eagerly—all of which keep the creative process flowing. Parents who are mindful about the importance of creative expression look for ways to encourage their children to continue using their imaginations. (Kids and creativity will be explored in more depth in Chapter 17.)

You may also equate spirituality with creativity, especially if you've had an experience in which you felt your inspiration came from another dimension, God, the Universe, or whatever you choose to name that presence. Or maybe you felt you were awakened by a *muse*, which may have led to a creative breakthrough. Author Caroline Myss maintains it's impossible to separate creativity and spirituality. In her audio recording "Your Creative Soul," she says, "Spirituality is an expression of your spirit and you cannot have any form of creativity unless you understand the impulse of creation itself."

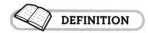
DEFINITION

> **Muse** is a term that originated with Greek mythology in which goddesses represented the arts, music, poetry, and science. A muse is cited in creativity as an unseen guiding force or spring of inspiration.

Creativity also is often associated with the business world. Beyond professions where creativity is apparent (such as graphic designers, fashion designers, and copywriters), scientists, engineers, architects, and a host of other professionals and entrepreneurs count on their ability to innovate in the workplace. In fact, today more and more businesses are demanding creativity and innovation from their employees to improve their bottom line, and research supports this need. Such advances can mean the difference between success and failure. (You'll learn more about creativity in the workplace in Part 4.)

Creativity as an Expression of Your Desires

I also think of creativity as the ability to manifest your desires. In other words, what do you wish to create in your life? For example, I once coached a woman whose dream was to live in Washington, D.C. She felt most inspired around the field of politics and believed it made sense to live and work near the nation's capital. She was in her forties and began to feel like if she didn't make the move soon, it would never happen. We began working together on how she could consciously create the right opportunity that would enable her to move from Florida to this area. Within one year, she accomplished her goal by using innovative thinking, putting her attention and intention on the life she wished to create, and taking action steps along the way. Within one year, she realized her dream.

What do you wish to bring to life? To be more creative and innovative in the workplace? To pursue a new hobby? To discipline your children more effectively? To develop a closer relationship with your Creator? To figure out a new recipe for a decadent dessert? To create a new mobile phone or tablet app? To improve an existing product? To finish what you start? (In other words, acting upon your best ideas instead of procrastinating.) The list of what you can create is endless.

You may not have even identified what you would like to engage in, and that's okay. There's a great likelihood that before you even finish this book, you will be inspired to act upon an idea you've considered before or possibly something that has never before crossed your mind.

Creative Play: What Creativity Means to You

The purpose of this activity is to help you "feel" into your creativity and appreciate all it has to offer.

Tools Needed: Paper, a writing instrument, and a memory that is positive

To begin, recall a time in your life when you participated in a positive experience that involved creativity. Perhaps you were part of a group effort or you were on your own.

Next, complete the following sentences:

- "The last uplifting creative project I engaged in was …"

- "While doing this, I felt …"

- "After completing this, I felt …"

- "Tapping into my creativity is good for me because …"

- "What I enjoy most about creating is …"

Once you have completed all of these sentences, close your eyes and take a moment to thoroughly experience the feelings you just described by quieting yourself, taking a few deep breaths, and releasing any tension in your body. Appreciate your participation and willingness to be part of a creative process.

Now create your own quote: "Creativity is …." This is not necessarily a definition, but a thought that has meaning for you that may serve as inspiration to you and others.

Is Creativity Learnable?

According to a study by George Land, it is our nature to be creative. One of the most obvious examples of natural creativity in action is observing children at play. Well-meaning, loving parents and grandparents buy their children what they think are educational, entertaining, or interesting toys only to see the kids toss them aside to play with cardboard boxes and pots and pans. Somehow they use their imaginations with these ordinary items and play for hours. As we grow older, however, we get away from our innate instincts.

CREATIVITY KEY

Adobe's 2012 State of Create global benchmark study showed that even though 8 in 10 people feel that unlocking creativity is critical to economic growth, only 1 in 4 people believe they are living up to their own creative potential.

Are you someone who has failed to own your creative spirit? Did you leave your creative instincts behind in elementary school? Perhaps you have been told by someone else that you aren't creative. Many people, particularly adults, have reached a point in their lives where they feel "I'm just not creative." Are you one of them?

I can't tell you how many times I have encountered people at an art gallery, a concert, or the theater and overheard them utter those very words. The sad part is that this statement—"I'm just not creative"—has become a belief for many people. That begs the question, "Is creativity learnable?"

Edward Glassman, PhD, former president of The Creativity College and former professor at the University of North Carolina in Chapel Hill, found in his research on whether creativity is inherited that most creativity skills appear to be learnable with training. His experiments put an end to the myth that creativity is largely inherited. This is great news if you don't think you're creative or you feel that you're not living up to your creative potential.

Like any skill, creativity takes practice, a certain way of thinking, and other imagination-building techniques.

Remembering What You've Forgotten

As a born creative, you already know how to be innovative and use your imagination. You may have simply forgotten or gotten out of shape. Just like you can't expect to run a marathon without first working out and building up to it, you can't put unnecessary pressure on yourself to create if you haven't focused on that or properly prepared yourself. It's all about "relearning" to tap into your creative self.

For example, when you're looking at the accomplishments of a successful entrepreneur or an artist's amazing work of art, you may say to yourself "I could never do that." Because they make it look so natural, it's easy for you to feel overwhelmed by their talents and use that to stop yourself or refrain from trying (see Chapter 6 for more on creative blocks like this).

However, you can't forget the fact that those people didn't come out of their mother's womb with the skills it took to create what you're seeing. If you take the time to speak with successful creatives, you will learn just what it took for them to achieve the level of success and creative output that you're witnessing. More than likely, you'll find they spent years developing their craft.

So instead of starting with lofty expectations, you have to start small and build your creative skills over time.

CREATIVITY KEY

The next time you're feeling you haven't been blessed with the ability to create, remember that creativity isn't a gift reserved for the select few. In fact, because creativity can be learned, it may be more accurate to refer to it as a skill, as well as a gift. While it's true that some folks may appear to be more "gifted" than others in specific areas, with practice and commitment, your own creative skills will become more refined. Once you have found a way to consistently express your creativity, you may feel like you've been given a gift. From that perspective, creativity is a gift you gave to yourself. For that, be grateful and give yourself a pat on the back!

Deciding to Be Creative

I started this book by saying "Everyone is creative." That has always been my personal philosophy, and it has been proven to me through the years time and time again. I haven't worked with a single client who didn't display some degree and form of creativity. It's a matter of choosing whether to proactively engage in your creativity. It may seem to come more naturally to some than others, but that's only because those people have *decided* to be creative. Yes, creativity is a decision! And fortunately, it's one that you and I can make at any time.

As with any other skill, creativity can be cultivated. Think of creativity as a garden. You plant some seeds in a conducive environment, you water them and make sure they're getting enough sunlight, you monitor their growth and remove the weeds that don't belong, and eventually you reap the benefits of the harvest. The seeds are your initial thoughts and ideas. In the beginning, those thoughts and ideas might not seem like much. However, with further exploration, using your imagination, experimenting, and nurturing yourself along the way, eventually you will hit upon the creative expression you are seeking.

So how is deciding to be creative learnable? An obvious example is with the playing of a musical instrument. It's a skill that takes practice, and the more you practice, the better you'll get. While some people may seem to have more of an *aptitude* for learning to play an instrument, most people who really focus and apply themselves will be able to learn at least the basics. They may not become the next Mozart, but they can continue to perfect the skill by practicing and just playing for the fun of it.

Just knowing there is no "creativity gene" may already bring a sense of relief to you! You also can feel supported by the many methods, tools, and techniques that will help you improve your creative expression. It begins with a commitment and your decision to start right now.

 **DEFINITION**

Aptitude is having a natural ability or inclination to do or learn something. It's not required to partake in a creative activity, but having an aptitude for it might make it seem to come more naturally and easily.

Creative Play: Creativity Commitment

This task asks you to make a commitment to your own creativity in a fun, yet meaningful, way. Have a good time making your own pledge in writing and take the meaning of it seriously.

Tools Needed: Paper, markers, and decorating materials

Copy the following text onto your paper:

> I, _____, on this ____ day of _____, 20____, do creatively dare (no solemnly swearing allowed) myself to do what it takes to enhance my creativity through the generation of ideas and the exploration, experimentation, evaluation, and execution of them. I see creativity as a necessity—not a luxury—in both my personal and professional lives. I am committed to Unlocking My Creativity and I pledge to apply myself, get the support I need along the way, and have fun in the process!

Once you've written it out, decorate your Creativity Commitment and post it in a place where you'll see it daily.

The Least You Need to Know

- The arts are a wonderful example of creativity in action, but the initiation and execution of original ideas is not limited to any one particular area. There are acts of creation everywhere—in business and at home, with parenting, spirituality, and beyond.
- Creativity is not genetic—it's a quality we all have that can be learned and developed with training and practice.
- Creativity does not discriminate. It is available to everyone!
- Creativity is a decision and a commitment. Decide and commit today to advance your creative nature!

The Benefits of Creativity

Is there a value to creativity, or is it just some buzzword that gives people an excuse to play? While creativity can be playful and fun, which in and of itself is important, there are several ways in which creativity may be beneficial.

You may look at your own creative actions and think "No big deal"—that is, if you even recognize when you're being creative. But creativity is a big deal—to you and all of the lives you touch. Exercising your creativity can make the difference between an uplifting day and a disheartening day. It's about learning as much as you can to put it into practice and thoroughly enjoying the benefits. So what is creativity worth? Plenty.

In this chapter, I help you tap into what creativity means to you and the world at large and how you can benefit.

In This Chapter

- How creativity can improve your work life
- Strengthening your relationships through creativity
- Gaining a better understanding of yourself by creating

The Value of Creativity in Business and Beyond

Whether you are self-employed or work for a mom-and-pop shop, governmental agency, non-profit organization, or large corporation, activating your creativity can lead to an increase in business. Your ideas may result in more profits or fewer expenses, a new product with huge appeal to your customers, a more efficient way for employees to function, or improved office morale. Businesses and those who make a living in the creative arts can speak to the monetary value of creativity and how it can affect the bottom line.

Take the story of how Hallmark, which relies on creativity, began. As a teenager from Nebraska, little did J.C. Hall realize that a couple of shoeboxes filled with postcards would eventually become a $4 billion business. His dream began with greeting cards and a patented type of card display rack that became an industry norm. Add to that Hallmark's first licensing agreement with Walt Disney, gift wrap, collectible Christmas ornaments, new brands of cards, ecards, cable television networks, recordable storybooks, and Interactive Story Buddy characters, and you can see what one person's dream can become as others joined in this creative journey.

Hallmark is just one example of many success stories of how creativity enhances business. More than ever today, CEOs now recognize that value, but it doesn't stop there. Those who are passionate about improving the education system, entrepreneurs competing for customers, home-makers enriching their lives with hobbies, parents striving to raise creative kids, advocates of older Americans, and individuals who want to create just for the sake of creating are all in the creativity mix.

Benefits extend well beyond dollars and cents. Creativity can result in more practicality and efficiency in your everyday life. One of the most apparent ways to illustrate this is in the field of technology. Before personal computers, people used a typewriter to compose letters, business documents, and other correspondence. Making a mistake required the use of correction tape or fluid, which was time consuming and sometimes noticeable. Then personal computers came along and you can correct a mistake literally in a second with the stroke of the backspace key.

There are additional benefits to using your creativity on the job, as follows. You may even discover that you'll reap these same payoffs when you're creating at home on your own, collaborating with others just for the fun of it, or volunteering to help a great cause.

 INSPIRATIONAL INSIGHT

"There are no dreams too large, no innovation unimaginable and no frontiers beyond our reach."

—John S. Herrington

Gaining Satisfaction and Recognition

When restrictions are imposed by your job and you're not given the opportunity to examine and pursue your own ideas, you can feel discontent. Depending on the limitations, your creativity may be stopped before it can even start.

On the flip side, working within an organization that supports and encourages creativity allows you to feel free to open up and innovate. Smart companies recognize the importance of developing a creative climate and encouraging their employees to effectively use their creative skills. If you're given the freedom to exercise your creativity at work, you are bound to feel more satisfied (see Part 4 for more on creativity in the workplace).

For some, being given opportunities to innovate and have their ideas accepted is a reward in and of itself. Sometimes, however, acknowledgment can come in the form of an industry award or a monetary reward. So being creative is a way for you to stand up and be recognized.

Feeling Motivated and Productive

When you are motivated to create on or off the job, a funny thing happens. You follow that drive and start to act on your ideas, which inspires you to create even more. In other words, motivation begets more motivation (an idea that's fully explored in Chapter 3). Once you are "on a roll," or consistently creating, your productivity naturally increases, making you that much more successful.

This burst of creativity can even inspire your co-workers or even friends. Oftentimes, others become interested and motivated to join in your creation and the productivity increases even more. Have you ever been part of a creative process in which the idea started slowly and then, little by little, started to capture others' attention? That's known as the "bandwagon" effect. Everyone enjoys being part of a winning team; sometimes winning means being part of a collaborative effort where there are no literal winners or losers. It allows you to be part of a greater whole, doing your part to contribute the overall effort.

Having a Greater Appreciation for the Process

Creativity is not simply the creation of ideas and executing them. There are steps in between, and each stage comes with its own challenges and rewards. Sometimes, your original intentions don't play out as you had intended. Perhaps you come to the realization in the middle of the process that your idea isn't going to work and you either begin again or scrap it altogether. Or your idea may take off in a way that exceeds your wildest expectations. Either way, your creative efforts as you go about your job should not be judged as success or failure.

Judging your efforts, especially in haste, is one of the quickest ways you can kill your own and others' creativity. The more productive view is to appreciate the process as a learning opportunity. If you're creating just for the sake of obtaining a certain result at work, you're missing out on what the process is teaching you along the way that you can apply to your next creative endeavor, whether job related or personal, and overall in your life.

CREATIVITY KEY

There may be many steps in between your initial idea and the realization of it. Recognize that each stage of your creation is part of the process and leads to your desired results, which may be nothing more than allowing your light to shine.

How Creativity Benefits Your Relationships

Creativity serves as a pipeline to connect you with family members, friends, God or a higher power, and even strangers if you're willing to share your efforts outside of your normal circle of support. For example, have you ever written a card or a letter that was so moving, you made someone's day? That kind of connection carries a value that some would say is priceless.

When you are happily creating, your personal relationships can become stronger and more refreshing. As you're breathing life into a new creation, it can translate into a breath of fresh air for your relationships. Whether it's your spouse, your significant other, your children, your fellow workers, or your friends, by being creative and sharing with those people, you're setting a good example and potentially inspiring them to walk their own creative path.

Touching others with your creativity can even extend beyond your normal circles. For example, in the last few years, Oprah Winfrey and Deepak Chopra, both prolific creators on a large scale, co-created the 21-Day Meditation Experience. It's designed to help people all over the world tap into their inner being to find peace and other internal gifts, as well as energetically connect them with others who are participating worldwide. While it's not necessary to create on that grand of a platform, it's just another way creativity can help you feel connection to others.

Creative Play: Valuing Your Creative Gifts

This exercise will help you appreciate the value of creativity both in what you've given and what you've received.

Tools Needed: Paper and a writing instrument

Think of examples from your own life where you made a difference in someone else's life due to your own creativity. Perhaps you made a gift such as a personalized card, photo book, jewelry, or clothing and gave it to a friend or loved one. Consider work examples, such as making a presentation that resulted in your company securing a new client. Write them down and appreciate your giving, creative nature.

Now think of those times when you were on the receiving end of someone else's creativity. What were those experiences and how did they make you feel? Write them down. Sometimes going through the process of writing helps you to capture memories that might otherwise be forgotten.

What's in It for You?

The value of creativity isn't just about how it helps others; unlocking the door to your creativity has plenty in store for you, too! For example, as a child, I can remember sitting down in the basement with my two older sisters and drawing people. It didn't matter how crude the drawings were; we were fully engaged in the process. It brought feelings of connection with my siblings and also a sense of accomplishment. Think back to a time when you were absorbed in a favorite creative interest. Did this creative activity produce an overall good feeling?

 CREATIVITY KEY

Think of a time when you were experiencing a "creative high" and see how many of the personal benefits speak to you. Anytime you are creating from a space of desire, you will benefit in numerous ways, whether they are measurable or not.

I have coached a number of people who have been able to break through their blockages and excel with their creative expression. The differences they've experienced in their lives are nothing short of amazing. At the very least, they feel an inner joy and a sense of freedom when they truly let themselves go. So while creativity can have those external benefits I've discussed, at the core, it's about what it can do for you.

Feeling More Energetic

One of the benefits you may notice when you're actively creating is an increase in your energy level. If you're doing something of which you've grown tired, your energy levels start to drop. The excitement is gone. You may even feel bored and that what you're doing is like watching grass grow. You are no longer feeling motivated to produce, which leads to lackluster results. Most everyone has been in this position at some point in their lives when they feel drained or even burned out. This feeling is not conducive to being creative.

Now what happens when you are actively engaged in your creativity? For example, have you ever had the experience of driving down the road or taking a shower—two activities that are often done on autopilot, without much thought—and suddenly an idea pops into your head, seemingly out of nowhere? The idea may relate to a problem you have either at home or in the workplace; a piece of artwork you've been thinking about creating; a topic for a song, poem, or blog post; a new business; or a thought related to an activity you've never done before. That single idea can awaken you from a weary or humdrum state of being and give you a surge in energy.

When you're really focused and excited about making an idea of yours a reality, your *adrenaline* kicks in. You can literally feel your heart beat faster, and you feel more awake and alive. The 86,400 seconds that comprise each day may not change, but when you find yourself in the midst of a creation that really matters to you, it feels as if there is no time—no time but the present, that is, and you're soaking up each precious minute.

 **DEFINITION**

Adrenaline is a hormone secreted by the body's adrenal glands, especially during stressful or stimulating circumstances, that can cause increases in bodily functions, such as heart rate and blood flow. You may experience this in the excitement of creating.

Whether it's in the initial stage of creativity when you first get an idea or later on as you come up with ways to turn that idea into a reality, your creativity gives you that special surge to drive you on. You are operating at a high energy level—and it feels great!

Embracing Your Freedom and Independence

As a creativity coach, it's not about me telling clients what they should do or say with regard to their creative challenges. They look to me for guidance, and through a series of asking them powerful questions, they uncover the answers themselves and feel more empowered as a result.

It's a basic human need and desire to be independent. Pursuing your creative interests brings about a feeling of greater independence, a feeling of knowing that you can count on yourself and trust your creative instincts.

Some of your restrictions may have been put upon you early in life, like when your mother, your father, a sibling, or a teacher told you that you couldn't create what you had in mind because that would violate "the rules." Other times, constraints don't come from anyone but yourself. But when you give yourself the go-ahead to create in a way that speaks to you, that's a freeing experience.

 INSPIRATIONAL INSIGHT

"We need to learn to love ourselves first, in all our glory and our imperfections. If we cannot love ourselves, we cannot fully open to our ability to love others or our potential to create. Evolution and all hopes for a better world rest in the fearlessness and open-hearted vision of people who embrace life."

—John Lennon

The importance of feeling self-empowered through creativity can't be overstated. It's about giving yourself the authority to pursue and produce what's in your heart, what you know will make a difference. By trusting your natural creative instincts and harnessing your own creative clout, you become a powerful creator!

Lowering Your Stress Levels

When you're truly involved in the magnificence of a creative project, one that you're passionate about and engaged in simply for the sake of doing it, you will feel more relaxed and less stressed. You become swept away in the project itself. It may even be a temporary escape from a difficulty you're facing at home or at work.

Plus, sometimes nothing reduces stress more than finishing your project and experiencing a sense of accomplishment. Just as children delight in the small wonders of learning to tie their shoelaces or ride a bicycle, you are happy when you achieve what you've set out to do. Sometimes, you may feel downright thrilled! Can you think of something you created in your life that led to this feeling of triumph? Think big. Think small. Think of any creative act at all!

Each creative act you engage in that you can see and appreciate will help you to build your creative spirit and keep that stress down. Anytime you complete a task, particularly a demanding one in which you doubted yourself along the way, you can and should celebrate. This gives you a sense of renewal, an affirmation of your creativity, and keeps you in the spirit of wanting to create again.

Making Your Life More Meaningful

The more you consciously create, the more aware you become, and the more tuned in you are with your inner being and outer surroundings, the more meaningful life becomes. That's because as you create, you are accessing your mental, emotional, social, spiritual, and physical well-being—some might call it your soul's yearning.

Regardless of what creative activity or direction you choose, as long as it's a reflection of who you really are—your genuine self—you will begin to notice how life begins to give back to you. This means making choices that are in alignment with your values and expressing your creativity because it's something you desire to do. By being true to yourself through creativity, you gain appreciation and gratitude for the overall beauty in the world that goes beyond your specific creation and get a better understanding about yourself through your own creative expression. Who wouldn't want that?

Creativity is like a bountiful harvest that gives back and feeds you and adds its own beauty to the world. Its value can't be overstated. Continue to plant your own seeds, water with love and attention, experience the growth, and reap the benefits!

Creative Play: Exploring Your Personal Benefits

It's time to get a taste of what it feels like to derive the benefits of acting upon your next creative project.

Tools Needed: Two sheets of paper that are at least letter size; markers, colored pencils, paints or crayons; stickers; and other decorative materials of your choosing, which may require glue

Pick one of your creative goals. It could be finding a new solution to a growing problem in the workplace. Perhaps you've been considering a new hobby or picking up on a previous interest you left behind. If you have more than one, pick the one that you are most interested in pursuing right now.

Next, imagine how you would go about acting upon your creative idea and achieving the result you're after by closing your eyes and visualizing it (see Chapter 4 for more on the process). Take your time! Keep going until you can see in your mind's eye the outcome you desire.

Now take one of your papers and quickly write down how this made you feel. Use single words, phrases, or complete sentences, such as "on top of the world," "smiling from ear to ear," "confident," and "successful."

Once you've written down your feelings, consciously think about all of the ways you felt you benefited from allowing yourself to create in this exercise. Understand that this creative play gave you just a tiny feel for the benefits you will actually experience when you're fully engaged in a creative project.

Finally, take your other sheet of paper and tap into your inner artist by drawing, sketching, or painting your benefits in whatever form, symbols, or images that come to you. You can even decorate your masterpiece with stickers or other materials you feel drawn to include. There is no right or wrong way to do this! If you're feeling uncomfortable with this part of the activity, know that you are doing this for your eyes only. You also have the option of sharing your artwork with others when you're done. Your choice!

 INSPIRATIONAL INSIGHT

"Always be on the lookout for the presence of wonder."

—E. B. White

The Least You Need to Know

- While it's true that creativity can lead to innovations that improve the bottom line, monetary value is but one slice of the pie.
- Creating and sharing your creations with others can breathe new life into your relationships.
- By embracing the desire to create, you can gain a better understanding of yourself and the world around you.

What It Takes to Create

Do you know why you have a desire to create and what motivates you to follow through with your creative expression? Some people describe this feeling as an undeniable urge to communicate their individuality and originality. This can be done through either the written or spoken word, by using your hands, or through body movements. In this part, you start to examine the "why" behind creativity.

This part also teaches you that being creative is far more than coming up with innovative ideas. You see the difference between immediate inspiration and the stages involved in the creative process. You also see how creative thinking works with both sides of the brain, the differences between convergent and divergent thinking, and the wonder of "accidental" creations. I then delve into the lives of famous creatives, their traits, and creative strategies, and how you can apply them to your life. You even get a chance to explore some creative thinking practices. Finally, you closely examine the blocks that are keeping you stuck.

Motivation and Creativity

If I asked you, right now, what motivates you to create, could you answer me without thinking about it? And just how strong is your drive? Is your motivation so pure and solid that you jump at every opportunity, or do you find yourself ignoring or delaying what's in your heart to create? Either way, you are not alone.

In this chapter, you have an opportunity to learn about the different types of motivation and closely examine what's behind your own inspiration.

In This Chapter

- Responding to your creative urges
- Exploring intrinsic and extrinsic motivation
- Considering what drives you

The Urge to Create

Do you ever get a feeling that something is gnawing at you? You may not be able to put your finger on it, but you know something is there, calling you, practically doing cartwheels in front of you to get your attention. Eventually, like a point-and-shoot camera trying to fixate on a horizon, the picture comes more into focus. It's an urge to create.

What do I mean by calling it an urge? Besides the traditional definition of *urge* being an impulse or desire, in the context of the word *urgent,* it can also indicate a need for immediate action.

 CREATIVITY KEY

Creative expression can serve as a form of therapy. Allow yourself to explore your unlimited potential, go beyond your boundaries, and reveal a part of yourself. Reflect on this without judgment or expectation and be open to what comes to you. The actual creation can come later. Begin with a conscious exploration.

This urge can range from an impulse—a thought or feeling that suddenly strikes you, which says "I must do this now"—to an idea that starts slowly and steadily develops more and more over time until you can no longer ignore it. For example, perhaps you've had a wish to visit Italy for years; it could simply be something you've thought of for a long time with little definition or direction, or something that suddenly drives you to book a flight at that very moment. One artist I know describes the urge to create as an inner voice that insists that she practically drop whatever else she is doing at that moment to start painting right here, right now. For me personally, it usually means I'm yearning to write a new song or pick up my Native American flute and play whatever notes come to me. Regardless of how it manifests, it's a feeling that won't go away.

Sometimes the urge is easy to miss because it starts out as soft as a whisper. This undercurrent may remain for a while and then at some point, as if someone outside of you is controlling a volume dial, the sound becomes louder and louder and eventually expresses more like a lion's roar.

Acting on your creative urges gives you a sense of satisfaction, accomplishment, realignment with your true self, and more than likely you will be teeming with energy. Not acting means you risk feelings of regret, bitterness, dissatisfaction, or even grief—if the urge is tied to a limited opportunity that passes you by.

But what can drive you not to act? Sometimes it's unrealistic to start on a project right when you think of it. You could be driving, working, or doing something else that makes it difficult or impossible to break away for the new creative pursuit. Many times, however, when that call is never or seldom answered, it's due to a lack of motivation.

Getting motivated to create means finding what inspires you. Once you understand what really inspires you to create, you will be better equipped to answer that call. It's time to tap into your inner voice now to see what might be trying to get your attention.

CREATIVITY KEY

Ignoring the voice, or not taking any action toward it, can also be due to fear. This fear may come from being uncertain of what to expect or having done something similar before with no success. If you think this is the case for you, check out Chapter 6, which talks more about creative blocks.

Creative Play: Understanding Your Urges

In this exercise, you center yourself to become more aware of what is calling you to action. Is it a loud, relentless voice or a soft, sweet nudge? Because you start out with your eyes closed, read all of the instructions first before actually doing this task.

Tools Needed: A pad of paper and a writing instrument

1. Sit in a comfortable chair with your pad of paper and writing instrument next to you.

2. Close your eyes and rest your hands, palms up, in your lap.

3. Breathe in and say silently to yourself, "I open my mind and heart." As you breathe out, silently say, "And I let go." Do this at least 10 times or until you feel that your mind and heart are wide open to receiving guidance.

4. Now, keeping your eyes closed, ask your inner guide questions such as, "What have I been longing to create in my life but haven't acted upon yet? Why haven't I pursued this? What is required for me to take that first step toward this creation? How will I feel if I continue to ignore this call? How will I feel during the process of this creation? How will I feel once I complete this creation?"

5. Keep your eyes closed as you contemplate your feelings to these questions. When you feel you have gained some valuable insights, open your eyes and write down your answers.

Did this exercise bring more clarity to you? At the very least, your awareness should go up a notch or two. If not, repeat this exercise in another day or two. It's best to do when you are feeling relaxed and can take the time to listen without any distractions. And be gentle with yourself if nothing really came to you … yet. You're already committed to becoming more creative (you did sign your Creativity Commitment in Chapter 1, didn't you?), so now it's a matter of learning more about yourself in the creative process.

How Are You Motivated?

Which comes first—the chicken (the idea) or the egg (the motivation)? Are you naturally motivated to create, perhaps because you've tasted how sweet the fruits of your creativity can be? If so, you've probably experienced how you become even more inspired to continue the creative process, as each stage builds upon the previous one and offers its own reward. If you're waiting for motivation to strike you, as if a genie arises from its brass lamp to awaken your creativity, you may never experience an increase in your drive to create because you're lacking motivation in the first place.

How can you become more motivated? Is it even possible to "make" yourself be motivated? The answer is "Absolutely." As with anything else, you have to desire it enough to be willing to learn, grow, and apply what you discover on your path. That driving force can come from your inner being or from outer sources, known as *intrinsic* and *extrinsic motivation,* respectively.

 **DEFINITION**

According to psychologist Teresa Amabile of the Harvard Business School, a leading researcher in the field of creativity, **intrinsic motivation** is an internal drive to create due to your commitment or passion for the activity itself. **Extrinsic motivation** comes from outside forces such as rewards, awards, promotions, money, and grades.

Intrinsic Motivation

The saying "Create art for art's sake" applies to intrinsic motivation. In other words, the enjoyment of the task itself is enough to drive you to create. You have an internal zeal, a passion for the work, and are fully committed to it without the need of an external reward. You may find the task at hand challenging or interesting, or you believe you will grow personally from the experience. The focus is on the activity itself and the creative process rather than the finished product. You feel fulfilled regardless of the outcome, as you are not attached to any result in particular.

The following are some different forms of intrinsic motivation:

Desiring personal growth: In some cases, the motivation to create extends from an inner need to grow as a person. For example, after 65-year-old Judy went through her second divorce, a quiet thought came to her about writing a memoir about her life. At first she ignored it, thinking, "Who would want to read about my boring life?" But the voice persisted, and once she realized there was no need to share her words with anyone, she became motivated to begin writing to gain a better understanding of herself. That was reason enough to write. She had no plans of publishing her story, although she was open to it. Her only motivation was to grow from the opportunity of creatively expressing herself.

Being intrinsically motivated by personal growth can be about wanting to feel like you matter and what you're doing matters. In his book, *Coaching the Artist Within: Advice for Writers, Actors, Visual Artists & Musicians,* creativity coach and author Eric Maisel says passion is what motivates us. This means engaging in pursuits you love, as they are meaningful to you and make you feel more alive. Making art, trying new recipes, inventing games with your children, or learning to play the instrument you've always dreamed of are all examples of creative activities you may choose because you're passionate about them. It makes you feel good. It makes you feel like you matter. And you do!

You may also be motivated to create in order to respond to a calling you believe is coming from deep within, as if your soul is leading you on a spiritual adventure. You're not sure where your creative expression will take you, and that's not your focus—it's the journey and not the destination you care about. Your motivation is to learn more about yourself in the process and to get closer to who you really are.

Sometimes with intrinsic motivation for personal growth, all you need to motivate you is to engage in a task that will open your heart—one that will move you past the walls that have been protecting you and allow you to experience the open feeling of creating. You are being driven by a desire to express yourself creatively because you know it will move you into a more heart-felt space. Or you feel motivated by the longing to stretch yourself beyond the usual boundaries. It's not about others assigning a task to you and pleasing them. No, you are motivated to create because in challenging yourself; you are giving yourself a chance to learn and grow. Or you may like the idea of being productive because it gives you a feeling of accomplishment. No reward is necessary. Engaging in the process is a reward in and of itself.

 INSPIRATIONAL INSIGHT

"If I create from the heart, nearly everything works; if from the head, almost nothing."

—Marc Chagall

Creating to satisfy a curiosity is another example of how this type of motivation works. Have you ever gone to an art show that features hundreds of artists and crafters? You stroll along the rows of booths, taking in all of the colors, textures, sizes, and shapes. You watch as the different vendors interact with the guests and you become curious what it would be like to paint, draw, work with wood, or make jewelry. You become so motivated by your curiosity that you rush to your nearest art store, speak with one of the store employees who recommends what materials you should buy, and purchase the basic necessities to get started. You have no goal other than to have fun with this new project and to satisfy your curiosity. Where it goes from there ... well, go for it and you'll find out!

Balancing your life: You may be motivated to take on creative projects because you're feeling like your life is unbalanced. This could be due to your life being all work and no play, where even your home activities seem to be more focused on doing laundry, dusting, vacuuming, weeding, cleaning out the garage, or other household chores. You know that if you don't introduce a new activity in your life, the imbalance will only get worse. You are now internally motivated to initiate a new creative project, one that will offset work and routine chores with fun and pleasure. That could be anything from taking a ceramics or woodworking class to getting back to a routine you had gotten away from months ago, such as writing in a journal. Regardless of what you choose, this inspiration is coming from a place inside of you.

Improving your overall health: This refers to how you think creating makes you feel better mentally, physically, and emotionally—and that's enough to drive you. For example, many people who exercise with the purpose of losing weight find it difficult to continue. Why? Because they're in a hurry to shed the pounds and they'll only feel good about themselves if they do instead of enjoying the workout itself. If your motivation to exercise is because you take pleasure in the activity itself, however, you know you're being intrinsically motivated. The same applies to a creative project.

Connecting with others: Upon first glance, you might think this one is more extrinsic because it involves other people. What I'm referring to is the feeling you get when you share a common interest with others—a sense of bonding and connection. For example, whenever I have facilitated small groups of 10 or fewer people in my creativity classes, I am always amazed at the amount of intimacy that takes place. I'm not talking about the kind of intimacy you experience with a spouse or mate; instead, it's the shared experience of creating as a group. I enjoy observing how the individuals in the group come together. Each group has a different energy about it, but the common denominator is a kind of love, empathy, and respect for one another. Feeling motivated in the presence of others provides a wonderful bonding opportunity!

Creating beauty in the world: You may simply be driven to create to give form to your personal expression. As I've already discussed, there really is no limit as to what kind of form you can create, as there are countless examples found in nature and everyday living. You may wish to create artwork that illustrates your heritage, or you may want to bring a certain culture to the forefront. In this type of intrinsic motivation, you believe your creations add a touch of beauty to the world and wish to share them, not so others may judge them, but because you are driven to do your part in adding your own personal garnishes. This, in turn, contributes meaning to the world and allows you to let your light shine because it makes you feel good!

Extrinsic Motivation

If you are extrinsically motivated, you are focused more on the end result rather than the creative activity or process. You're inspired by a goal that is external to the work itself, such as winning awards; getting a promotion, salary increase, or bonus; satisfying your customers; finding a solution; improving your social status; or, if you're a student, getting good grades.

CREATIVITY COMPASS

During a creativity coaching session, Bobbi, who was retired, explained that she enjoyed drawing and painting, but she found that she was more interested in having a sense of completion rather than appreciating the creative process. Her desire was to have more fun while actually doing her artwork. We discussed ways that would allow this, and in the end she decided to set a reasonable time frame to complete each piece to eliminate a feeling of needing to rush. She also meditated and wrote in her journal to move into a space of gratitude. By committing to these steps, she noticed how she became more deliberate with her art and began to thoroughly enjoy the actual process rather than worrying about the end result.

A great example of extrinsic motivation is a friend of mine who is a writer. She once declared, "I hate to write but I love the feeling I have once the article is finished." She is paid to write and has received accolades and recognition from her boss, co-workers, and readers. That is what drives her to write—not the process of writing. That's not to say that this applies to all writers. Unlike my friend, I enjoy the process of writing—in particular, researching and writing this book. At the same time, I am being motivated by the end goal—the publishing of this book.

As you can see, they are both extrinsic, but one is simply about the external, while the other is a combination of the internal and external. According to psychologist Teresa Amabile of the Harvard Business School, these differences can be classified synergistic and nonsynergistic motivators:

- **Synergistic motivators:** This type of extrinsic motivation moves the person to complete the work in combination with intrinsic motivation. An example of this would be an artist who is inspired to paint because she loves the feeling it gives her but also is motivated by the end goal of selling the piece. She derives both a monetary benefit and a feeling of appreciation that she was able to enhance that customer's life with beauty.

- **Nonsynergistic motivators:** These give a person more of a feeling that he's being controlled by external incentives that are not in harmony with intrinsic motivators. For example, when you were a child, your parents may have pressured you to get an A in each of your classes. If there was a subject you really disliked, such as math, your nonsynergistic motivator to study and do well would have been due to your parents' demands, not because you had a desire on your own to learn more about arithmetic.

In one of Amabile's studies that involved college women, she concluded that "the intrinsically motivated state is conducive to creativity, whereas the extrinsically motivated state is detrimental." How so? If you're simply extrinsically motivated, someone is sitting in judgment of you. If they deem your work to be "less than," you may not feel as inspired the next time you take on a creative project unless your motivation is coming from within.

That doesn't necessarily mean that if you're motivated extrinsically that you can't or won't be creative. It just means, ideally, your motivation should be synergistic, which allows you to rely on both your inner resources and outside forces so you can have the most rewarding creative experience. For example, if you're a scientist who is motivated to find the cure to cancer, it goes without saying how life-changing that discovery would be not only for yourself, but also for millions of other people. In this case, the primary motivating force may be the end result (extrinsic) and also ties into the scientist's passion (intrinsic).

Do not judge yourself if you are more extrinsically motivated. There is nothing wrong with striving to get good grades or wanting to be recognized by your boss with a healthy raise. You just need to combine that with some intrinsic motivation so that nothing is necessarily required of anyone or anything outside of you to find joy in creating.

Understanding Your Own Motivations

In the end, it's important to be aware of what it takes for you to move forward. There has to be some kind of connection to a feeling within yourself, an external reward or a person, or both. Amabile believes being motivated by a passionate heart will result in the most creativity. That simply means you have a deep caring for whatever it is you've decided to pursue; it matters to you. If you can identify your primary motivators, you can use this information to help you the next time you may be feeling stuck or ambivalent about an idea you have. Yes, it is possible for you to search for ways to increase your motivation. If you know what drives you, you'll be able to recognize what's missing and see if you can you fill that void with one of your motivational prompts. The following questions will help you do that.

Are you in touch with your intentions and talents? In an online article, professor Jane Piirto, who wrote the book *Creativity for 21ˢᵗ Century Skills,* addresses motivation by saying that regardless of the creative activity, those who are creative must have motivation with an intention to make something. They have to want it and have "a certain amount of obsession." Knowing what you want and taking the time to clearly articulate your intention—whether you write or record it—will help you to maintain your motivation. If your motivation begins to wane, revisit your original intention. See if anything has changed within you or with outside circumstances and if any modifications need to be made.

Having talent in your chosen area and receiving support also may be important. If you really want something and are willing to do whatever it takes, you can develop a talent in a given area.

At the same time, if engaging in an activity frustrates you time and time again, you may want to shift your focus to something that feels better. But don't give up too soon. Sometimes just when you feel like quitting, you're on the brink of a breakthrough, so keep that in mind! That's where getting the encouragement and support of others could help you get motivated again to continue.

When was the last time you took on a project or decided to do something new? Think about it, and then, with that situation in mind, determine if any of the following statements apply, using "I was motivated to do this because …" to begin:

- I knew it would help me grow personally.

- I felt it would balance my life.

- I thought it would lead to making personal and professional connections.

- I wanted to create beauty in the world.

- I felt it would bring me more prosperity.

- I figured, if done superbly, my work would be considered for an award and recognition, which would help me advance my career.

- Serving others makes me feel good inside.

If there are other factors that motivated you, write them down. This way, you can revisit them when you feel like you're running out of steam. They will help you get back in touch with what drives you.

Are you motivated by positive or negative reinforcement? When facing the prospect of a creative request or demand, do you respond better if it's prefaced with a positive statement, such as "I know you can do this," or do you like to be challenged with statements, such as "You'll never be able to do that"? Those words would come as a crushing blow to some and would be the perfect motivator for others. I, myself, take those kinds of statements on with a type of rebellious "Oh yeah? I'll show you!" attitude.

Do you consider yourself to be an overachiever, underachiever, or average? If you have ever labeled yourself as an overachiever, you probably have a relentless drive that extends to most areas of your life, including creativity. Where does that drive, that ambition, that desire to constantly create come from? Is it a need to gain approval from others? Are you motivated to go nonstop because you feel your contributions make a difference in the world? Or is the act of challenging yourself and then meeting that opportunity head on enough to keep you motivated? There are no wrong answers here. These are questions to ask and answer yourself to gain a better understanding of how you function.

If you've ever referred to yourself as an underachiever, ask yourself what's missing and what will it take to inspire you to take action. Sometimes people get labeled as "lazy" when what's really lacking are their motivational drivers. This is why it's so important to realize what propels you to move forward. If you consider yourself to be an average achiever, are you comfortable with where you are or do you wish to have more energy to engage in more opportunities? Again, look to what really matters to you.

If you had to rank your motivation to create on a scale of 1 to 10 (with 10 being the most motivated), how would you rate yourself? Why did you give yourself that ranking? What did you base it on? Did you compare yourself to others, or did you base it on the fact you haven't created in a long time? If you gave yourself a higher number, is it because you are consistently creating? The purpose of this ranking is not to berate or applaud yourself. It's to simply be aware of where you're at and whether you want to increase what you're doing, scale back, or stay right where you are.

Know that it's normal for the forces that drive you to go into neutral at times. Even the most motivated people in the world don't always have their gear shaft in D for Drive. Even they put on the brakes or go into reverse at times as they stop to reflect and reexamine where they're at creatively and where they need to go from there. Resist the temptation to label yourself as lazy or not ambitious enough just because you haven't exercised your creativity in a while. Just like your car has to be maintained on a regular basis, you also must undergo a process of refueling and recharging your battery before continuing.

Creative Play: Becoming Motivated to Create

While it's possible it never occurred to you to think about it, after reading this chapter, you should have a better grasp on what motivates you. In this creative play, you are going to consciously consider your driving forces, which will help you the next time you decide to create something. This exercise works best when you have about 45 minutes to an hour of free time.

Tools Needed: A good pair of walking shoes, comfortable clothes, paper, and a writing instrument

Start off by taking a walk by yourself. It doesn't matter if you live in a small town, a city, or the country. Your only task now is to walk where you feel safe. You may choose to walk during the day or evening. The purpose of this walk is to tune in to all of the things you see that have been created and to see which, if any, serve as inspiration.

As you're walking, start observing everything and everyone around you with the wonder of a child. If you're in the country, notice the trees, flowers, insects, and the sounds of a dog barking in the distance or birds chirping. If you're in a busier area, such as a city, observe the people who pass you by. Are they wearing interesting shoes, outfits, hats, or jewelry? Look at the structure of the tall buildings, the flashing neon lights, and other surroundings and listen to the sounds of cars honking, police and ambulance sirens, and other noises. Mentally note anything that piques your curiosity, makes you wonder, or inspires you.

After 20 or 30 minutes, head for home. Once you arrive, it's time to select a creative project you wish to undertake in the next month. It may relate to something you observed on your walk—or not. It never hurts to get a little exercise to stretch both your physical and your mental muscles. Either way, write down what you want to create.

Fill in the blank:

I chose this project because _____.

Before completing the next sentence, consider the intrinsic and extrinsic motivators that were discussed in this chapter, and then list your motivator(s). (You might want to refer to the sample statements in the "Understanding Your Own Motivations" section.) The following factors will motivate me to create this: _____

_____

_____.

CREATIVITY KEY

Remember, there are no right or wrong answers—no rules! Even though the more recent research conducted on motivation by and large shows that creativity is driven primarily intrinsically, it doesn't make you wrong or less creative if you are motivated more by the end result, or the goal itself, be it a promotion, salary increase, or better grade. Only you know what truly works for you. But if you think you've been motivated extrinsically in the past and have not been pleased with your creative output, it's time to take another look at what really drives you and makes you want to answer that urge to create right now!

The Least You Need to Know

- The urge to create can present as a thunderous bang or a barely audible murmur that eventually grows louder. Either way, it's something that tugs at you until you finally heed the call to create.

- The forces that inspire you to create can come from the task itself (an intrinsic motivator) or from the end result (an extrinsic motivator).

- The more motivated you are to create, the more you will want to continue to create. The more you create, the more motivated you will be.

- Only you hold the key to what truly motivates you. Tap into your driving forces on a regular basis. This awareness in and of itself will help keep you motivated to create.

The Process of Creativity

Setting out to generate creative ideas or having inspirational thoughts strike you unexpectedly is but one aspect of the creative process. Remember in Chapter 1 when I posed the question "What good is an idea if it isn't implemented?" In this chapter, you learn that creativity is a process that requires motivation and goes beyond ideas.

While it's true that sometimes you have no conscious goal of creating anything and then an idea shoots through like a bullet headed straight for the bull's-eye, you still have to decide if you're going to act on it. After learning about the process, I show you how it relates to different types of creative thinking. I close with examples of how everyday products came about "accidentally" when the creators' intention or thinking changed.

In This Chapter

- Learning and applying the stages of the creative process
- The difference between divergent and convergent thinking
- How mistakes often lead to creative results

From Idea to Execution

Chances are, you've experienced an "out of the blue" idea, or one that seems to come from nowhere. Maybe it came as you were dining alone, just appreciating your meal and not thinking of anything in particular. Or maybe you were in the shower and suddenly thought of a solution (believe me, I've heard many people reference how ideas came to them while in the midst of applying shampoo and soap!).

What happens when you get that idea? You've probably heard the analogies of an idea striking you like lightning or a light bulb coming on. Or perhaps this concept brings images of a wacky scientist with his "Eureka!" moment. As for me, I tend to make my right hand into a fist and exclaim, "Yes!" with a big smile on my face when an idea or insight suddenly hits. Whatever the case, it's possible for ideas to come in an instant and give you that sudden rush of inspiration; however, that doesn't necessarily lead to any follow-through.

Sometimes, the ideas live to see another day; they are cultivated, placed in an incubator, and evolve as they go through different processes until the end goal is finally reached. Other times, the ideas never see the light of day; instead, they vanish as quickly as they appear.

Why do some of your ideas make it and others don't? It could be a difference in motivation. For the ones that don't make it, maybe the project isn't meaningful enough to you or you're feeling blocked, unable to take action for any number of reasons (I will explore these reasons more in Chapter 6). However, for those ideas you choose to pursue, they go through a process. It's possible you've taken your thought from idea to implementation in a way that flowed so smoothly you didn't even realize there was an actual method you employed.

That's the creative process, or CREATE:

- Clarify your intention
- Round up ideas
- Explore and experiment
- Analyze and act
- Take a breather
- Execute, evaluate, evolve, and enjoy

At times, you may glide through this process easily; other times, you may have difficulty keeping to it. Like a boat on rough waters, at those difficult moments, you decide to jump ship before you reach your destination. So how can you stay focused when you go from that "Eureka!" moment to something you've implemented?

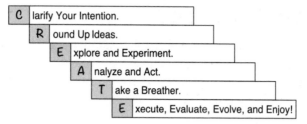

C	larify Your Intention.
R	ound Up Ideas.
E	xplore and Experiment.
A	nalyze and Act.
T	ake a Breather.
E	xecute, Evaluate, Evolve, and Enjoy!

The stages of the creative process.

The following takes you through each stage of the creative process. As you read through the various stages, you may recognize which ones have presented the biggest issues for you in the past and which ones are your strengths. With that knowledge, you can improve upon those weaknesses and embrace your strengths, giving yourself that extra push to get your ideas off the ground.

CREATIVITY KEY

While the process I'm about to describe serves as an effective model for how creativity unfolds, it in no way means you must apply the stages exactly as described. The more you create, the more you will develop your own style and process that works for you.

Clarify Your Intention

I'll begin with the premise that started this chapter—that ideas can materialize without any intention. Imagine you're having lunch with a friend for the simple pleasure of reconnecting and catching up on each other's lives; the thought of creativity isn't even in the background of your mind. During your conversation with her, however, she says something catchy. You think to yourself, "Hmmm, that's a great line! I could do something creative with that." What do you do with it? Is your intention to write a song using her words as the hook, paint a picture that conveys the feeling, or write a funny poem using that line? Whether an idea comes to you suddenly or you have yet to begin the idea-generating stage, the creativity process doesn't really take off until you figure out your intention. For this example, let's say you decide to write a funny poem using her line; that's the intent you have for the idea your friend inadvertently gave you.

Sometimes, like with the funny poem, you deliberately decide you want to create all on your own. You may already have an idea, however sketchy or firm, or want to spend some time developing some ideas. Your intention to create on purpose could be due to a creative urge that's been vying for your attention, because you're feeling inspired and want to experience more beauty in your life, or out of a motivation for gain (such as a promotion at work). What you intend to do with your decision to create, in turn, ties into your inspiration or motivation. Therefore, the more you can clarify your intention, the more success you are likely to achieve. This success could mean anything from "I just want to experience more feelings of appreciation and beauty" to "nothing short of a promotion will satisfy me."

But what do you do when you're being asked by someone else to create? For example, imagine you're working for a membership-driven organization and your boss wants you to come up with ideas to increase membership by 20 percent within six months. That's a specific expectation, and as a result, you define your intention based around that expectation. In this case, it could be to create a new membership benefit or perhaps a whole new program.

So whether or not you already have an idea or you have yet to generate one, clarifying your intention can help you understand what you want to do and why.

 INSPIRATIONAL INSIGHT

"When I say artist, I mean the man who is building things. ... It's all a big game of construction—some with a brush, some with a shovel, some choose a pen."

—Jackson Pollock

Round Up Ideas

The next stage in the creative process is to gather ideas or further develop the one with which you started. This may involve working with other people in a collaborative process or using people as a sounding board so you can bounce ideas off of them. In turn, ideas may come to them, and you can continue to play off of each other. You also can round up ideas by going online and doing an internet search on your topics or going to the Pinterest website, which features images that may lead to more ideas. This stage can actually present you with the most opportunities for fun and using your imagination if you allow it (for more on idea-generating techniques you can try out, see Part 3 and Chapter 14 in the workplace section).

When in this stage, resist the temptation to limit yourself to one or two ideas. This is especially important when you're taking on a new challenge. Have you ever been involved with a committee of volunteers or co-workers and in the middle of the discussion, someone blurts out, "That'll never work" or "We've always done it this way"? It's like riding a bicycle and enjoying the scenery, appreciating all of the new and different surroundings you never noticed before, and then suddenly getting a flat tire—your progress stops right then and there. The same happens with statements such as these; they limit the natural progress of an idea or ideas.

You also may find you need to let the ideas you've gathered sit for a while. Take your time and allow them to continue to develop.

Explore and Experiment

So now that you've gathered enough ideas to play with, it's time to do just that. This is a testing stage, one that can be a lot of fun as you go from one idea to the next trying them out. It's also an important stage because if you bypass it and act hastily, you may find you waste a lot of time, money, or other resources if the quickly selected idea ends up not working out.

How you specifically explore and experiment with your ideas depends on the nature of the project, but here are some suggestions:

- Look at the ideas from different points of view, especially if other people are involved. If the project is not confidential, this is a good time to bounce the ideas off of other people for their feedback.

- Share your thoughts with a friend or two to see if the topic or your approach to the subject sounds interesting. This is particularly helpful if you're considering ideas for a creative activity that doesn't involve other people, such as writing a book.

- Do some hands-on work. For example, if you're a sculptor, you may want to play around with clay, modeling different shapes to get a better idea of which direction to go.

- Select a test market. For example, if you're working for a restaurant, before adding a new dish to a menu, you may offer it first to a select area to gauge the response.

Analyze and Act

Once you've tried out your various ideas, the next stage is to analyze them and formulate your action plan. After careful analysis, you may decide to go no further because you've determined your idea is not cost effective, you aren't able to pull together the proper resources, the timing is bad, or another sound reason that tells you to go back to the drawing board. While a simple modification may be all that's necessary, you may need to start fresh or trash the idea altogether.

Sometimes your exploration reveals that you have a great idea worth pursuing but you stop progress in its tracks. You may love generating ideas and experimenting with them as you imagine the joy they might bring to other people, but for some reason, you don't follow through. It could be due to a lack of motivation or one of the many blocks outlined in Chapter 6. For example, I have spoken with plenty of folks who have talked about writing a book. They come up with ideas, try them out, and then single out the book's primary purpose. And then ... they never write. Their dream of becoming a published author dies with their unexecuted ideas.

Therefore, for those ideas that survive the first three stages, you must begin to formulate your action plan. This involves everything that needs to happen for your idea to become a successful reality. Such actions include determining the various steps that need to take place and who's responsible for them, setting realistic deadlines, and tapping into existing resources or buying the necessary tools and components.

CREATIVITY COMPASS

At the beginning of a 13-week creativity course I facilitate, I ask participants to state their intention. One young man with an entrepreneurial spirit spoke up and said the reason he was there was because he had a lot of ideas but he rarely acted upon them. His intention was to get better at finishing those projects he started. At the course's midway point, he missed two classes in a row, another example of not following through. I contacted him and once he confirmed he was okay, I reminded him of his intention. Fortunately, all it took was a gentle reminder of his stated purpose and he returned to finish out the course strong. Today, he is a very creative, successful entrepreneur.

Take a Breather

If you've gotten this far, it means you've set your intention, explored your ideas, analyzed those ideas, and come up with an action plan. At this point, it's always a good idea to step away from your project and literally and figuratively take a breather. Putting some distance between you and your project can shed new light on it when you return. How much time you take varies, but generally speaking, step away long enough to refresh yourself without taking so much time that you become disconnected or unenthused when you return.

It's possible you may not see a need for any changes once you come back to it. On the other hand, you may get more ideas that make you feel even better about what you're doing. Depending on the length of your creative endeavor, you may want to give yourself more than one timeout throughout the process.

Execute, Evaluate, Evolve, and Enjoy!

This is the final stage in the creative process. When you execute, you are fully engaged in your actual creation and doing whatever it takes to complete what you started.

However, as you go along, it's important to continue to evaluate your progress as a kind of "check-in." Are you sticking with your original plan, or is there a need for changes? This is where "evolve" comes in; even this late in the game, it's possible your project will need to be altered in some way to meet your current needs. As long as your venture continues to move forward, you are on the right road!

Hopefully, you are enjoying yourself during this process, even if your main focus is on the end goal. (Remember, your motivation can be both intrinsic and extrinsic, as I discussed in

Chapter 3.) Still, once you have completed your creative process, don't forget to celebrate. After all, if you find joy in what you've done, you'll be ready to take part in the creative process all over again!

Creative Play: Tapping Into the Process

Each of us has our own strengths and weaknesses. The idea of this exercise is to get familiar with going through the creative process as outlined earlier using either an actual creative project you're considering or the fictional situation described here. If you feel too daunted by this task, remember that this is called *creative play* for a reason. Have some fun with it while trying out the different stages. There will be no short quiz or test that follows! And if you don't feel into it at the moment, you can always come back to this when you're feeling ready.

Tools Needed: Your imagination, paper, and a writing instrument

Stage 1: Clarify your intention. You have committed to being a volunteer on an events committee for your local animal shelter, which is celebrating its fiftieth anniversary. The nonprofit organization's president has asked the committee to create a festive event that will raise both awareness and funds. Begin by writing a statement of your intention, such as "Our intention is to create a commemorative, fun-filled event that elevates our shelter's image in the community while raising at least $200,000."

Stage 2: Round up ideas. It's time to have fun! Get wild and crazy. No idea is too outrageous—at least not at this stage. Start with ideas for a theme. What would entice supporters and the public at large to attend this event? Looking at your own community, what kinds of events are other charities hosting? You can play off of their ideas to springboard you to different schemes. Will the party be formal or casual? Can you take the idea of a black-tie event and put your own spin on it? I know of one nonprofit organization that decided to have an "Un-Event" in which they spared their supporters of having to attend any kind of event and instead asked for a donation to be mailed. Keep the ideas flowing and see what comes up.

Stage 3: Explore and experiment. Now you can try out the ideas you generated in step 2. In this fictional situation, you are sitting with other committee members, so if you want to fully play with this exercise, involve some of your friends. Otherwise, look at all of your ideas and imagine how they might work. At this point, you're not scrutinizing them as much as getting a feel for them. Which ideas bring excitement? Which go beyond the usual charitable fundraising event? Which ideas motivate you?

Stage 4: Analyze and act. This is the time to take a hard look at what will work and what won't. For example, your idea may have a million-dollar price tag, but you only have a $10,000 budget, meaning it's not practical. In addition to your budget, you'll be looking at all of your resources, including personnel (staff and volunteers), location (questions pertaining to convenience, safety, parking, how many people it holds, and how well it fits the theme), expertise needed, decorations, admission cost, and all of the logistical details. You won't really be able to ascertain such details and write a complete action plan for this fictional animal shelter event, but for the purposes of this exercise, select one of your ideas and list all of the logistics that come to mind. See how different this stage feels compared to generating ideas and exploring them.

Stage 5: Take a breather. If you're in the middle of planning a special event, you may feel like you don't have time to breathe, let alone stop long enough to consciously breathe! But it's at this time when you should allow yourself to take a step back to prepare for the final stage. Let everything you've been working on sink in. Sometimes taking a breather leads to new insights that will make your ideas even better. Given this fictional situation, you may not be able to take any more than a day or two, perhaps a weekend, to step away and come back to it. The idea is to step away long enough to stay fresh and avoid burning out before the event but short enough that you don't forget key details. So go ahead—take a break from this creative play before returning to the final step!

Stage 6: Execute, evaluate, evolve, and enjoy! Now it's time to put all of your ideas, planning, logistics, and creativity into action. Again, for the purposes of this creative play, imagine what this stage would be like for you. Picture yourself doing your part to make this happen. Remember, you are one of many volunteers, so you are not alone. One of your first action items might be to determine a theme for the event and the admission cost. Other tasks might include working with a graphic designer or a qualified volunteer to create invitations, tickets, flyers, and a program that emphasize the theme; booking a band and strolling entertainment; selecting a caterer; arranging a valet service; promoting the event to the media; approaching local businesses to donate to a silent or live auction and securing an auctioneer; and approaching a local celebrity to emcee your event. These are all considerations for this fictional example.

Of course, you will get an even better feel for the creative process when you're engaged in a real experience and not just an imaginary one, but did you get a sense for how you felt while going through the various stages? Can you identify where you felt most comfortable and confident in the creative process and where you felt resistance? The next time you engage in a creative activity, you will be that much more aware that creativity goes beyond having a light bulb moment. It doesn't mean you won't have those occasional "a-ha" moments; it just means you will know what to do with them now.

 **INSPIRATIONAL INSIGHT**

"Imagination is everything. It is the preview of life's coming attractions."

–Albert Einstein

Embracing Your Roles in the Creative Process

As you read through the six stages of the creative process, did you find that you identified with one of them more than the others? For example, are you good at coming up with ideas but find it hard to act upon them? Or do you feel generating ideas is your weakness—that you would rather play the role of analyzer instead? Everyone has their strengths and weaknesses, so it's likely you feel you're better at some stages more than the others. That's why it often works to be part of a creative team in which the members play to their different strong points.

For example, the immensely imaginative Walt Disney, who created an entire entertainment mecca filled with fantasy and fun, described creativity as "imagineering," or a mix of imagination and engineering. Without ideas that spring forth from imagination, creativity won't manifest; without the engineering or executing of those ideas, creative expression also will die. In order to make his ideas come to life, he had to adopt many different roles.

Two of Disney's animators referred to the following as the three roles he played in the creative process:

- **Dreamer:** The one who uses visionary insight to come up with ideas for different ventures.

- **Realist:** The one who produces what's needed to turn ideas into reality.

- **Spoiler (or critic):** The one who uses evaluation skills that polish the dreamer and realist's productivity.

As you can see, each one demonstrates a different type of thinking strategy. Just like you may have felt more comfortable in certain stages of the creative process, you may identify more with one of Disney's three roles. Are you comfortable as the dreamer? Do you take pleasure in getting lost in the "island of ideas" and actually delight in tossing silly and serious notions around? Do you enjoy brainstorming sessions, in which you rattle off a list of thoughts, however crazy they may seem at the time? If you relate best to the dreamer role, you derive excitement from this process of generating ideas. But what if you're more interested in taking those ideas that will work and turning them into reality? If that's true of you, you relate best to the realist role. You thrive on figuring out how to make ideas concrete creations. Or maybe you're the one who likes to question and find reasons why the ideas won't work or how they can be improved; if that's the case, you're more comfortable with the spoiler role. For example, as the spoiler, Disney was known to scrupulously analyze every piece of work to ensure his projects were as close to perfection as possible.

As you go through your own creative processes with each project you pursue, you will probably find yourself enacting some version of these perspectives. If you're feeling weaker in one of these areas, you can work to strengthen it by first becoming aware of your discomfort and then seeing if you can identify what's behind your uncomfortable feelings. For example, if your strength is as the "dreamer" but you're not as skilled in executing the ideas (the "realist"), perhaps it's due to a lack of experience or confidence. This could be addressed with more training or working with a mentor. By honing in on the reason and getting the support you need, little by little, you will begin to feel more at ease with the other role. As previously mentioned, you also can balance the process by teaming with others who complement your skills.

 CREATIVITY COMPASS

If you like to work independently, as I do most of the time, it still pays to find at least one partner who can take the pressure off you in your perceived areas of weakness or to help with any parts you simply don't enjoy. For example, at a time before every company had a website, I looked into creating my first website for my public relations company. I had plenty of ideas for its content, look, and feel, but I lacked the technical skills to create it. I partnered with a graphic designer and a webmaster and spared myself a lot of aggravation in the process. In the end, I was very happy with my decision, my partnerships, and the finished product.

Engaging in Whole-Brain Thinking

Much has been written about the differences between the left and right hemispheres of the brain. While the left side of the brain is considered to be for things that are logical, linear, analytical, detail-oriented, practical, and organized, the right side is considered to be aligned with imagination, images, sensual, big-picture thinking, passion, and appreciation. Therefore, the truth that was being presented for many years was that those who possessed more of the right-brain characteristics were said to be more creative.

More recently, however, cognitive neuroscientists have been researching what actually happens when the brain is engaged in the creative process, and according to a *Scientific American* Beautiful Minds blog post by Scott Barry Kaufman on "The Real Neuroscience of Creativity," they are discovering that these standard explanations are outdated.

Their findings are showing that the typical left brain–right brain perspective falls short of providing the full landscape of how the creative process actually unfolds in the brain. In other words, creativity is not simply a right-brain process.

You can probably see that for yourself after reading about the creative process, which requires both imagination (right-brain) and analytical (left-brain) functions. This means both hemispheres are important for creativity because they are both involved, depending on the stage of creative development. While this doesn't negate the differences between how the brain's left and right hemispheres process information, it does mean the creative process requires "whole-brain thinking," or use of both sides of the brain.

Still, that doesn't mean each stage of the creative process is both analytical and imaginative. There are actually two different ways of thinking that can help you with stages that require clear-cut thinking and stages that need a more open approach. They are known as *convergent* and *divergent thinking.* Let's take a closer look at what both types of thinking are and how they can help you in the creative process at different stages.

Types of Thinking

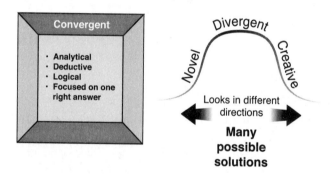

An illustration of the convergent and divergent thinking processes.

 **DEFINITION**

Convergent thinking is analytical, deductive, logical, and usually focused on one right answer. **Divergent thinking** is novel and creative, and looks in different directions and at many possible solutions.

Convergent Thinking

When faced with a problem, consider how you think much of the time. If you find your tendency is to take bits of information and look for a single solution, you're thinking convergently. You're using logic, analysis, scrutiny, and judgment to find a clear-cut answer. This type of thinking makes sense when one answer will do the trick. For example, if you're taking a multiple-choice test or a true-false test, you're looking for one correct answer, meaning convergent thinking is what's needed.

In terms of the creative process, convergent thinking is useful when you're focusing in on your intention during the first step of the creative process. It also works when it comes time to analyze your ideas (stage three) and formulate and execute your action plan (stage six). However, convergent thinking would hamper a situation in which you're wanting to look at multiple solutions. For example, if you're looking at ways to drum up new business, you wouldn't want to limit yourself by thinking there's only one answer. Once you've thought of many ideas, you can put this type of thinking to work and begin weighing the pros and cons.

Divergent Thinking

One way to remember how to define divergent thinking is to think "divergent = diverse." This way of thinking contrasts with convergent thinking because it requires you to think more abstractly and openly, which yields a variety of solutions, ideas, and thoughts. In the creative process, divergent thinking works well when you're rounding up your ideas, as well as when you're exploring and experimenting. For example, if you're writing a novel, there is no end to the number of story lines and characters you could consider; there is no one answer to the type of plot and people your book contains.

The brainstorming process or anytime you want to open up to something new and different also capitalizes on using divergent thinking. Have you ever participated in a creativity starter that asks you to write down how many ways a cotton ball can be used? You probably can rattle off some of the typical uses first, such as removing makeup or nail polish, but coming up with the more obscure answers requires divergent thinking. Thinking divergently allows you to go beyond the obvious and can lead you to innovative solutions.

However, keep in mind that just as creativity should no longer be viewed as solely a right-brained process, neither should it be defined as only needing divergent thinking. The creative process capitalizes on convergent thinking as well.

Creating by Accident

When you make a mistake, do you see it as an opportunity to learn from it or a failure, a letdown? Some people have such high expectations that when some type of gaffe is made, they berate themselves for not doing better. What if you make a mistake and rather than criticizing yourself, you look at the situation in a different way? Making mistakes has actually led to making millions for some when a shift in point of view occurred. Some of the most popular products people use came about this way. The creation of the Slinky toy is an example of divergent thinking in the face of an accident. In 1943, navy engineer Richard James was looking to create a meter that could monitor power on navy ships. He inadvertently knocked down one of the springs used to stabilize the meter and watched that now famous, end over end, gentle walk. Once he demonstrated to his wife, Betty, what happened, she got the idea for a new toy and ultimately named it the Slinky. Had she gotten stuck on her husband's original intention, the thought of a toy would not have even entered her mind. This exemplifies what can happen with open thinking and a little ingenuity.

Kellogg's corn flakes cereal, penicillin, the microwave oven, super glue, Post-it notes, Velcro, the pacemaker, Coca-Cola, potato chips, Play-Doh, champagne, saccharin, chewing gum, popsicles, and chocolate chip cookies also are examples of discoveries that came about "by accident" through the use of divergent thinking. This is where keeping your mind open to more than one possibility can lead to unique solutions.

 INSPIRATIONAL INSIGHT

> "Go and make interesting mistakes, make amazing mistakes, make glorious and fantastic mistakes. Break rules. Leave the world more interesting for your being here. Make. Good. Art."
>
> —Neil Gaiman

The Least You Need to Know

- Creativity is not limited to the generation of ideas, which can strike suddenly or may be hatched over time. Rather, it's a process that involves many stages.

- You may favor or feel more comfortable in one of three roles in the creative process: dreamer, realist, or critic. This is why teamwork often works well during creative ventures.

- Convergent (logical) thinking and divergent (more innovative) thinking are both used during the creative process, which requires whole-brain thinking rather than strictly right-brain thinking.

- When you're willing to change your original intentions and thinking, you open yourself to the possibility of creating something you never imagined. There are dozens of examples of how accidents changed intention and blossomed into great creations, such as Velcro and Post-it notes.

Characteristics of Creatives

While you know everyone is creative, there are certain traits typically found in people who create on a regular basis. In this chapter, I discuss the common stereotypes surrounding those who are perceived as creative. You also get to look at some of the more universal characteristics that are common to those who create regularly, determine which attributes you possess, and learn how you can develop more of these creative traits. You then get an opportunity to look into the lives of some of the better-known creatives to glean strategies for creative success.

In This Chapter

- Stereotypes surrounding creative people
- How opposing traits can work together
- Twelve common creativity traits
- A look into the lives of some famous creatives

Common Stereotypes About Creatives

In the first chapter of this book, I established that everyone is creative—artists and nonartists alike. Yet why is it that many people still limit their views of those whom they deem creative as being "out there"? That may mean they have spiked hair, tattoos covering much of their body, or wear wild-looking clothing. That's just one stereotype that continues to exist. In particular, it seems that those who express their creativity in the arts have gotten a bad rap through the years. Impressionist artist Vincent Van Gogh, who led a troubled life and even cut off his own ear, prompted many people to refer to him as a "mad genius." Some other labels that have been placed on both famous and everyday working artists are lazy, weird, sloppy, self-centered, irresponsible, gay, loners, and broke. You've even probably heard the phrase "starving artist" more than once.

Take a moment now to think about your own views and then bring to mind the most creative people you know. Do they seem "different" to you, or do they fit the "social norm"? What makes them stand out to you? For example, think about how they dress. Do they wear business suits, wild-looking outfits, or something in between? Are they independent thinkers or crowd-followers? Are they risk-takers, or do they play it safe? Get out your idea journal and list the top three to five creative people you know. Next to each name, make a list of their characteristics—both positive and negative. Once you finish with all of their attributes, see if you notice any commonalities.

How you view creative people you know and even those you don't personally know may be a direct reflection of how you see yourself. Or you may fear that if you fully express yourself creatively that others may perceive you in a way that is less than flattering. Perhaps you have a friend who is an artist and while you cherish the friendship, you and others view him as quirky and even foolhardy at times. You might want to emulate his artistry but may subconsciously hold back from your own creativity due to the labels placed upon your friend.

For example, I know someone who held back from painting because when she engaged in that activity, her husband viewed her as being selfish, indulging in an optional activity, and taking time away from the family and him. After explaining that painting helped relieve her stress and that she would actually be more available to her family if she could have this quiet, creative time once a week, he changed his perception and she began pursuing her passion again.

See if there are shifts in your own thinking that need to be made when it comes to your perspective of creative people and yourself as a creative. Your views may already be positive, and if so, good for you! Optimistic, affirmative thoughts will always serve you better. Just make sure to stay aware of any negative stereotypes you might encounter when it comes to creativity.

Common Traits of Creatives

While there is no single recipe for highly creative people, they do share some common "ingredients." Productive creators benefit from having their own creative, colorful traits, starting with an active imagination. As you read through the descriptions of these common traits, take a look at some of the things you do every day and when you're creating to see which characteristics speak to you. You probably have more of these qualities than you realize! You also may notice that there is some overlap among these traits.

Additionally, you may feel you possess some of the opposite traits, and if you do, you fall right in line with the research conducted by author Mihaly Csikszentmihalyi. Csikszentmihalyi has spent more than 30 years researching how creative people live and work and ascertained that most productive creatives appear to be *paradoxical,* which means they exhibit traits that are in extreme opposition to each other. Csikszentmihalyi boils down this observation to one word: complexity.

In other words, you're not alone if you consider yourself to be both spontaneous and a planner, playful and serious, or rebellious and compliant. So keep this contrast in mind as you read through these common creative traits. Regardless of these paradoxical traits, Csikszentmihalyi said the most important quality that creative people consistently express is inherent joy of the creative process for its own sake. I'm guessing that includes you!

 **DEFINITION**

> **Paradoxical** is a way to describe highly producing creatives who display characteristics that are contradictory.

Curious

Curiosity is important to creativity because it expands your way of thinking, opens you up to new possibilities, and invites you to look at the same thing in a new way. When you are curious, you may ask a lot of questions because you're interested in the details—the how and why behind things. You take it upon yourself to investigate matters for the sake of learning and gaining a better understanding. One answer might lead to another question, and another, and another— and the process continues. For example, I think it's safe to assume that anyone who has surfed the internet has had the experience of starting with one web page and then seeing another link and clicking on it, which leads to another and another—all out of a sense of intrigue!

You can cultivate your own curiosity by getting in the habit of asking questions. Practice in both work and personal situations. Listen intently to the answers, which may prompt more questions. Your curiosity will grow with practice, which will help you feel more relaxed as you move out of your comfort zone and into the home of curiosity. You might think asking questions will mean others will judge you as ignorant. Let go of that fear. What it really shows is your interest. Another technique is to not allow yourself to make assumptions. Enter into conversations, books, hobbies, business meetings, and other areas of interest with an enthusiasm to learn as much as you can.

What areas of interest will grow your curiosity? Think about all of those things that light you up like a child—areas of life you truly wonder about—and like a kid, go on a continual quest of asking and exploring. As a truly inquisitive creative, you can take what you learn from your exploration to come up with new ideas, which you can then use as inspiration to pursue creative projects. Don't underestimate your own curiosity!

Risk-Taking

Can you think of occasions when you shared a dubious idea with friends or family members and were discouraged from pursuing it? They may have said words of caution, such as "I'm not sure I'd do that," "You could be opening up a can of worms," or "There's too much risk involved." But you pursued it anyway and found it was the best decision of your life—or not, and you're still willing to step into ambiguity. This kind of risk-taking is among the top traits of highly creative individuals. When you have this trait, you're willing to fail and go beyond the limits of your comfort zone. You know you're putting yourself out there in a way that could be characterized by others as crazy, reckless, or even stupid. However, you also know that if the risk pays off, you could reap plentiful benefits.

Taking risks opens you up to a whole new realm of possibilities, which will enhance your creativity. You can cultivate your risk-taking ability by starting small—engaging in interests or taking action that falls outside of your normal routine. Such behavior may increase your anxiety and stress levels but only to a small degree. For example, if you consider yourself to be the worst dancer in the world, take an introductory line dancing class. You may find it's easier to have friends go with you as an encouraging presence. On the other hand, you may want to go where no one knows you. Either way, if it gets you out of your comfort zone, you'll be strengthening your risk-taking skill.

Taking risks keeps you on your toes compared to being occupied with the "same ol', same ol'." When you push your limits, you have to pay more attention because you're dealing with the unknown. This process can lead to those "a-ha" moments, which will help your creativity come alive. Taking risks can apply to anything you wish to create. For example, one of the greatest risks many people consider at some point in their lives is leaving a job in which they have stability and security to change professions entirely and enter a world of the unknown. What are you willing to do when faced with uncertainty—play it safe or take a leap of faith? Taking risks gives you the opportunity to experience anything from a small success to a whole new chapter in your life. If you always play it safe, you'll limit yourself and your creativity.

INSPIRATIONAL INSIGHT

"Since I reached the conclusion that the essence of the creative person is being in love with what one is doing, I have had a growing awareness that this characteristic makes possible all the other personality characteristics of the creative person: independence of thought and judgment, honesty, perseverance, curiosity, willingness to take risks and the like."

—Paul Torrance

Adventurous

This trait can tie into risk-taking in that you have the courage to explore unfamiliar territory. When you are adventurous, you are not only willing to open yourself up to new experiences, you also thrive on the adrenaline it gives you. This can be important in the creative process. It keeps you enthused and energized and presents you with new ideas and perspectives.

Be proactive in seeking new experiences. Rather than waiting for an invitation from others, spend time with people who have an adventurous spirit. Does anyone come to mind? If you can think of several people, perhaps you could form a "creativity adventure group," whose purpose is to identify new adventures you can enjoy together.

Another idea is to revisit past yearnings you either abandoned midstream or never started. Maybe the timing wasn't right and now's the time to pursue them. If you have a "bucket list"—those things you wish to experience in your lifetime—see if you can do any of the items now. Part of being adventurous is setting the intention to be so and then taking action. All of the thinking and planning won't get you anywhere unless you act.

You don't necessarily have to do something bold like climbing Mount Everest or skydiving. You just need to have a willingness to go beyond your normal boundaries to explore. For example, if you're in a relationship, married or otherwise, make an adventure out of an activity you do on a regular basis, such as going out to dinner and add untried elements to make it different. New adventures often lead you to fresh inspiration, which liberates you to express your creativity in a way that satisfies you like never before.

Resourceful

Most productive creatives are naturally resourceful. Sometimes this trait grows out of a need. For example, if you've ever been short on cash to buy the necessary supplies to make your ideas happen, you find a way to improvise when you're resourceful. You're able to use your ingenuity by thinking divergently to find alternatives that will work just as well, if not better (see Chapter 4 for a refresher on divergent thinking). Beyond that, you use your make-do, can-do attitude to come up with clever ways to meet whatever creative challenges are before you. Whether it's finding suitable substitutes for ingredients in recipes or making purses out of blue jeans that no longer fit, you find an alternative way to make things happen when you have this trait.

To increase your resourcefulness, don't wait for a problem to happen; anticipate different scenarios, especially if you see signs of trouble or undesired outcomes looming. Start viewing problems as opportunities to create solutions. Also, reach out to others. For instance, I've become somewhat of a Mac geek because whenever I encountered a problem with my computer, I called tech support. Through the years, I've learned so much by working with the various technicians that frequently I can figure out the answer myself now.

Being resourceful often means thinking unconventionally, which can lead to innovative solutions. It also can spare you a lot of frustration. There will always be situations that arise that either require or desire a novel approach. The more resourceful you can become, the more this will aid your creativity by giving you more options to explore.

Spontaneous

When you're spontaneous, you're allowing yourself to respond to your impulses, a trait found in many productive creatives. Others may not understand your spur-of-the-moment decisions and may actually label you as irresponsible because you appear to be unstructured in those moments, yet it's often those unplanned instances that lead you to your most creative output. If you feel you are more of a planner and have trouble being spontaneous, take heart. Just as with the other traits, it's possible to develop this one as well.

Fear of making the wrong move or decision is what might keep you from being spontaneous. Try to get to the bottom of your fears and know that you don't have to do anything perfectly (more on that in Chapter 6). Also, examine any beliefs that may be holding you back, such as thinking that planning everything is the responsible thing to do. This will enable you to think more quickly and try more new things.

One way to test this spontaneous mind-set is to give yourself a time limit. For example, if you're the last one to figure out what you want to eat at a restaurant, decide ahead of time that you have two minutes to make your selection and then place your order. You can apply it to different situations, too, such as choosing your outfit for the day, buying a pair of shoes, or answering your co-worker's email. By taking your normal time frame for making decisions and cutting it down, you allow yourself to make decisions without questioning every aspect of them.

There's no question that planning is important to the creative process. However, being spontaneous gives you the freedom to instantly respond to your instincts and whims, which can prove beneficial. You may be breaking from your original plan, but the payoff is often well worth it.

CREATIVITY COMPASS

Cindy had planned a camping vacation in North Carolina. The day came to leave, and she drove from her place of work to the airport. When she got out of her car, she grabbed her purse and then inadvertently locked her keys in the car with her luggage still inside. With her plane departing soon, she didn't have time to have a locksmith unlock her car, so she had to decide on the spot whether to still go on her trip. Even though all she had with her were the dress clothes on her back, her purse, and a boarding pass, she decided to go anyway. This went against her "planning nature," but in the end, she was happy with her decision.

Energetic

Most people who are in the mode of creating on a regular basis are highly energetic when in the midst of a project. When you're feeling vigorous, you're full of life; always on the move; and in shape physically, mentally, and emotionally. Your creative initiative seems to feed itself.

When you're energetic, your mind is usually very active, oftentimes spinning with ideas and how you might advance them. You get lost in what you're doing and it's easy for you to lose all track of time. Sometimes you have to force yourself to take a break because you have so much energy that you find it hard to slow down. You're on a creative roll!

The way you can feel more energetic in the context of creativity is to discover your passions and then embrace them (see Chapter for 11 for more on passion). Doing what you love helps you to feel more alive and vibrant and willing to try new things. Also, taking care of your physical needs—eating properly and getting enough rest—are important to help sustain your energy.

Ambitious

Productive creatives usually demonstrate a high degree of ambition. This means you have a strong desire to pursue your innovative interests and be successful. You're willing to do what it takes to achieve your creative goals and make your dreams come true. You focus on what you want and go after it.

Ambition comes in many forms. For example, I had a friend recently say to me that she didn't think she had much ambition. That's because she was comparing herself to other people who, on the surface, appeared to be more ambitious because of their careers. When I pointed out how enthusiastically she pursued painting and piano lessons, decorating on a regular basis, and trying out new activities, she realized she was more ambitious than she thought. Ambition doesn't always have to relate to a career—just a strong determination to succeed.

This trait overlaps with being energetic because your ambition can stem from finding your passion and then having the exuberance to pursue it. Identifying your passion will help you develop your ambition. If what you're doing is meaningful, you'll be more driven to become absorbed in everything it involves. There are different pictures of creative success. Start by visualizing a mental image of what that means to you and then write down your thoughts to bring clarity to it. Once you have a defined idea of what you want, you can then focus on your creative goals.

 CREATIVITY KEY

Are you ambitious because you're trying to prove to yourself or someone else that you're worthy? This is the dark side of ambition. The bright side of ambition is responding to your motivational drivers and doing what it takes to answer your creative calling and achieve creative success. Your passions fuel your creative ambition.

Rebellious

When you are rebellious as a creative, it's usually because you're striving for originality, which often means ignoring rules, directives, restrictions, instructions, and standards. It's because you want to go to a place where no one else has gone so you can express your creativity in a way that's real and true for you, even if it means standing up for yourself in a way that comes across as headstrong and uncooperative. You break away from others' cherished beliefs in an effort to express purely from your own heart and mind.

In this regard, rebellion is a positive aspect of creativity. To further develop this trait, practice speaking out against something you don't agree with. You can do this respectfully while at the same time maintaining your position, which may be counter to the norm or the other person's point of view. It's a statement that your individual perspective has value. Rebellion is about establishing boundaries and actively saying no to someone's attempt to influence or change you. This is especially valuable when it comes to your own creative expression.

Independent

Not surprisingly, being independent is another common trait of creatives and can overlap with being rebellious. The key difference is rebellion has a lot to do with resisting social norms and outsiders' points of view, whereas being independent is more focused on the freedom to express your creativity in your own way that doesn't necessarily involve opposition. It simply means you take charge of your own life. You enjoy working alone when that's what the situation calls for and when you work within a group, you're still able to maintain your own creative voice.

Being independent means you have a sense of who you really are. You choose to be different as a way to declare your individuality not necessarily in a rebellious fashion, although that's possible. It's more about finding your creativity style and feeling confident and comfortable with what and how you've developed it. This may show in the decisions you make, your work and artwork, and perhaps your personal choices (such as clothing, hairstyle, and overall appearance).

As you begin to work more with your creativity, you will probably begin to feel more independent—not looking so much to others for validation—although feedback can be helpful. A truly independent creative can withstand feedback that is in opposition to his way of doing things because he believes that much in his own creative expression. Independence is about having the freedom to create exactly how you desire.

Sensitive

If you've ever been told "You're so sensitive," you may have felt the need to defend yourself because usually what the other person means is that you are overly sensitive. But there's really no need to apologize or explain. Simply say "thank you," because what this really means is that you easily tune into the beauty that surrounds you, which can translate into magnificent pieces of creativity.

Being sensitive can fill your soul with appreciation and also gives you a greater understanding of others, which again, can only help your creativity. Sensitive creatives can also take their feelings and transform them into inspiring works of art, heartfelt songs, motivational talks, dramatic movies, and more.

One way you can advance this trait is to practice becoming present. This means releasing thoughts about the past and worries about the future and tuning into what's in the here and now. Be in the moment by quieting your mind and becoming aware of your inner feelings, as well as your external surroundings. This allows you to pick up on even the slightest changes in your environment and the people around you. You might pick up on other people's feelings just by observing their body language or facial expressions. Other observations may have to do with sounds, colors, the room temperature, or scents. You can then see if any insights come to you from the sensory information you've gathered. Perhaps they can be applied to a creative project.

Another way to increase your sensitivity is to observe your own feelings in response to what's going on around you. Even if you're not an artist or feel you have little to no artistic ability, draw or paint your feelings. Sing or chant. Write in your idea journal. It's this relaxed, open state of awareness that can lead to innovation. And finally, becoming a better listener—that is, listening to others intently and without judgment—will help you be more empathetic, which ties directly into being sensitive.

Passionate

One reason most active creators have so much energy can be summed up in one word: passion. When you are passionate about an idea, activity, or cause, your emotions light you up. Like a magnet drawing you in, you're attracted to involving yourself as much as possible. Your strong feelings mean you are willing to devote your time, resources, and energy into advancing your passion. It's so important that I've even devoted an entire chapter to the subject (see Chapter 11)!

This passion usually comes from an inner wellspring of feelings that may be related to a past experience, which may have been painful, and therefore something you wish to change for yourself and perhaps others; or your passion may arise from a happy memory that you wish to further enhance. Or you develop a passion for something you've experienced for the first time and you can't wait to learn even more about it. It's like someone just lit a fire underneath you, prompting you to get up and go!

To intensify this trait, notice how you feel about one of your passions, and then see how your feelings change if you could double or triple the feeling. Exaggerate and act it out. For example, if one of your passions is creating art programs for children of single mothers, imagine how you would feel if one of your local programs was so effective it got replicated statewide. Not only would this be an honor, it would probably provide you with even more fuel to continue embracing this passion. Ideas begin in your imagination. Once you've captured that passionate feeling, as long as you're willing to dedicate yourself to the work that's involved with it, there's no limit as to what can happen in the creative process! Also, commit yourself to learning as much as you can about your passion. This could involve speaking with others who share your passion and experts in the field, reading books and articles, researching the topic online, and getting actual hands-on experience.

Playful

Most productive creatives have a keen sense of play. When you're being playful, it's easier to tap into your imagination. When partaking in fun activities, you may even personify the zeal of a child. You're not afraid to act silly and you'll seek out things that make you laugh.

You may have found that when you're all work and no play, your creativity gets thrown off because you're feeling an imbalance. Life has gotten too serious and your inner child is nagging you to come out and play again. If you want to get back on the creative track, you'll listen to this little voice (see Chapter 9 for more on the power of play)!

If you'd like to become more playful, think of what you liked to do as a child and see which activities you can apply to your life today. You can then schedule in playtime in the same you make business appointments. This could mean having a game night and playing board games or more physical games such as Twister, picking one of your favorite sports, or taking your kids or grandchildren to the park. Being playful helps you to loosen up, relax, and not be so serious, which can lead to new insights.

 CREATIVITY KEY

As with everything, there is no one set formula to blend that guarantees that a person will be highly creative. The traits I've listed have risen to the top of various studies, but the beauty of creativity is that regardless of your personality, you have the capacity to be as creative as you allow yourself to be through a level of commitment that you select. I have said or implied repeatedly in this book—you get to decide!

Creative Play: Realizing Your Own Attributes

By now, you have a much greater idea of what traits lend themselves to creativity. In this exercise, you will examine your own attributes.

Tools Needed: Poster board, sticky notes, markers, and decorative materials (such as stickers)

At the top of your poster board, write these words with your favorite-color marker: "Celebrating My Attributes." Make a line down the middle of the board. On the left side of the line, using a different-colored marker, write "Creative Strong Points" and underline it. On the right side of the line, using another-colored mark, write "Areas to Improve" and underline it.

Using yet another-color marker (if you have another one available), write down each of the attributes that best describes you on your sticky notes (write only one trait per square). Include both the positive and challenging traits (those that might be deemed negative or have a downside). You don't have to spend a lot of time thinking of your traits. You know yourself well, yes? Now place the characteristics that you feel best support your creativity on the left side, and place the traits that could detract from your creative efforts on the right side.

Decorate your poster board and then place it in a visible spot at work or at home. Look for ways to strengthen the right side of your board. Eventually, you may feel some of your sticky notes on the right side can be transferred to the left side. Keep working to develop those traits you wish to strengthen and add any attributes you may have inadvertently left out the first time. Now go and celebrate the creative you!

A Look into the Lives of Famous Creatives

Now that you've read about some of the more common traits of creative people, you have a better idea of your own characteristics and what it's going to take to further strengthen them. Because creative people who have become famous share some of these same traits that you and I do, for additional inspiration, I've included a few examples of famous creatives—two modern-day and two from yesteryear—to close this chapter. See what insights you can gain from a brief look at their stories.

Oprah Winfrey

I'll start with one of the most recognized faces and names in the world who can be identified by first name only—Oprah. The multitalented Oprah Winfrey has brought to life more creations than you can even count. Her creativity transformed the basic talk show format where she dared to explore what were once considered "taboo" topics, which falls right in line with the risk-taking trait. She also facilitated the improvement of millions of people's lives as she, along with her expert guests, helped them grow and heal. Her sensitive nature allowed her to make people feel as though they were in the comfort of their own living room, despite the fact that millions of people were actually watching. Her creative juices also opened new avenues in the world of book, online, and magazine publishing, and she has not been afraid to present new, sometimes unpopular, beliefs pertaining to spirituality.

What has made Oprah stand out? Among her attributes are her unrelenting drive to create—representing both ambitious and energetic traits—and her upbeat, positive focus that she extends to others. At the same time, she remains open in her quest to gain a better understanding of others' points of views, whether or not she shares their perspective. As popular as Oprah is, she has had to endure some pretty ugly attacks publicly, which is common among celebrities, yet it hasn't stopped her from creating what she believes in.

Clearly, Oprah exhibits a passion to find and create more beauty in the world. Her worldwide influence is undeniable and yet she was quoted in an article on her own website as saying she didn't think of herself as creative. She acknowledged that she's usually not the one to generate the ideas but that her strength is in making a good idea even better. She also talked about how teaming with other creative souls boosts her creative senses and that her only limitation is within her own mind.

Like Oprah, maybe you don't see yourself as creative, but as you know, taking risks and asserting your independence are important creative traits. Without those, projects may never get off the ground.

INSPIRATIONAL INSIGHT

"This is what all great works of art do: resonate with the artist inside you, no matter how deeply buried that artist might be."

—Oprah Winfrey

Leonardo da Vinci

Now I'm going to take you back in time to the Renaissance period of the fifteenth century to observe the life of Leonardo da Vinci, one of the most prolific and influential creatives ever. As an artist, da Vinci produced two of the most recognized and greatest paintings of all time: the *Mona Lisa* and *The Last Supper*. He generated a vast collection of drawings as well, but his creative talents didn't stop there. His tremendous ambition, energy, and passion allowed him to excel as a sculptor, architect, military engineer, inventor, and scientist, pioneering many discoveries along the way. da Vinci serves as an excellent role model and possessed creative traits you may already have or can develop.

In exploring da Vinci's life, Michael J. Gelb, author of *How to Think Like Leonardo: Seven Steps to Genius,* spoke of da Vinci's traits and ways of being that made him such a creative genius. According to Gelb, da Vinci displayed the following qualities. He had an insatiable curiosity and a continuous quest for learning. As a risk-taker, failure didn't stop him because he was willing to learn from his mistakes, test knowledge through experience, think independently, and persist in his pursuits. He was comfortable with uncertainty and fully examining what appeared to be logically unacceptable. The fact that he was able to make connections among diverse phenomena that were not apparent to others further points to the trait of being independent.

Read through each of those traits again, slowly, and see if you feel in alignment with any of them. Think of how each of them may apply to your overall life and then specifically to your creative interests and efforts. You don't have to be a genius to take ownership of these attributes; you just have to be willing to open yourself up to the possibilities they hold and to pursue them.

J. K. Rowling

J. K. Rowling's *Harry Potter* books are now the best-selling series in history, according to an online article in *The Telegraph*. In 2008, she delivered a Harvard commencement address, "The Fringe Benefits of Failure, and the Importance of Imagination," that revealed some of what makes her tick. During the talk, she showed her sensitivity by admitting her struggle between her own aspirations and what her parents expected of her.

Not surprisingly, her only interest was in writing novels, and if you've read any of them, you know that her sense of adventure comes through in dramatic fashion. During the address, she went on to say that her parents appreciated her "overactive imagination" but were concerned that she wouldn't be able to financially make it as a writer due to their own financial challenges and lack of a higher education. However, Rowling's greatest fear wasn't being poor—ironically, it was failure, a creative block that will be fully discussed in the next chapter. Seven years after she graduated, she actually described her life as failure on an "epic scale"—the "biggest failure I knew." She hit rock bottom.

Rowling was able to start her upward creative climb by getting back in touch with her true passion by pouring all of her energy into writing. Despite her parents' concerns, she took a risk, which everyone now knows paid off handsomely. According to an online article in *The Telegraph*, she wrote her initial Potter ideas on a napkin on a delayed train from Manchester to London in 1990, which shows her resourcefulness. Ambition and energetic traits also are apparent with the success she had and continues to enjoy.

One important lesson from her story based on her creative traits is that those who don't use their imaginations remain in their own comfort zone as opposed to those who dare to see new images and conjure up new thoughts. Doing this may invoke fear, but it's well worth the journey.

 INSPIRATIONAL INSIGHT

"We do not need magic to change the world, we carry all the power we need inside ourselves already: we have the power to imagine better."

—J. K. Rowling

Albert Einstein

For a final look at a famous creative, consider Albert Einstein, one of the most influential, brilliant physicists of the twentieth century. He never stopped questioning due to his unquenchable curiosity. It was this passionate thirst for knowledge and answers that helped lead him to his success. In an article on the HealthResearchFunding.org website, Einstein was also described as a playful man who sometimes presented as mischievous as well. His playfulness manifested as a violinist (since age 6) and how he preferred performing to practicing.

He also depended largely on music for his scientific insight and intuition and saw a connection between music and science, which points to his independent thinking. Had he not been a physicist, he would have loved being a musician, as he saw his life as music, according to Michele and Robert Root-Bernstein in a *Psychology Today* online article. When asked about his theory of relativity, he is quoted as saying "The theory of relativity occurred to me by intuition, and music is the driving force behind this intuition."

An obvious risk-taker, Einstein said, "Failure is success in progress." In his initial stages of finding solutions to problems, he used visual images rather than logical symbols, words, or mathematical equations, another example of his independent thinking and resourcefulness. Only in his secondary translation step did he try to express his findings in words.

As you can see, imagination can apply to anything and everything. What can you take away from Einstein's perspectives? Does it change your view of how to think about systematic or technical subjects?

The Least You Need to Know

- There are many stereotypes about creative people. Take the time to examine your own views to see if these are based on any facts or simply your own perception.
- Highly creative individuals are a study in paradox. They often exhibit traits that contradict each other. In a word, they are complex.
- Productive creatives, whether they are well known or not, possess a lot of the same traits, including being insatiably curious, adventurous, spontaneous, imaginative, passionate, playful, and willing to take risks.

Locked in the "Creativity Closet"

There are countless numbers of reasons why you may feel stuck in the "creativity closet." Perhaps you're feeling a lack of confidence, time, or resources. Maybe your thoughts are preventing you from taking action. Or it could be you're feeling too old, too young, too vulnerable, or too inexperienced.

While it's still possible to create with walls surrounding you, you will enjoy your creative journey much more and fulfill its potential once you break through them. Better yet, replacing your blocks with keys to that closet will be even more pleasant and productive! In this chapter, you learn about some of the most common reasons that prevent creative flow, which will help you identify your own blocks.

In This Chapter

- How the "lack mentality" can limit you
- Obstacles based on fear
- Going beyond the negative voices

What's Keeping You Stuck?

You now know that creativity can be learned and is not reserved for the elite few. However, there may be times where you feel that something is holding you back from being creative. Perhaps you have experienced bursts of creativity in the past and feel stuck now. Or maybe you feel you have yet to tap into your true, creative nature. There may be one primary reason driving your blocks or multiple reasons. Your challenges may be temporary and recent or feel more permanent and date back to your childhood. Situations vary, but what remains the same for every one is the importance of identifying your blocks. Consciously recognizing your obstacles is the first step in moving through the clutter in your "creativity closet" before finding your way out.

Some suggestions will be made to begin working to eradicate your blocks, but the primary purpose of this chapter is to first recognize them by being honest and authentic with yourself. As you explore some of the more common reasons for feeling uninspired, take notes on those that resonate most with you, as this will help you get in touch with your barriers. In some cases, you may find yourself feeling defensive and making comments such as "Oh, that's not me." Beware of any "knee-jerk" reactions. While it's possible your initial reaction is accurate, it's also possible the words have revealed a sore that needs healing, like a bandage that's fallen off and causes you to look directly at the wound.

Once you've identified your blocks, you can then explore the ideas, techniques, and tools to overcome your obstacles found in later chapters. In the end, it's all about freeing yourself to be creative. I promise—I won't leave you locked in the creativity closet!

When What You Have Is Not Enough

This grouping of possible blocks has one thing in common: perceiving or actually lacking what you need to be creative. It even could be that you, yourself, perceive you aren't good enough. I call it the *lack mentality*. A good example of this is the cliché of seeing the glass half empty instead of half full. Instead of seeing the possibilities of what you can do, you look at what you can't do because you think you don't have enough time, money, ability, confidence, or any number of other things you think are necessary for creativity. See if any of these blocks strike a chord with you.

The Time Trap

Whether your creativity happens within your job, at home, or both, poor time management can become a real stumbling block. This creative block has a lot to do with perception. The truth is, everyone has the same amount of time each day. It's a matter of how you use your time and being aware of how you manage—or mismanage—it. (After all, most of us know what it feels like to waste time!) Saying you don't have enough time can be a way to excuse yourself from not engaging in the creative process. Therefore, I suggest you take a deeper look at these time traps and see if they apply to you.

One major time thief for a large number of people these days is technology. Engaging with social media—such as Facebook, Twitter, Pinterest, and Instagram—can quickly become an addiction. Pouring through an overflowing email inbox also can consume an inordinate amount of your time. So it's crucial to check in with yourself to see just how much time you spend online, whether it's with email, surfing the internet, or making and reading posts.

Another way people waste time is with mismanaged downtime. Watching television, spending time with family, gossiping, reading—the list is endless. Not all of the things on your list are time-wasters, particularly spending quality time with family; however, even family time may require setting boundaries. It's also possible that your daily life is so packed there is no room left to add anything more. You may be at a point in your life when it's not practical (for example, perhaps you just had a baby).

Time also becomes an issue when you're dealing with personal problems that go beyond the usual everyday challenges. Examples are dealing with a divorce, a serious health matter, or money issues. Your time and attention can become wrapped up in your emotions, which makes it difficult to prioritize your creative interests.

If you feel a lack of time serves as a block for you, I recommend you seriously explore where you're spending your precious moments by keeping a time log that tracks your time and then evaluating your findings. By taking an honest inventory of how you spend your day, you'll probably see that you find the time to do things that are really important to you. Make being creative one of those important things. Also, taking on a new activity may be the very thing that will help get you out of your rut. I know for myself, when I'm in the midst of a personally troubling situation, the worst thing I can do is nothing. Taking action helps move me forward, even if it's just taking baby steps. That doesn't mean I'm at my creative best, but it does mean I'm going in the right direction. And for those stressful issues that eat up a lot of time, it's important to seek the support of family and friends, a therapist, or a spiritual counselor. If you can get enough support, you will begin to shift your focus and create the space you need to engage in some form of creativity, however small.

 CREATIVITY COMPASS

> Over the course of a summer I spent outside of my home state, I wrote the first draft of a book by longhand. When summer ended and I returned home, I knew the next step was to type the handwritten pages. I enthusiastically began this process, but rather quickly, I told myself I didn't have enough time due to having too many other responsibilities. Later, I realized that wasn't the problem at all. It actually was resistance to editing and rewriting, which I knew would surely become part of the process and could consume me. Like me, if you want to get past your creative barriers, always explore what's really at the core of them!

Fighting with Finances

Do you ever catch yourself saying "I can't afford that" or "I'd love to but I don't have the money"? Sure, if you want to make jewelry and start off with platinum and diamonds, those statements may actually be true. In reality, creativity doesn't have to cost a lot of money or any cash at all. Of course, that depends on your creativity goals, interests, and most importantly, your beliefs. Did you grow up with the belief that you should only spend money on things you *need*—that something like art supplies is a luxury? If that's the case, is it possible for you to trace this belief to someone or something in your past? Perhaps you grew up in a household where scarcity thinking was commonplace or deep down you don't believe you deserve to spend money on creative pursuits.

For example, I once had a client tell me that he really wanted to take guitar lessons but they were too expensive. I asked him how much the lessons cost and he couldn't tell me because he hadn't actually made calls to any teachers to find out. He made an assumption that he couldn't afford lessons. During our next coaching session, he told me he contacted a teacher and learned the lessons weren't as pricey as he had thought, and he booked his first lesson.

As you can see, sometimes it just takes that little nudge to go beyond your assumptions or beliefs. This block is no different than the others. Get to the root of it, rip it out, and plant new seeds!

Perfectionism = Procrastination

Expecting perfection is actually a form of procrastination because it can paralyze you in your tracks. You won't even take the first step if you tell yourself "I'm not good enough," "I haven't been formally trained," or "I need to practice more until I can wow my supporters." Your rational, logical mind knows that perfection isn't really possible, yet you may find yourself placing these unrealistic expectations upon yourself.

Even if you don't consider yourself to be a perfectionist, or perhaps you're a "recovering perfectionist," you may still hear these voices or similar declarations in your head as you seek to have your high standards matched by your present capabilities. You feel there's a gap between the two, and this alone can hold you back. For example, if you find yourself picturing a project in your mind's eye and you don't think you have the skills to achieve that vision, chances are you won't even take the first step. On the other hand, it's possible you allow yourself to create but upon finishing the project, you are so dissatisfied with your results that you destroy your creation entirely.

If you consider yourself to be a perfectionist, it may seem counterintuitive to lower your standards. The question is: Is it more important to create something—anything—that you can continue to work on and improve, or would you rather not create at all if it can't be perfect? Embracing the former gives you the freedom to keep working, because you're not holding out for an idea that's perfect from the get-go. It's not about making something subpar; it's about holding yourself to reasonable standards so you can accomplish your goals.

> **CREATIVITY KEY**
>
> Strive for excellence, not perfection. In doing so, you can still aim high and at the same time set reasonable expectations for yourself. If you know you are truly doing your best, you can't top that!

Colliding with Confidence

Whether you're a professional creative or a hobbyist, you may suffer from a lack of confidence. The causes vary, but if you don't believe in yourself or feel uncertain of what you are capable of undertaking, these feelings may be enough to immobilize you and keep you locked in the creativity closet. This block could be tied to the previous one of perfectionism because you set expectations of yourself so high that when you don't achieve that level, it dings your confidence yet again.

It's important to look at the reasons behind this block. You may doubt yourself because you don't have formal training with the creative interest you wish to pursue. For example, if you have a desire to paint but have never taken the first painting class, you may feel too blocked to purchase the necessary supplies because you're not even sure what you should buy! Or perhaps you're a self-taught musician and are afraid someone may ask you about your musical background. You don't want to admit that you haven't taken any lessons because you're afraid the person may view you differently than they would a trained musician. In actuality, you may be a better musician than those who have been taught by instructors; however, because your confidence is low, your creativity suffers.

It's normal to question yourself from time to time—it's when these insecure feelings are so strong and frequent that they jeopardize your creativity. In order to be creative, you must learn to find that confidence and accept that while there will be times when you don't know everything, that's okay.

"I'm Too (Fill in the Blank)"

How did you fill in this blank? Too old, too young, too inexperienced, too fat, too thin, too stupid, too poor, or something else? In this case, the "lack" has to do with not having or no longer having what's necessary to be creative. This is one of those blocks that really is more a matter of the mind than a rock-solid block.

For example, I once had a friend who was interested in photography tell me that she was too old to learn how to use computer software to retouch her pictures. I asked her, "How old will you be in a year if you take a class to learn this program?" She replied, "I'll be 60." I continued, "And how old will you be in a year if you don't take the class?" I made my point. That old saying—"Age is a matter of the mind. If you don't mind it, it won't matter."—applies here.

Or take the case of singer Susan Boyle, who could have told herself "I'm too shy to perform publicly" or "I don't have the looks to be a singing star" but didn't. Instead, she took to the stage to sing on the UK television show *Britain's Got Talent* and stunned the judges with her modest appearance, powerful voice, and heartfelt performance. Within days, videos of her surfaced on the internet and she became an overnight sensation. Apparently her desire was stronger than her self-described shyness.

So take a hard look at the "I'm too" excuses you are telling yourself. You deserve to pursue your dreams!

 CREATIVITY COMPASS

Louise Hay didn't let age stop her from following her heart's desire. She founded a publishing company at around age 60. Today, her company, Hay House Publishing, is one of the leading publishers of spiritually oriented books and materials. It just goes to show you're never too old to strive for your goals!

Facing Your Fears

The thread that ties this group of blocks together is fear. As you go through these creative blocks, consider the acronym FEAR: False Evidence Appearing Real. In each case, the fear is "false evidence" that has been generated by yourself and those who influence you with their own fears (such as family members and even well-meaning friends). Read through each one and see if any of them hits you right in the gut. That's a sure sign it's a block that needs removing.

Fear of Failure

Fear of failure ties directly into some of the challenges that I have already addressed. It can stem from a lack of confidence, comparing yourself to others, perfectionism, hanging onto past letdowns, and being critical of yourself. This block of fearing what will happen if you don't succeed can happen at any stage of the creative process. If it happens at the beginning, you may not even get started. Fear may also strike right in the middle or near the end of your project and make you put all of your tools away and stop. Or after working through your doubts along the way, the fear may return as you are just completing the finishing touches, stifling your final step.

It's one thing to recognize you have fear; however, it's critical to get to the bottom of where the fears are coming from. Are the fears rational and tied to one or many experiences from your past? Do they involve other people, or are you trapped alone in the "critic's corner"?

One way to look at your fear of failure is to ask yourself, "What is the worst that could happen if I did, indeed, fail with this effort?" In my experience, the worst usually doesn't happen; the fear itself tends to be greater than any failure. Another way to think about failure is to consider how it can be a learning experience. If you can learn lessons to apply to your next creative effort, a failed project will not have been done in vain. Finally, get a handle on your definition of success and failure. Are you setting yourself up for failure because you've set your expectations exceedingly high?

Sometimes it's a matter of how you view the situation that determines whether you've succeeded or failed. For example, prolific inventor Thomas Edison is credited with over 1,000 patents, but he also went through more than 10,000 attempts to produce a commercially acceptable light bulb before finally succeeding. To that experience, he is quoted as saying, "I have not failed 10,000 times. I have not failed once. I have succeeded in proving that those 10,000 ways will not work. When I have eliminated the ways that will not work, I will find the way that will work." As you can see, if you don't fear the worst and treat any failure as just another step toward your goal, you can find great creative success.

CREATIVITY KEY

Eliminate the word *failure* from your creative vocabulary. Recognize when things don't go as planned, the unanticipated result is just another step in the creative process.

Fear of Success

The flip side of the failure block is fear of success. You may be inhibited before you ever come close to achieving your potential because the fear alone stops you from creating or executing your ideas. This could come from being afraid you won't be able to handle what you imagine comes with success, such as less privacy and high expectations that could be placed upon you by others. You may also fear some will see you as a fraud or that others will become jealous of you and stop being friends with you.

Your fear could also come from enjoying early success; you want to continue pushing forward but wonder if the best is already behind you. For example, you've probably heard the saying, "one-hit wonders," when referring to bands or singer-songwriters who become well known for a smash single, only to have no commercial success that follows; they weren't able to capture the same success as that first hit. Another example of this is authors who have had best-sellers who worry that their next book won't be able to live up to the expectations of their readers. In both cases, it's based on fear of being a disappointment since the previous success was so great.

Whatever the case, success really is a matter of definition. If your goal is to perform on Broadway and you never make it past community theater, will you see yourself as a failure for not having accomplished that goal or as a success for giving it your all and enjoying the process? It's important to define what success means to you and avoid allowing outside forces to determine your level of accomplishment.

Risk or Routine?

Uncertainty is built into creativity and falls right in line with fear of success or failure. Ambiguity goes with any new territory you're exploring because you're venturing into the unknown. Do you look at that unfamiliar landscape as challenging but exciting, or does it present too much risk for you, so much so that you don't pursue your idea or project? How much assurance do you need before you can begin? Perhaps you get started with your new project but you falter a bit when risk rears its ugly head once again.

Part of why taking risks can be uncomfortable is because it's easy to get married to your daily routines. They feel safe because you do them every day and you know what to expect. How can you get past this? As discussed under fear of failure, you can play the "What's the worst that can happen?" game, knowing the negative outcomes you imagine probably won't happen. You can also change your perspective on failure to be more like Thomas Edison and start making small changes in your routine so when change presents itself, you will be more comfortable. After all, getting comfortable with uncertainty is part of the creative process (see Chapter 7 for more on this concept).

Rejection ... Again

Rejection can tie into failure and success and comes in many forms. You bake what you think is the most scrumptious dessert, only to notice that your guests leave most of it on their plates. You interview for a job that ends up being offered to another candidate. You direct a ballet that gets panned by the local newspaper's critic. You present your boss with an idea you're excited about, only to have it shot down.

These examples and countless others are a part of life. It's your reaction to rejection that counts. Are you letting past criticisms stop you from pursuing new ideas because you're afraid you'll be dismissed again? If you stop being creative because of those rejections, you're stifling your true self. Rejection doesn't have to be the end; instead, it can be a stepping stone to a better opportunity.

All About Anxiety

As psychotherapist, creativity coach, and author Eric Maisel once put it, "The greatest block to aliveness is anxiety." Regardless of where you are creatively, you've probably experienced a certain amount of anxiety in your life. Anxiety can manifest in different ways. For example, Grammy Award–winning singer-songwriter Carly Simon has suffered for years from stage fright so debilitating that she once reportedly collapsed in front of 10,000 fans at a concert in the 1980s. She went on to perform publicly, but it's a safe assumption that her anxiety has limited her public appearances. Your own nervousness may have revolved around a creative effort or around something unrelated, such as health. However, like all creative blocks, anxiety is only a block if you don't know how to manage it.

 INSPIRATIONAL INSIGHT

"In its negative aspect anxiety blocks the artist, causes her to limit her scope or create second-rate work, and more. In its so-to-speak positive aspect it is like the itching that accompanies the healing of a wound: horribly uncomfortable, but proof that creativity is happening."

–Eric Maisel

Again, recognition is key. Noticing that you are experiencing anxiety will allow you to take the first step in quieting your concerns. Delve into the root of your worries and think about how you have dealt with them before. Does your anxiety revolve around a specific creative task or does it pervade your entire existence? There's a key difference, and knowing the answer to this will help you move through it so your creativity is not threatened as a result. In the end, Maisel believes anxiety is an expected part of the creation process and that you must actually invite it in. So if anxiety is your block, you goal shouldn't be to completely eliminate it; you should work toward creating in spite of it.

The Comparison Game

One of the most deadly games you can play in thwarting your creativity is when you start comparing yourself to others. There are several ways in which this can work.

The first way is in observing another person's creativity and thinking that you couldn't possibly attain their level of achievement. When you compare yourself to others and are feeling "less than," it's easy to forget that you have talents of your own and may have been recognized for them. Comparing yourself to someone who has less skill or experience also can lead to damaging outcomes. You may develop a false sense of security and then get knocked down when you enter the comparison game again and encounter someone you perceive is better than you are. It doesn't matter if you're comparing yourself to those you feel are "more than" or "less than"—either way, this becomes a diversion and takes you away from confidently filling your own creative space.

Another part of the game is being critical of those who are actually out there creating. You may go to an art show and view an artist's work and think, "Well, that's not very creative. I could do better than that." And you may be right. You then realize the difference is that person had the courage to create and share her work and you're still feeling stuck and not doing anything to further your creativity. If you find you are comparing yourself to others through judgment, take note. It's just another way to prevent you from exercising your creativity.

The truth is, there are a variety of skill levels. If you continue to compare yourself to others, you will remain blocked, either in the sense of not creating at all or not feeling good about what you are creating. So while it's a common practice to look at what others in your field are doing, observing and taking notes on their technique or their tools is different than comparing. If you can learn from them or be inspired by them, that's positive. It's when you monitor another person's talents, weigh hers against your own perceived abilities, and use that as the decisive measure of your abilities that you become the pawn in this game. Remember, opt for observing over comparing. You don't have to be at the level of Ludwig van Beethoven or Meryl Streep to appreciate your own creative talents!

 CREATIVITY COMPASS

During a creativity coaching session with my client Austin, he expressed how inadequate he felt as a guitarist while watching other musicians perform. "They make it look so effortless as their fingers run up and down the fret board," he said. "Then I think to myself, 'Why bother? I'll never be that good.'" It took some time to work through his doubts, but eventually he got to a place where he remembered that many of his fans have approached him after a performance and complimented him on his singing and songwriting talents. He also realized that comparing himself to others only diminished his creativity.

The Past Hasn't Passed

In my experience of facilitating creativity classes with small groups, there are always a few people who have allowed themselves to be stuck for years because they remember a parent, teacher, classmate, or friend who once told them they weren't creative or criticized their work in some way. Take Nathaniel, who completed what he felt was a work of art at the vulnerable age of 8 and couldn't wait to show his mother, who said, "Oh honey, that's a nice try, but you're not the artist in the family. Your brother is." From that moment on, Nathaniel stopped creating, until decades later, when he worked through this memory.

Can you recall a time in your life when your creative spirit was dampened because of a discouraging or derogatory comment that someone made to you about something you created? Search your memory bank to see if you are still carrying around any negative childhood experiences. Next, check in to see if more recent memories are clogging your creativity. In the end, you'll find it's not the actual memory of what happened; it's your judgment of that memory that has blocked you creatively. Your history doesn't have to be part of your creative biography. The sooner you can let those harmful memories go, the sooner you will emerge from the creativity closet!

Critic's Corner

Ah, yes, the critic's corner. This block has to do with fear based on criticism. It is comprised of both the outer critic and the inner critic. Let's start with the outer critic, who is good at judging others' creativity output even though she may not have the first clue about the particular project or subject. Sometimes the outer critic comes disguised as a friend. You would think the "jealous" sign on her forehead would give her away, yet somehow you fail to see it and you let her criticism bother you. Maybe someone else then comes along and tries to advise you how you could have handled your creative project differently. The feelings of disapproval are enough to shut you down.

Hearing constructive criticism from a qualified person is another matter altogether, but negative feedback can still be hard to hear, especially if you're new to creating. The question for you to answer is whether you have allowed criticism from others to stop you or slow you down from creating.

The other part of the critic's corner is the inner critic, or that familiar place that resides inside of you where you do everything from censoring to chiding yourself. How many times have you condemned yourself for not living up to your own expectations or someone else's? While "condemn" may be too strong of a word for you (or it may fit what you do to yourself perfectly), at the very least, you've probably figuratively slapped yourself on the wrist thinking you should have known better and done better. The inner critic repeats the old adage, "Woulda, coulda, shoulda," using 20/20 hindsight to tell you what you accomplished wasn't correct or good enough.

However, telling yourself "I should have" after the fact doesn't help you unless you can take what you've learned from the experience and apply it to your next effort. You must learn to recognize the difference between beating yourself up and recognizing the hidden jewels in the mine that you just unearthed in order to quiet that inner critic.

CREATIVITY COMPASS

I remember submitting one of the most heartfelt songs I had ever written to an online radio station. I went into it feeling anxious because the song had such personal meaning to me. When I found out the song had not been accepted, I reviewed the reasons. One was simply a personal opinion and the other had to do with recording quality. I knew I could correct the latter issue, but there was nothing I could do about this person's opinion. Initially, this held me back, but ultimately I did not allow that experience to keep me from continuing to write highly personal songs and sharing them with others.

Creative Play: Breathing into Your Awareness

This exercise will help you to calm down and become more aware of what's keeping you stuck. The ideal time to do this is when you think about starting or continuing a creative project and do not take action. Before you begin, read through the instructions, because you will be conducting the first three steps with your eyes closed.

Tools Needed: Paper, a writing instrument, and a willingness to be still and honest with yourself!

1. Close your eyes and begin taking deep breaths. Slowly inhale and hold for three seconds before exhaling slowly. Do this at least five times.

2. Once you get to a place of stillness and peace, continue to be conscious of your breath while inhaling and exhaling normally.

3. Begin to notice what feelings come up. Fear? Your inner critic? A voice from your past? Continue until you feel you have tapped into the real reasons that you are not taking action.

4. Once you feel complete, write down everything that comes to mind, making sure to be as specific as possible. Remember, awareness is one of the first keys to unlocking your creativity!

Keep this list handy because you will be using it to find solutions when you go through Part 3 of the book.

Getting Beyond the Negative Voices in Your Head

As you can see from the different creative blocks I've presented, a lot of what keeps people stagnated is contained within their own heads. While you may have one voice telling you that you're good enough, at the same time, another voice may be discouraging you by saying, "That's great, but you're too busy to take on that creative project." There are two ways you may develop your negative thoughts:

Self-imposed: This is when you trick your mind into thinking negative thoughts that lead you astray because they are based on assumptions that hold no truth. You continue to repeat the same old story in your head, and possibly aloud to others, and it becomes an illusion. An example of this is Mary and Michelle. Their parents praised Mary for being smart and Michelle for being pretty. They never told Michelle that she wasn't smart, but she made an assumption that she couldn't be both pretty and smart. That negative thought became her self-imposed illusion, and the voice in her head continues to tell her "I may be pretty but I'm not smart enough to do that."

Influenced by others: This is when you develop negative thoughts as a result of what other people from your past have said to you or taught you, such as parents, siblings, teachers, well-meaning (or not so well-meaning) friends, or childhood bullies. Take the example of Jed, who was brought up in a family where only his mom and sisters spent time in the kitchen cooking and baking while his father taught him how to repair cars. Jed formed a perception that only girls cook and he dismissed his secret dream of becoming a chef. The voice in his head says "It doesn't matter if you want to be a chef. Girls belong in the kitchen. Not you!" Perceptions also can form based on society's views.

Do you recognize these types of voices? When you hear them, how much credibility do you give them? You may not always know if your thoughts were solely self-imposed or influenced by others because it's impossible to know what may be hidden in your subconscious mind. In fact, it's possible the negative voices come from a combination of the two. To start getting beyond these illusions and perceptions, I think it's important to understand how deeply rooted they are and then trust in yourself and get help from others, if necessary, in order to banish those thoughts.

Deep Rooted or Temporary?

Which of the creative blocks were most relevant to you? Could you relate to more than one? Can you name other reasons that were not discussed here that are preventing you from creating? Exploring the different areas is important, as is determining if your challenges are deep rooted or temporary. Deep rooted means you've gone beyond the negative voice in your head into more serious issues that include phobias, panic attacks, or feeling physically ill whenever you think about a particular endeavor, such as public speaking. Or your block may date back to your childhood and you notice certain memories trigger a strong sensation, either emotionally or physically, that is hard to overcome. Working through a more profound block may require the services of a therapist or a professional who is trained in assisting with clearing the subconscious mind.

A temporary block is more situational and feels lighter, more fleeting, and easier to work through. When a creative opportunity is presented to you, you may initially feel you're not capable, you are too stressed, or you don't have enough time. The thought may overwhelm you, but eventually you're able to work through those feelings and move forward. It's common for a fear to pop up here and there. It's also not unusual to procrastinate at times. It's when any of these barriers keeps you permanently locked in the creativity closet that it's time to take a serious look.

I Admit It When I'm Right!

I hope that line brought a smile to your face. It's a statement that my brother-in-law, Ed, likes to say, and it usually strikes people as funny because they're expecting him to say "I admit it when I'm wrong!" This small bit of humor makes the point that you do not have to buy into other people's beliefs about you or the self-imposed illusions that have plagued you. You know what's right for you—now admit it. And smile when you say that!

There are several ways to start ridding yourself of negative voices and getting more of a sense of what's right for you. Expect to go through a trial-and-error process as you work through your blocks and engage in new and different creative activities. Don't automatically cast away a project that doesn't go smoothly. Frustration may enter into the picture, especially if you're learning something new. If you can work through that, you may feel a tremendous sense of accomplishment once you do. If your creative endeavor is giving you energy rather than taking it away from you and no block emerges (or if one does, you quickly work through it), you'll likely hear a positive voice whisper in your ear. In the end, the most important thing you can do to dismiss those negative thoughts is to trust yourself.

 INSPIRATIONAL INSIGHT

"Keep away from people who try to belittle your ambitions. Small people always do that, but the really great ones make you feel that you, too, can become great."

—Mark Twain

Creative Play: Breaking Through Your Barriers

This is a method you can use when you want to get a handle on your blocks to creativity.

Tools Needed: Paper and a writing instrument

First, pick an idea, interest, or project you have been thinking about doing or have already begun but are feeling stuck. Once you've done that, make a list of the barriers you believe are keeping you from moving forward. (You can refer to the blocks outlined in this chapter or write down others you have uncovered.) Next to each block, write down the reasons you feel this is a block, regardless of how insignificant or unreasonable they seem. If you're feeling them, they're real to you.

Next, using the logical or left side of your brain, think of rational ways of dealing with your fears, anxieties, or other blocks and write them down. Now step away from your list and go do something fun that has nothing to do with this project. It could be as simple as putting on your favorite piece of upbeat music and singing along into a hair brush that serves as your microphone (one of my favorites) or going for a walk in nature.

When you've taken some time away, return to your list, and off the top of your head, write down all of the thoughts that come to you. Next, write down ways to overcome your blocks, even if they seem "outrageous." If you're a parent, think about how you would encourage your child. Or picture yourself as an elementary school teacher compassionately helping a student. In other words, be gentle with yourself!

Finally, weigh in to see if you feel differently now and have been able to decrease or eliminate the reasons that were keeping you stuck. Better yet, are you now inspired to begin your creative process? Note that this exercise, in and of itself, is a creative process. That's a start!

The Least You Need to Know

- Identifying and getting to the root of your barriers is the first step to breaking through them. They may be temporary or deep rooted.

- Beware of any defensive reactions when looking at your blocks. You may not want to admit to yourself that you haven't overcome a particular challenge, yet getting to the bottom of it may be the key to getting you to move forward.

- Appreciate where you are with your creative efforts presently without comparing your level of skill, energy, and talents to others.

- Don't be surprised if a block you dealt with in the past surfaces again later. That's a normal part of the creative process. Notice it and deal with it as quickly as possible to continue moving forward.

PART

3

Finding Your Keys to Creativity

Now that you have taken a closer look at what's keeping you stuck in the creativity closet, you will be given various keys to unlock the door. In reality, there is only one key—and that lies within you. However, that key is not always easy to find. Sometimes it gets lost in the twists and turns of your internal labyrinth with all of its secret and unexpected passageways. Part 3 is all about finding a comfort level with your creative expression and making new discoveries.

This part begins by offering suggestions on how you can overcome your blocks, such as by reframing your viewpoint and considering the different ways to accomplish that. You also learn tips to open your mind to more innovative possibilities; that way, you can get your wheels turning about how you can establish your ideal creative space. I also give you a smorgasbord of appetizers to give you a taste of what creativity feels like when you incorporate simple practices in your life. You then get to try out some unusual as well as common creative thinking techniques that you may have forgotten about or stopped using. This part also gives you ways to tune in to your passions and explores how hobbies can advance your creativity. This part ends with the benefits of creating with others. After all, creativity is often enhanced when shared with a partner, a group of people, or the community at large.

Reframing Your Viewpoint

You can breathe a sigh of relief now that you've made it through that last chapter and identified your blocks. But you can't stop there; it's time to start working through them. By doing this, you prime yourself to experience the wonderful world of your own creativity!

In this chapter, I give you tips for getting past your personal blocks. I also take you through how you can foster creative freedom and how to understand the beliefs surrounding your own creativity. I finish by giving you ways to bolster yourself with some affirmations.

In This Chapter

- Suggestions for overcoming your blocks
- Getting in the right frame of mind to be creative
- How to use affirmations to shift your thinking
- How creativity redefines your life

Overcoming Your Obstacles

Becoming more self-aware is sometimes a process people avoid. It can bring up painful memories that many don't wish to revisit. However, if the last chapter triggered unpleasant, forgettable, or regrettable stories from your past, that's actually a good thing. Why? Because they're tied into the obstacles on your path to creativity. Being aware they are there is the first step. Now that they've risen to the surface, it's time to sweep them away entirely! The following are some suggestions for getting past your blocks.

Setting Your Priorities

If I had to identify one statement I've heard more than any other in my creativity coaching practice and in my own head, it would be "I wish I could but I don't have enough time." As I pointed out in the last chapter, the number of seconds in a day remains constant. What it really boils down to is the choices you make, which are based on your priorities.

Sometimes the things you deem as most important are done so out of a need. For example, in this physical world, everyone needs a certain amount of money to pay his bills. Unless you have achieved financial independence and have all the money you'll ever need, doing what it takes to generate income is probably a high priority. Choosing to work is the responsible thing to do. However, you may also have priorities that aren't necessarily critical to your most basic needs of food and shelter but are highly important to you. For example, if you're a parent, caring for your children would be high on your priority list. Or maybe staying physically fit or spending time daily in prayer is essential to you.

Where does your creative expression fit in? Only you can make that determination. However, don't think of creativity as something to slot into a schedule; instead, think of it as something you either give (or don't give) priority to. If one of the ways you would like to express yourself creatively is painting but you're not doing it because you don't think you have enough time, shift your statement from "I'm not painting because I don't have enough time" to "I'm not painting because I have chosen to spend my time on other things." That's what is really true—not that you're lacking time. Sure, a lot of people wish there could be more hours in a day, but even if that were so, chances are, you would still be wishing for even more time.

 CREATIVITY KEY

Stop telling yourself the lie that you don't have enough time to be creative. If it's important enough to you, you will find the time. That's what commitment is all about. Even if it means squeaking out 15 minutes here and there, that's a start!

Once you've reframed how you see time in terms of priorities, take a hard look at all of the things in your life that are essential. Are you filling your time with these priorities? Or—and this is a significant question—are you spending time on things that really aren't all that important? Again, you're the only person who can answer that. Just know that bypassing your creative opportunities is not because you don't have time; it's because you have chosen to prioritize other things above it, whether they're actually meaningful and vital or not.

The same principle applies to the other areas you perceive are lacking. In keeping with the painting example, it may be true you don't have the money to go buy an expensive set of artistic painting supplies, but what can you afford? What is really necessary to get started? Maybe it doesn't have to cost you anything if you pair up with a friend who would be willing to share his materials. Bartering—where you exchange something of value that you have with another person and they, in return, give you something they have that you desire—is a great way to get you started and perhaps keep you going. Or if you feel you lack the skills necessary to pursue your creative interests, how much is it worth to you to develop your abilities? Are you willing to give up or spend less time in another area of your life to do that? Again, it comes down to your priorities. No matter what it is you feel you're lacking, none of it will change unless you place a high-enough value on your creative expression. Simply put: think priorities, not time.

Creative Play: Examining Your Priorities

Tools Needed: Paper and a writing instrument

First, think about the top five priorities in your overall life and then write them down. Now assess how much of your life is being spent on each of your priorities. For example, your relationship with your spouse or significant other may be on your list, but in reality, you may be spending 80 percent of your time working, 10 percent gardening, and the other 10 percent watching television. You may even discover that you're not spending any time on one of the priorities that you listed.

Did you discover you are putting the most time into your defined priorities or is there an imbalance? Write down solutions on how you can get back in alignment with what's most important in your life. For example, you may have listed engaging in hobbies such as scrapbooking as one of your top five priorities but find you are taking care of the kids and doing household chores most of the time. To start acting on that priority, you may decide to write scrapbooking into your schedule and treat it like an important meeting. Or perhaps you noted family time as a priority yet you spend most of your time working. To achieve a better balance, you might consider establishing a family night where you take turns deciding your activity, such as having a game night. Whatever the case, make it a priority to implement them!

Being Willing to Be a Beginner

Did you identify with fear of success and fear of failure in the last chapter? If fear (whether temporary or deep rooted) is one of your primary creativity blocks, one shift you could consider is being willing to crawl before you walk, which will eventually allow you to run—in other words, allow yourself be a beginner. Are you willing to start slowly? Agreeing to be a beginner at something throughout your life will keep you open to newness, support brain functioning, and invite growth.

Sometimes learning a new skill or spending time engaged with an unfamiliar activity can be frustrating, especially if you fall into the comparison game and watch other people do the same activity and make it look so easy. When playing that game, it doesn't seem to matter that those people have been perfecting their craft for years because you're so fixated on what they can do that you can't. It's easy to forget they didn't shoot out of some cannon with instant know-how and magical perfection.

If you're afraid you'll look like a failure because "you're not good enough," is that really true? Good enough in whose eyes? If it's due to a lack of experience, take baby steps and get the support you need. You can work with a mentor or role model, take lessons, attend related workshops or conferences, or simply practice your craft more on your own (the last of which you can do with the creative plays in the chapters and Appendix C). By being patient with yourself, avoiding comparisons to others, and taking small steps, your fear will begin to diminish.

Dealing with Mistakes

Mistakes—everybody makes them. They've been around since the beginning of time. Even if you don't consider yourself to be a perfectionist, I'm guessing you would prefer not to make any blunders. But there are positive ways of dealing with mistakes. The most common advice is to learn what you can from them. Naturally, some have a higher price to pay, and those expensive lessons are usually the ones that offer you the most personal growth. But how do you deal with everyday mistakes—those on a smaller scale in which you catch yourself in the moment? Do you laugh it off or berate yourself? What if someone else points out that you made a mistake? Do you become defensive or do you thank the person?

In his book *Fearless Creating*, author and creativity coach Eric Maisel suggests that mistakes should not be ignored, defended, or left uncorrected. They also should not be accepted as something you deserve nor mourned forever. So if you're in the middle of a creative project and it doesn't go exactly as planned because you didn't properly execute the step or made some other gaffe, you can fix or modify the work, complete it, start over, or quit. By accepting that you are human, hopefully you will forgive yourself, work through it, and continue.

CREATIVITY COMPASS

Benjamin Zander, conductor of the Boston Philharmonic Orchestra, tells a story about dealing with mistakes in the *Art of Possibility* (co-written with his partner, Rosamund Stone Zander) that I love. He speaks of how mistakes in performances help the performers and him realize what requires more attention. Recognizing this value, he trains his students to deal with their mistakes by hoisting their arms in the air, smiling, and declaring "How fascinating!" Are you willing to give this lighthearted approach a shot?

Allowing Yourself to Be Vulnerable

To be vulnerable means you're subjecting yourself to physical or emotional attack. Neither of those things may happen, but the possibility is there. Allowing yourself to be vulnerable means you're willing to leave yourself "wide open," and that can be a scary place from which to operate. It's what keeps people from sharing their creative works. I know that feeling personally; I was a closeted singer-songwriter for more than two decades! Yet "vulnerability is the birthplace of innovation, creativity and change," according to researcher Brene Brown, who is an expert on the subject of shame and vulnerability.

You may think of vulnerability as a weakness, but it's actually a strength. Give yourself a pat on the back for being courageous enough to show your true colors and risk judgment from others. Over time, you'll realize that your vulnerability is what enables your creative expression to fully flourish because you're allowing others to see the real you. Sure, you risk criticism from others and in Chapter 18, you'll learn different ways of dealing with feedback from others. For now, though, start with being aware that vulnerability is part of the creative process. It's a matter of acceptance and being comfortable and confident enough in your own skin to breathe through what can feel like personal attacks. For example, I realize there could be critics and readers who may criticize certain aspects of this book. I could let that stop me, or I can accept the possibility is there and write regardless. (Obviously, I'm doing the latter!)

INSPIRATIONAL INSIGHT

"I spent a lot of years trying to outrun or outsmart vulnerability by making things certain and definite, black and white, good and bad. My inability to lean into the discomfort of vulnerability limited the fullness of those important experiences that are wrought with uncertainty: Love, belonging, trust, joy, and creativity to name a few."

—Brene Brown

Reclaiming Your Power

What does it mean to be self-empowered? It means taking control of your life by making what you think, believe, and feel matter more than the opinions of others. If you can master that, you've found one of the biggest keys to unlocking your creativity.

You may have experienced times when you have felt others were unduly judging you. This can happen because of their own feelings of insecurity, arrogance, or even jealousy. In order to reclaim your power, start to pay attention to how you feel during and after an interaction with a friend or family member, especially if you've just shared one of your creative projects. Whether it's a poem, song, or book you've just written; a painting you started or completed; or an idea for how to decorate your child's room, if you don't get the reaction you were hoping for, will you still be okay? Will you still feel proud of your accomplishment or will you withdraw?

Even if you're not sharing a creative project, it's still important to notice how you feel when spending time with others. Do they zap your energy or leave you feeling invigorated? Does it happen every time with certain individuals or only on specific occasions? These observations may prove to be valuable to your creative process. If you hang out with a friend who inspires you, setting up a lunch date may be just what you need to get your started on a new creative project! By the same token, you can learn to limit your time around those who bring you down. Hanging around with such individuals can suck the life right out of you; however, rather than cutting the "energy vampires" out of your life, you may decide to give them a chance by being open and honest with them by sharing your feelings. Only you can stand up for yourself. That's reclaiming your power.

This is not to say you shouldn't ever listen to feedback from others. Sometimes their comments can be very helpful, as long as they're constructive and delivered in a way that is supportive. You can do your part by letting people know what you want from them up front. If you're looking for them to voice their honest opinions and give advice, tell them that. If you'd rather have them just listen quietly and not comment, let them know that, too. That way, others will be more likely to give you what you want and need in the moment. For example, I had a friend who had a very nice way about her whenever I would discuss a matter that concerned me. Before launching into giving me advice, she would preface her feedback with a question: "Would you like my support on this?" That always made me relax and feel comfortable because it made me realize from the outset that her concern was genuine, even if what she said afterward wasn't what I really wanted to hear. In most cases, it was what I needed to hear!

One last thing you should consider when reclaiming your power is the effect you have on others. Do you come across as encouraging, caring, or understanding? Or are you critical and judgmental? Sometimes what you're getting back from people is a direct reflection of what you're putting out. You may not mean to come across negatively, so that's where more self-awareness is necessary. By telling people what you need in a manner that invites feedback in a way you desire, you can truly reclaim your power.

Creative Play: What Color's Your Traffic Signal?

This is a quick mind workout to check in to see who's in charge of your creative control and to make any necessary adjustments.

Tools Needed: Paper and a writing instrument

Do a quick scan of everyone in your life to see if you allow their words, thoughts, or actions to stop or delay you from pursuing your creative interests. Write down their names.

If you are allowing others to stop you from creating, your traffic signal is red. If they delay you, it's yellow—you're being cautions. And if it's already green, good for you! That means you're already in motion. For example, let's say you want to make a career change. You discuss it with your spouse and he says, "Now isn't a good time. It's way too risky given our financial situation." That signifies a red light, and you decide to put your plans on hold. A yellow-light response would be "I wouldn't jump right into it but if you hear of the right opportunity, I support you to explore it further." A comment like that may slow you down but not stop you.

Now it's your turn to direct your own traffic. Use the following words to start as many sentences you can think of: "I give myself the green light to …." For example, you can write "I give myself the green light to draw at least 15 minutes per day."

If the image of a traffic signal works for you, you can start using it as a quick visual reference whenever you're considering taking action on something. If a yellow light pops into your head, there's something that may intuitively be trying to tell you to proceed slowly. Also, observe who's in control of that light. If it's not you, you have the power to change it!

CREATIVITY COMPASS

Some people have a way of inspiring you to take action. I recall an experience when my late friend Sue and I sat on her dock and discussed our dreams. I told her I had always wanted to play classical guitar. She asked, "Then why aren't you taking lessons? Life's too short." She always seemed to motivate me, and the next day, I made some calls and found a classical guitar teacher near my home. I immediately began taking lessons. She was right about life being too short, as hers was cut short a few years later when she died suddenly. The memory of this conversation and Sue's overall being continue to inspire me to act on my dreams.

Setting Reasonable Expectations

One of the quickest ways to set yourself up for disappointment or perceived failure is by placing unreasonable or even impossible expectations upon yourself. If you're in the beginning stages of exercising your creativity or getting back in the creative game, it's especially important to let go of all expectations related to outcome. You'll do yourself a favor if you can make whatever it is you've chosen to do simply be about letting your light shine.

While you can always set long-term goals you can build up to achieving, in the meantime, set yourself up with manageable, enjoyable activities that may not have meaning to anyone else but you. In other words, if shaping modeling clay into animals or building a prayer altar in a corner of your room brings you pleasure, let that be enough!

Sometimes the tendency is to expect too much of yourself too quickly. When the outcome falls short, you may feel disappointed and discouraged to the point where you decide not to take on anything else. Rather than giving up, remove any expectations and instead focus on creating for the sake of illuminating your creative soul and spirit. Be authentic in the process, and you may just light up someone else's life, too, as you openly share what's in your heart and make a connection.

Not Being Afraid of Risks

Learning to take risks with your own creativity is an important aspect. Why? Because so much of creativity goes into unknown territory, which is precisely why and how many new concepts, products, artwork, and services are born. Each person has his own tolerance level for risk. On one end of the scale are daredevils who are willing to go as far as risking their lives, while on the opposite end are people who are literally afraid to leave their homes for fear something bad will happen to them. When it comes to your creativity, what feels like a risk to you? How expansive or narrow are your limits? Are the fears you have realistic or something you've told yourself due to a lack of self-esteem or confidence? For example, have you ever taken a risk that didn't pay off? Did you then "should" on yourself, become filled with regret, and say to yourself "I should have known better"? That reaction is a common one when the chance you took turned in a direction you may have anticipated but didn't think would actually happen. If you can look at these risks as learning lessons, you'll live with a lot less regret.

Even the most educated risks, where you weigh the true pros and cons of the situation to whatever extent that you can, can have good or bad results. This is no different than deciding whether to buy an extended warranty for a new car; you could impulsively decide to buy it or you might research the item in question to learn more about its failure rate and reputation. Whether or not you buy the warranty, you're taking a risk—of either not purchasing a warranty and ending up needing repairs or getting a warranty but your car never needing the fixes covered by it. It's the same with creativity; you are always taking a calculated risk.

However, that doesn't mean taking a risk typically results in something bad happening. You've probably also experienced coming out on the other side of risk. There are few things that feel better when that happens, which can only add to your feeling of self-empowerment. Expressions such as "Yes! I did it!" become the battle cry, making you much more likely to continue on creatively.

CREATIVITY KEY

The next time you feel your work has been harshly judged, you can either ignore it or learn from it. For example, if an artist completes a painting and then destroys it out of anger because he received negative feedback, that may stop him from painting for a while or perhaps forever. But if any of the feedback was indeed valid, instead of demolishing the painting, the artist could have applied the lessons learned from that piece of artwork, painted over the canvas, and focused on how to improve the next piece. That's the difference between the self-critic and the pupil.

To help yourself feel more at ease with taking risks so you can have those "I did it!" moments, start noticing when you feel discomfort in situations that are unfamiliar to you. Tune into the reason behind your hesitation. This may require some deep contemplation, depending on the situation. Are you reluctant to get started on a creative project because it's risky? One example of this is a person who decides not to pursue his dream of becoming an artist because he thinks it would be too financially risky as a career. Instead, he becomes a graphic designer at an agency. Another example is a writer who has fictional story lines running through his head since childhood but determines there's not enough security in becoming a novelist. He therefore opts to work toward a career in journalism. Ask yourself if the risks can be calculated and if it's worth it to you. What kind of meaning does it hold? If it's part of a lifelong dream, do you treasure yourself enough to move forward?

You can start building your risk muscle by starting small. For example, you may have the dream of owning and operating your own business but you don't feel ready to quit your current job. As long as it doesn't present a conflict of interest, you could work toward that goal by taking on some freelance jobs on the weekend or at night. This not only allows you to reduce the risk, you'll also get a taste of whether being on your own is for you. If you've been making crafts and giving them as gifts to friends and family, you may decide you'd like to begin selling them but you're not ready to invest in buying a tent, showcases, and other supplies necessary to display your work at juried shows. Instead, start with local church fairs and other events where the requirements are not as demanding and the entry fees are less. These types of smaller risks can help you make friends with uncertainty.

Being Open to Getting Help

Whether you feel stuck or are ready to dive in to your creative expression, it's always a good idea to surround yourself with supportive and loving people who truly believe in you and accept you for who you are. If you have a trusted friend who can serve as a confidant, that may work. However, if your creativity blocks are deep rooted, you may consider getting help from a professional. Value yourself enough to get the help you need if you are finding it difficult to move forward on your own. This could be your local clergy person, a spiritual counselor, therapist, or doctor. Getting help doesn't necessarily mean it will require months of your time. Sometimes a trained professional can hasten the process by helping you get to the heart of the matter quickly.

The following are some tips to help you know when to seek professional counseling:

- Talking with friends hasn't worked and you are still feeling very depressed or anxious.

- You're feeling withdrawn and are spending more time alone. This is especially a crucial sign if you are normally very social.

- You feel like your emotions are out of control. Anger, sadness, or mood swings dominate your state of being, and these feelings are getting in the way of your responsibilities and interests.

- You have a lot of difficulty concentrating.

- You've lost interest in important things that used to engage you and feel lethargic.

- Friends or family have noticed a major shift in you and have suggested getting help.

- You're absorbed in habits that are detrimental to your well-being, such as using drugs and alcohol to excess, and this behavior is interfering with your daily life.

- You're grieving a loss—due to a death, divorce, job loss, or something else—and you wish to move on but find you can't do it on your own.

- You have thoughts that go round and round. Your thinking has become obsessive and you don't know how to let go.

- You are having flashbacks to traumatic events.

Ways to Foster Creative Freedom

Now that you've been given some suggestions on how to overcome your blocks, it's important to realize that working through them is a process that may take some time. These obstacles didn't just appear instantly; they took time to develop. It's like making a snowball. If you form a snowball in your hand and keep adding to it, eventually it will become large enough to place on the ground, where you can give it a push and watch it roll while it takes on a life of its own. That's what happens with creative blocks. But just as with snow, they can melt away given the right environment and resolve.

Fostering creative freedom involves being gentle and patient with yourself as you navigate your way out of the creativity closet and into your creativity calling. There are many ways to find your way out to enjoy the wide-open field of creative expression, but I've provided a couple suggestions to get you in the right frame of mind. If you discover a strategy that works for you that goes beyond these, pat yourself on the back and by all means follow your intuition.

There's No Such Thing as Trying

Have you ever noticed that when someone uses the words "I'll try," it usually has a negative connotation? For example, when you invite friends to a party and ask if they can come, and they respond "We'll try," 9 times out of 10 they don't attend because they really weren't planning to come in the first place. Rather than tell you "No" up front, they felt it was easier to let you down easy. As you can see from this example, there is no such thing as trying; either it happens or it doesn't happen.

 CREATIVITY COMPASS

Consider this example from my own experience at author and speaker Neale Donald Walsch's retreat, where he demonstrated the concept of "try" when I questioned him about it. He told me to try to take off my shoe, and I responded by taking off my shoe. With a sly look and a smile upon his face, he said, "I didn't tell you to take off your shoe. I told you to *try* to remove your shoe." Point well taken!

When it comes to creativity, are you "trying" to be creative—gently letting yourself off the hook due to one of your blocks? Maybe you tell yourself "I'm going to try painting someday," but you never actually do it because "trying" automatically gives you leeway or freedom to escape. In order to get away from this mentality, when you start thinking about whether to partake in one of your creative interests, let go of the word *try*. In fact, removing or decreasing the use of that word from your vocabulary isn't a bad idea. I've tried that (kidding!). In all seriousness, I set that very intention when I realized there is only doing or not doing—creating or not creating.

As you think about or are involved in a creative pursuit, think twice whenever you catch yourself about to say the word *try*. Do you see the difference in telling yourself "I'm setting an intention to paint someday," as opposed to "I'm going to try to paint someday"? The difference is subtle, but the word *intention* carries with it more of a focus and may actually prompt you to think about a game plan of when you might actually do the activity, rather than the vague *try*.

Giving Yourself Permission to Create

Sometimes people put off creating because they're waiting for someone else to give them permission—in other words, they're seeking approval. Do you ever find yourself in this position? This can happen when you feel others view your interest in creative projects and activities as superfluous or low on the priority list. Perhaps your spouse has asked you, "How can you spend time drawing when you have all of that laundry stacked up?" or "Don't you think you already spend enough time on your own stuff? After all, you're working and going to school." That can make your guilt set in and cause you to put off something you love one more time. You're putting the opinions of others before your own, even though you know creative activity really feeds your soul.

Give yourself permission to create on a regular basis, rather than wait for someone else to give you the green light. This will not only have a positive effect on your inner being and overall outlook, it will probably extend to those around you because you will feel so much more contentment. I'm not suggesting you shirk your responsibilities; rather, it's about finding a balance. If you find yourself surrounded by loved ones who don't understand your need and desire to create, perhaps you can sit down with them to explain just what it means to you and how your creative expression can actually benefit everyone, rather than pull away from spending time with them. If taking time to create ultimately makes you a happier person, the quality of time you spend with others will improve as well.

It Begins with a Belief

When I was in middle school, the thought "Those who believe achieve" came to me, and it's a phrase I've held onto ever since then. What is a belief? I describe beliefs as thoughts people form based on what they've been told, what they've experienced, and what they've read. They are not necessarily based on any truths. Oftentimes, these convictions are based largely on assumptions. Some people believe without seeing (which can be described as faith), while others must see to believe. When it comes to your creativity, do you already believe you are creative, or do you need to see evidence of that first?

In my opinion, there are two ways people view themselves creatively. Quite simply, there are those who believe they are creative and those who do not. What's your *paradigm*—in other words, how do you view yourself? Do you believe in your own creative abilities? If you don't, what will it take to begin changing that belief? If you already believe you are creative, do you wish to be even more creative? Believing in your creative self is crucial but does not guarantee you'll act on your creativity. In fact, some who believe they're creative do not take advantage of their skills and talents for reasons they may or may not realize. Are you one of them? I have yet to meet anyone with the desire to be less creative. But what does "being more creative" actually look like to you? What does it feel like? Being more creative may mean the following:

- Starting projects or a creative initiative you've thought about but haven't moved forward with

- Following through on projects you started but never finished

- Taking your creativity to the next level by evaluating your creative efforts and determining how to improve upon them

- Taking a class or getting more training in your area of choice

- Working on your own or with a coach to remove your creativity blocks

- Discovering new creative outlets and acting upon one or more of them

- Getting back in touch with your original enthusiasm to create

- Gaining a better understanding of your creative process

These are all possibilities that tie into being more creative. See if you can identify any other ideas for yourself that would mean "being more creative."

 **DEFINITION**

> A **paradigm** is a set of beliefs that drive your thoughts and actions. Sometimes paradigm shifts are necessary if your belief structure is getting in the way of your creativity.

Another thing you should consider when it comes to your beliefs about your creativity is whether you view your creative pursuits as a luxury or a necessity. Your answer to this also will affect your creative output. As a luxury, your belief would be that creativity may add an element of pleasure but it's not essential; it's more of an indulgence. Maintaining that belief may result in you putting off taking any action toward one of your creative interests. This is especially true if you believe you don't "deserve" much time to play. On the other hand, seeing creativity as a necessity means it's not optional; you feel it's a requirement in your life. Otherwise, it feels like you're missing a key, meaningful ingredient. This belief alone can make the difference between tapping into your creativity or not. You wouldn't dream of allowing your creative dreams to lie dormant if you view creativity as a necessity.

For example, I know if I go too long without at least dipping into one of my many creative interests, I start to feel a void. If I ignore that feeling, the gap widens and the only way I can close it is to allow my creative sensibilities to take over. For me, that's primarily singing, songwriting, playing an instrument, photography, or writing. What is it for you? Is it any of those things I just named, or perhaps it's cooking, sewing, quilting, designing jewelry, acting, sculpting, making greeting cards, finding solutions to problems, painting, drawing, poetry, teaching, public speaking, praying, planning, inventing, or training your dog to do tricks? There is no end to creative possibilities. They are only limited by your beliefs.

Creative Play: Examining Your Beliefs

This exercise helps you get a better handle on the beliefs you have fostered regarding your own creativity.

Tools Needed: Paper and a writing instrument

First, evaluate the following statement with a ranking of 1, meaning "not at all," and 5, representing "absolutely or wholeheartedly": "I believe I am creative."

Think about why you ranked that statement with the number you selected. If your ranking was anything less than a 5, what will it take to shift your belief up the scale to a 5? If you're already a 5, good for you! That's a great start! Write a paragraph (or more, if you're so inclined) that explains your viewpoint and how you wish to improve or maintain it.

Now, using the same scale, select a ranking for the following statement: "Creativity is a necessity in my life." Write a paragraph that provides insight about your belief.

You do not have to share your answers with anyone! This prompt is to help you get in better touch with your beliefs about creativity. Anytime you stop to consciously consider how you view yourself, you are taking steps toward a better understanding and awareness, which will direct you on how to further proceed.

Changing Your Attitude with Gratitude

Although there are many examples of creativity that have emerged from a space of heartache and sorrow, it's not a place most people wish to stay in for long. Living with an attitude of gratitude will not only give rise to your creative expression, it also will sustain your entire life. One of the quickest ways you can adjust your attitude when you're feeling sad, angry, bored, jealous, depressed, confused, or any emotion you wish to transform into joy and peace is through appreciation. Many negative emotions are fear based, making it impossible to be in fear and gratitude at the same time.

There are different ways to put gratitude into practice. One way is to verbally express your appreciation to others. Not only does it make them feel good, it can make you happy to see them happy! Another way is to keep a gratitude journal in which you write all the things for which you are grateful on a daily basis. Perhaps your friend treated you to lunch, a stranger let you go ahead of him in the grocery line, or your boss let you leave work early. You can even write about every-day happenings, such as the unconditional love your dogs give to you and the weather—whether it's rain watering your garden or sun helping flowers blossom. In order to keep your journal from becoming repetitive, you can challenge yourself to make every journal entry unique. Whatever you decide to do, find new things every day that fill your gratitude cup. The more you can come from a space of appreciation, the more likely your creativity will flow.

Affirming Your Creativity

Now that you've learned some ways to overcome your creative blocks and get into the right frame of mind for creative freedom, it's time to *affirm* your creativity. An affirmation is a positive statement that helps reinforce a belief or attitude. It's the opposite of the negative voices that sometimes take up residence in your head. Writing down your affirmations and then putting them in places you'll see every day can help to support your creative process. Take a moment now to think about the various negative phrases about your creativity that have passed through your consciousness. Some of the statements may be "I'm too old," "Learning to play the piano is too hard," "No one will ever want to read what I have to say, so why write?", or "I'm just not creative." How often do you make kind, loving, and supportive statements to yourself? Well, here's your chance.

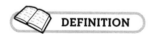 **DEFINITION**

> An **affirmation** is a positive declaration that uplifts, encourages, and strengthens a particular feeling or viewpoint and can be helpful in bolstering your creativity.

The following are some tips for writing your own affirmations:

- Focus on your desires—what you wish to have or experience rather than what you don't have or aren't accomplishing.

- Keep your language positive. For example, it's better to say "I am prosperous and enjoy all of my gifts in life" rather than "I no longer struggle for money in my life."

- Leave out all doubt, even if you feel uncertain about what you're writing. Write in the present tense, as if you already are or have what you want.

- Aim for words and phrases that are simple and easy to remember and recite. A simple way to begin is with the words "I am" or "I feel," followed by what you wish to be, do, have, or experience. In fact, some people have expressed that saying "I feel" brings a deeper, more emotional attachment than saying "I am." Write it in a way that works best for you.

- Use language that is familiar to you so you can speak it with conviction.

While you may not believe what you're declaring right now, given enough commitment, dedication, repetition, and practice, you'll begin to notice a shift toward the positive.

Creative Play: I Am Creative!

You are going to form the habit of positive self-talk, starting with writing affirmations that counter your negative self-talk.

Tools Needed: Paper and a writing instrument

At the top of the page, write I AM CREATIVE! Once you've done that, draw a line down the middle of the page. On the left side of the page, write down 5 to 10 statements that are negative or do not support your creative life, making sure to number each statement. The following are some examples of negative statements:

I'm really not creative.

I'm too old to start painting now.

I'll never be as good as Fred at coming up with ideas.

My poetry sounds like a kid wrote it.

On the right hand side of the page, write an affirmation that counters the sentence on the left side of the page. Write the statement in such a way that totally supports you, even if you don't yet believe what you're writing (yet)! The following are some affirmations that counter the previous negative statements:

I am creative!

My youthful spirit supports me as I have fun painting.

I freely express my creativity, which leads to new insights.

I capitalize on my childlike imagination to inspire others through my poetry.

Place your affirmation list where you will see it every day and repeat each one at least five times per day. As an additional reinforcement, write the affirmations on sticky notes, one sentence per note, and put them in places such as your bathroom mirror, your car's dashboard, your computer monitor, your refrigerator door, or anywhere you will look daily. If you feel moved to write even more affirmations that help put you in a positive space, go for it!

Redefining Your Life

In Chapter 1, you were asked to sign a creativity commitment—to do what it takes to enhance and see your creativity as a necessity. You've made a pledge to devote at least a portion of your life to your creative expression. If you truly remain 100 percent dedicated to that promise and have started following the tips in this chapter to move forward creatively, you have already begun to redefine your life.

I can speak from my own creative experiences and say, with unwavering conviction, that my life feels more complete, more joyous, more free, and more life-giving to others and me when I allow myself to explore and express my creativity—in whatever form it takes. If I feel I'm having a bad day, sometimes all it takes is to pick up my ukulele and play a song before returning to my workspace. Other times, my creative pursuits are more involved and may take days, weeks, or months to complete. Either way, I am using my creative interests, skills, and abilities to enrich my life.

Your life will take on a new definition as you begin to really believe in yourself and all that you have to creatively offer the world. By consciously and intentionally allowing your creativity to redefine your life, you are living "on purpose." Reading about creativity and learning new ways to tap into your own "think tank" is just one positive step on your creative path. Engaging in this book's creative plays is another proactive step you're taking. As you use what you've learned in this and other chapters, you may begin to notice even the smallest shifts that occur in your attitude and behavior. Observe whether you react differently to the things that used to upset you, and see how quickly your feelings transform from a negative to a positive space when you're engrossed in a creative project. Through these actions, your life will begin to take on a new meaning. Perhaps it already has.

The Least You Need to Know

- Reclaiming your power and giving yourself permission to create are essential to realize your creative potential.
- While working through your creative blocks is entirely possible, it is a process that requires awareness, commitment, action, and time. Having the right mind-set will keep you moving forward.
- Believing in yourself, living in gratitude, and affirming and expressing your creativity will help redefine your life in a way you never thought possible!

Laying the Groundwork for Creativity

Creativity is no different than any other endeavor. Whether you're looking to run a marathon, ace an exam, or survive a hurricane, you will do better if you prepare yourself. This does not mean you have to plan every move you make along the way—that could actually inhibit the creative process. What it does mean is establishing the proper mind-set and supporting yourself in the best way possible.

The previous chapters helped to start your preparation by asking for your commitment and giving you ideas to ponder, tips and information, and hands-on activities all related to creativity. In this chapter, you are given additional food for thought and considerations to build the best possible creative space—mentally, physically, and emotionally. You get a chance to look at this not only through your eyes, but also through your other senses. So settle in and feel the inspiration work through you. The best is yet to come!

In This Chapter

- How to open your mind to the doorway of creativity
- Considerations for setting up an ideal creative space
- Using your senses to boost your creative expression

Opening Your Mind

As I said in Chapter 1, creativity is a decision. By reaching this chapter, I assume you have made your decision to continue to explore your creativity. That's great—even if you're not sure yet what you wish to create or where your talents lie. One of the keys to discovering that is by opening your mind to all possibilities. Many people have the tendency to box themselves in. They put limitations on themselves before they even start to consider the many options available to them. How open is your mind? Like a property's zero lot line, are your boundaries of what you're willing to consider so tightly defined that you have left no room for expansion? Or are you willing to explore? The following are three tips to help you open your mind:

Remove the ceiling. You've probably heard the reference of something having a glass ceiling. This has been typically used with women in the workplace who have been limited in how far they can advance within their organization. Of course, this concept can apply to men as well. And it could apply to you—but only if you let it. You are in charge of your creativity, so if there is a ceiling—glass or otherwise—remove it! There's no need to break through if it's not there in the first place. Think big. Think endless possibilities. Think beyond the sky! You could even build an affirmation around this, such as "My creativity is an endless stream of possibilities!" or "I open my mind to allow unexpected inspiration to flow through me."

Let go of judgment. While it's true you can judge something to be positive, typically your mind is focused on more of a scrutinizing, usually critical process when you're in judgment. This is not to say you should never evaluate your creative works. You already know that's part of the creative process. What I'm talking about here is the ability to keep an open mind so that when some kind of inspiration comes to you, you don't automatically dismiss it by finding all of the reasons why that idea won't work. Sometimes the best ideas end up being the ones in which your first reaction is "That's crazy." An open mind welcomes thoughts that appear to be crazy. They can always be dismissed later, but not without first giving them a chance.

Say to yourself, "If I knew I couldn't fail, I would …," "If I knew I didn't have to do it perfectly, I would …," or "If I knew others wouldn't laugh at me, I would …." As Chapter 6 identified, fear of failure, striving for perfection, and worrying about what other people think about you are all blocks to creativity. By prefacing your thoughts with these statements, you're dismissing those blocks and creating more of an expansive feeling within yourself. If you do make any mistakes along the way or things don't turn out how you had initially envisioned with your creative project, using the experience as a learning lesson also means you can't lose.

INSPIRATIONAL INSIGHT

"Every day we slaughter our finest impulses. That is why we get a heartache when we read those lines written by the hand of a master and recognize them as our own, as the tender shoots which we stifled because we lacked the faith to believe in our own powers, our own criterion of truth and beauty. We are all kings, all poets, all musicians; we have only to open up to discover what is already there."

—Henry Miller

Clutter, Comfort, and Creativity

Your physical environment—the space that surrounds you when you create—can enhance or detract from your creativity. You may have images in your mind of "the scattered artist," with paints, brushes, and other supplies appearing to be positioned haphazardly in an overly crowded small space. You also may have a vision of a busy executive with a pristine office and pictures hanging in perfect alignment to each other. These are both stereotypes that continue to be perpetuated, and while you may actually know people who fit these descriptions, you may be surprised to learn what research has revealed about how physical space affects your creativity.

Clearing the Clutter—or Not!

Some creatives negatively describe their clutter as procrastination, self-sabotage, and resistance, while others say their messiness stimulates creativity. When I first drafted the outline for this book and decided to include a section on "stuff" and how it affects creativity, I had the notion that clearing your clutter would equate to opening the way for creativity to flourish. I then began researching the topic and read some interesting studies that pointed to the opposite being the case. Although there's no consensus across the board among creatives, it's certainly worth thinking about where you fit into this scheme.

First, let's talk about people who need an uncluttered area to stimulate creativity. Neat freaks usually find it difficult to understand how clutter kings and queens can function in such an unkempt office or home. For example, I used to have a boss who maintained an orderly desk at all times. Whenever he would pop into my office, he would get a look on his face that made me think his brain was going to explode as he scanned the piles that sat upon both my desk and floor, not to mention all of the little gadgets, knickknacks, and artwork that adorned them. To a Tidy Tom or Neat Nancy, a person who functions with cluttered surroundings could be interpreted as being scatterbrained, disorganized, and unfocused. One study seems to agree with that. In an unclutterer blog post, career expert and author Jonathan Fields explained the brain must rely on increased levels of working memory when there is disorder, which taxes the brain's prefrontal cortex. In turn, this drains this part of the brain, which could cause you to act more on impulses and become distracted. A weakened prefrontal cortex also won't be as effective in allaying your anxiety or fear—two potential blocks to creativity—as much as one that is functioning at full power.

On the other side are people who thrive working in a cluttered space. I know for me, I struggle with keeping my workspace tidy, especially when I'm in the midst of creating. It seems the bigger the creation, the messier my space becomes. Yet I know there's a big part of me that thrives on order. (How many people do you know whose entire collection of hundreds of CDs is alphabetized within multiple music categories?) Now there's reason to celebrate for those who delight in disarray or at least aren't bothered by their messes. That's because a team of University of Minnesota researchers led by Kathleen D. Vohs conducted three studies showing evidence that working in a messy environment seems to bring out more imaginative ideas than a space that is neat, which fosters more traditional and conservative thinking. Professor Vohs noted that both environments made a huge difference in the participants' behavior. Being messy doesn't mean you'll automatically be creative; it just stimulates imaginative thinking to the extent of your existing creativity, according to Vohs. Meanwhile, those who prefer tidy spaces can rejoice in knowing the study also showed that working in an uncluttered space promotes healthy eating, generosity, and conventionality.

What are your own takeaways from this information? Regardless of what the studies and experts say, if you find that working in a space jumbled with your stuff creates an equally jumbled mind and prevents you from functioning at your best, your brain is probably seeking more organization. You will know you're not optimally working if your surroundings are distracting you to the point of interrupting your thoughts and your actions and causing you to lose focus. Or perhaps you're one who is not bothered in the least by working in a disheveled space and may even benefit by spotting an item you didn't know was there that inspires you. If you've never stopped long enough to notice either way, start paying attention to see what suits you best.

 CREATIVITY COMPASS

I used to live with a college roommate who was one of the messiest people I knew, yet she was not disorganized. She seemed to know exactly where she had put her things. If I moved one belonging of hers, she would immediately notice and start questioning me as to where I put it. Do what works for you—just make sure it really does work for you and that you're not using your untidiness as an excuse.

Creating Your Ideal Space

A tidy or messy space is just one aspect of devising your ideal creative space. You also need to carve out a specific space in your home—and if you work outside the home, an office space, too—that optimally supports your creativity. The following are some things you should take into account for your creative space:

Type of activity: Knowing what activities you are likely to engage in will help with your planning. You may even have to set up more than one area if your interests are vastly different and won't work in the same space. For example, if you have an interest in music and setting up your own home recording studio but also enjoy woodworking, the former would probably work better in a room inside your home, while the latter may be more suitable to an outdoor, basement, or garage setup.

Size: Set aside whatever space you have available that you can designate as a "creative zone." If you live in small quarters, you may only be able to devote a corner of a room. If your space doesn't allow for even that availability of space, perhaps you can organize a box of supplies you can stash inside a plastic container that can slide underneath your bed. That way, you won't have to pull your supplies together each time you want to create. I use part of my great room (mostly for music and art) and a small den area (mostly for writing and photo/video production) as my primary creative spaces. Sometimes my activities extend to the kitchen and even my bedroom, although when I get too spread out, I start to feel too scattered.

Comfort: Once you have decided on where you will set up your creative space, consider what it'll take to ensure it's comfortable. What kind of seating will be most conducive to your activities? Can you make do with what you have, or do you wish to add any new elements, such as a footstool or a cushion for back support? What color will your walls and furniture be? (Colors that support creativity will be discussed later in the chapter.) What can you hang on your walls that inspires you? Look at what you are currently displaying and see if you wish to make any changes. They need not be expensive. Think about hanging your children's finger paintings, one or more of the visuals you made as part of a creative play, or an old album cover that evokes good memories.

Tools and materials: Consider the tools and materials you'll be using in your creative space. For example, many of the creative plays in this book call for different types and sizes of paper, pens, pencils, markers, stickers, glue, and paints, so you'll want those available. You should keep these and any other creativity implements and props visible and handy. By having them in plain view, you'll be gently reminded of the gift of creativity. Perhaps seeing them will motivate you to take time out to create—either in the moment or later in the day or evening. For example, if you play music, will you display your instruments or put them away in their cases? If you keep them conveniently positioned in their stands, you might find yourself playing more often—they'll be front and center to remind you "We're here! Play us!"

Beyond your creativity tools, reference and inspirational books also may be essential to your space. Sometimes a quick glance at their title may bring an inspirational thought to mind. Or you might pick one out to thumb through it to awaken your muse. To capture any ideas on the fly, consider hanging a white board. Grab a marker and write them down while they're fresh! Magnetic white boards and bulletin boards are good for posting notes, too. If you prefer to dictate rather than write, a recorder would also be useful to keep nearby, though a cell phone with recording capability can work just as well.

 CREATIVITY KEY

Where can you store your supplies? A woven basket—available at your local arts supply store or department store—works well, as do plastic carts that contain multiple drawers. Some carts even move around on wheels, which is convenient.

Lighting and ambiance: Do you have windows or a skylight that bring in enough natural light during the day? In an online article by Leo Widrich on "The Science of How Temperature and Lighting Impact Our Productivity," he wrote about a recent study conducted by study scientist Mirjam Muench. The research exposed one group of people to daylight and the other to artificial light for several work days. The results showed that compared to the afternoon, the participants who were exposed to daylight were measurably more alert at the beginning of the evening, while those that had artificial light were considerably sleepier by the end of the night. Additionally, cortisol levels dropped appreciably under artificial or poor lighting conditions. Low cortisol levels can result in more stress and can lead to health issues.

So if you can create a way to allow more daylight into your space, that's a positive. You may still need to add lamps or overhead lighting for evening hours or if you can't get adequate natural light into your space during the day. If you don't have a window in your creative space, you can find artwork that is painted to look like a window, complete with beach or mountain scenery, to add to your ambiance.

Other touches you can add to your creative space include plants, shells, rocks, and knickknacks. Depending on whether you're okay with clutter, be sure these little trinkets don't take over your space. You want to have enough room to create! Generally speaking, environments that achieve a balance between too messy and too plain work well, but again, play around with what works for you.

Sensing Your Creativity

You will hear many people talk about experiencing their creativity through the five traditional senses: sight, sound, smell, touch, and taste. Some of them were incorporated into the previous passage on setting up your ideal creative space. Because your creativity can be stimulated through each one of these, I invite you to take a closer look now at how you can use these senses (plus one other) to kindle your creativity even further. When you start consciously connecting your creative flow in this manner, you will start to notice more opportunities for expanding and expressing your creativity on a daily basis.

Sight

Visuals are an important part of creativity. Even differences in color can potentially stimulate your creativity in different ways. For example, one study conducted by a team of German researchers from the University of Munich showed 65 study participants either a green or white rectangle during an online creativity test. Those who were shown a green login screen received a 20 percent higher score than those who didn't, and when the experiment was conducted three more times using green, red, gray, and blue, the green won out each time. The study's author reasoned that people associate green with growth and development. So are these results a conclusive finding? Not necessarily. But it gives you an idea of how the color green can potentially play a role in sparking creativity. Does thinking about this color bring up images of nature—tree leaves, grass, and plants—which all have to do with growth?

In another study, the effects on creativity were compared between the colors red and blue. The research team tracked some 600 participants who performed six cognitive tasks, which were primarily done on computers with a red, blue, or white screen. The activities included an orientation toward either creativity or details. Red improved performance by up to 31 percent on exercises that included proofreading and memory recall, while the participants using blue cues generated twice as many creative results as they did when operating with red prompts. So the results showed that red is good when focusing on details is important, while blue is better for thinking creatively. This is due, in part, to learned associations.

Take a few moments to think about what you associate with the color red in your environment. In terms of roadways, red means stop both in signs and traffic signals and emergency vehicles use red sirens. In terms of school, it wasn't a good thing to have your homework returned in a sea of red marks, indicating wrong answers. What comes to your mind when you think of the color blue? Perhaps the sky and the ocean, which connote an open and calm feeling. Like green, both red and blue contribute to creativity, possibly in different functions for your creativity.

So how can you use color to positively impact your creative expression? Before you start to paint the walls of your creative space a different color, start to notice the effect different colors have on you. Be aware of colors on everything from your clothing; to the different-colored walls in your home to your office; to spaces you visit for the first time, such as restaurants.

CREATIVITY COMPASS

Most people have engaged in some level of photography, such as taking snapshots at a party. One of the ways I express my creativity is as a professional photographer. On one hand, it feeds my creative spirit. But there's also an irony I've felt. Having my eye attuned to what's unusual in my surroundings may result in capturing a standout image, yet it can cause me to miss the experience of the moment. For example, at times I've been so engrossed in photographing my son's fast-moving soccer game that I've missed the best part because my focus was too narrow. Sometimes, the best way to experience creativity through sight is by using your very own eyes as the only lens.

Of course, when it comes to the senses, it's hard to isolate color as a lone factor of creativity, as the overall atmosphere—which includes other sights, sounds, and smells—has an effect. Therefore, think about how you can introduce color into your creative space beyond your walls. For example, you can mix things up by rotating different wall hangings. Or you may decide to hang a crystal prism in front of a window, which will reflect different colors; showcase awards you've received or other items that signify personal achievement; place meaningful photos on your desk; or display posters with inspirational sayings. It's really about surrounding yourself with things that will help you relax and keep your spirits high.

Experiencing your creativity using your sense of sight also goes beyond inanimate objects. The following are some other ways you can engage your sight in order to become more open creatively:

- Start paying attention to some of the smaller things in life to become a better observer. Do you know what color eyes your friends or co-workers have? What about the person who always waits on you at the post office or the checkout person at the grocery store? This not only involves what you see, but the feelings you associate with such a detail.

- Go into nature and find at least one item per visit you never noticed before. It could be the intricacies of a single leaf that falls to the ground or the construction of a flower bloom.

- Become aware of those views you most appreciate, such as watching the sun rise or set, the glow of a fireplace, or the waves of the ocean breaking against the shoreline.

- Place yourself into environments that rouse your muse in some way on a regular basis. If you draw inspiration from action scenes, go to a place where you can enjoy the hustle and bustle of a city, people watching, bright and flashing neon lights, or dancing.

Practicing these can feed your creative spirit and open your mind. You also may be able to translate some of your observations into creative opportunities.

Sound

When you think of sound in relation to creativity, what comes to mind? Perhaps music is the first thing you think of when you associate sound with creativity and it can, indeed, play a big role. Do you prefer to listen to music while you are creating, or would you rather have silence? If you like to have music playing, what kind? It may depend on what you're doing. For example, usually if I'm writing a magazine article and I'm on a deadline, I have classical music playing in the background; it has become my auditory signal that it's time to get serious about writing. However, when I'm editing photos, I often choose very upbeat music to keep me invested in my task. What about your tastes? What music, if any, supports your creativity? Instrumental or songs with words? Melodic or more ethereal? Easy listening or heart thumping? What about when you're not in a creative mode? What songs inspire you, move you to tears, or make you feel on top of the world? You can find select songs that can prime you either before creating or while you're in the creative process and play them.

Beyond music, experiencing creativity through sounds can come from natural sources. As I'm sitting here writing, I'm listening to what sounds like an entire chorus of birds singing. These kinds of sounds can stimulate your brain or cause you to associate what you hear with an uplifting experience. That alone may prompt a creative idea. If you live near water, the sounds of the sea or a babbling brook may move you because they're soothing and relaxing. You're bound to feel more creative when you're not stressed out. If you don't have such sounds normally close by, record them the next time you're in an area with them, or possibly purchase an electronic gadget that features a whole smattering of nature sounds. You might also consider putting a small water fountain in your creative space or in your front or backyard, where you can take in both the sight and sound of it every day.

In addition to music and nature, another familiar sound is someone's voice. Too much talking and not enough listening can limit your creativity. Remain open around others, particularly when the topic is about creativity. By being a good listener, you may gain a valuable tip or be stirred in a way that prompts you to explore something that you may have missed on your own. Listening intently also helps the other person to feel heard and valued. This can be a reciprocal process in which you both benefit.

Smell

You can probably quickly rattle off a list of smells you avoid. What about aromas that are inviting to you? Just like a bad smell can turn you off quickly, an enjoyable scent can help elevate your mood. Beyond food being cooked in the oven or on the stovetop, you've probably had the experience of walking into a store or someone's house and gotten a whiff of something unfamiliar yet you found it pleasing. Start to satisfy your curiosity by finding out what the smell is so you'll know and you can replicate it in your own space.

One option is burning different scents of incense or candles to enhance your creative space. There's also the option of using a diffuser that mists essential oils into the air. If that interests you, there are many websites and books that can educate you as to the different properties of the oils. Some are calming, while others are energizing. And here's an obvious one: Take time to smell the roses—and other flowers, too! Having plants and flowers in your creative space not only can enhance the fragrance, they can serve as visual triggers as well.

Touch

This sense can be experienced between people and with objects. Are you someone who likes to be hugged and give hugs? If so, reach out and touch! Hugs are a sign of support and may be just the thing you need before, during, or after a creative project.

Start to become aware of your surroundings, too, where touch is involved. Do you notice if certain types of clothing feel good or bother you? What works for you? The feel of your seating, whether it's in your home, office, or vehicle, can also make a difference in your comfort level. If you're not comfortable, it's hard to create. Do you prefer leather or plush? A stiff, more supportive seat or a flexible feel (such as a beanbag chair)?

You can also engage your creativity through touch. Getting back to the flowers, don't just stop and smell—touch them, too. Notice whether the petals have a soft or rough feel to them. Understanding textures like this and how they make you feel can really get your creative juices flowing.

Taste

"I want it so badly, I can taste it!" How many times have you uttered that phrase? Experiencing creativity through your taste buds can come in many forms.

CREATIVITY KEY

Eat a meal in complete silence. This can be done while dining alone or with friends and family. Concentrate on thoroughly chewing each bite (more times than you usually do) and really appreciating the taste. Sometimes eating meals is done so rapidly that the taste is lost in the process. Therefore, taking time to discern different flavors can be an art form in and of itself, especially if you're eating a cuisine that's not that familiar to you. By eating without speaking, you allow yourself to fully concentrate and be in a state of appreciation, both good practices for creativity.

With regard to your creative space, would it help to have a bowl of sweets on your desk to be used only as an occasional treat? Or would you find that too tempting, something that's too difficult to keep a disciplined attitude about? Perhaps a nearby bowl of fruit would work better for you. It doesn't even have to be food. For example, having a decorative jug filled with water and a favorite cup nearby can make drinking water an art form! You can even experiment with different flavors in your water through adding fresh fruit or vegetables to it. A drop or two of certain essential oils also can do the trick. (Be sure they're the kind that can be ingested.)

Outside of your creative space, taking chances with taste not only broadens your palate; it can even broaden your mind! Ordering a restaurant dish you've never tried before or cooking something yourself that falls outside of your typical menu engages your sense of taste with something new and gives you a creative learning experience, regardless of whether you end up liking the new taste.

The Sixth Sense

The five senses you just read about relate to the sixth sense: intuition. Some people call this getting a hunch or gut feeling, which may come through one of the five senses. Those who have polished this skill may define themselves as clairvoyant (clear seeing), clairaudient (clear hearing), clairsentient (clear feeling), claircognizant (clear knowing), clairgustant (clear tasting), clairalient (clear smelling), or simply psychic. Everyone has this ability to some degree, and your intuition plays a huge role in creativity when you tune into it.

It's those times when you have a suspicion or feeling about something or someone. For example, if you've been discussing the possibility of partnering with someone on a creative project and you notice you've been getting bad feelings that continue to grow, that's your gut telling you not to enter into this agreement. On the other hand, your intuition can prompt you to follow your heart's desire, whether that's a life-altering career change or taking a pottery-making class. Ignoring your inklings may mean you miss out on a great opportunity of creative expression. Learn to listen to what your body, mind, and spirit are seeking to tell you. Your sixth sense will tell you when it's wise to wait and reflect, dismiss an idea, or take action.

Creative Play: Uncommon Sense

You've probably been told before, "Use your common sense." In this activity, you'll be looking at ways that are special to you (which may be uncommon to others) that will help you enhance your creativity using the six senses.

Tools Needed: Paper and a writing instrument

At the top of the page, write the word "Sight" and underline it. Underneath the word, make a list numbered from 1 to 5. Do the same with the other of the four senses: Sound, Smell, Touch, and Taste.

Under each of the five senses, come up with five ways you can use that particular sense to encourage your creativity. For example, under Smell, you might say the following:

> I will go into a candle store and find several smells that inspire me. I will then burn them one at a time while I'm in my creative workspace.

Now write the word "Intuition" and underline it. Underneath it, write a paragraph on how you have used your sixth sense in the past and how you can tune into your internal guidance even more.

If you can't think of five things for each sense or what to write about the sixth sense right away, take a breather; you come back to this creative play and add to it later. Once you've completed it, refer to your list often to implement as many as these ideas as possible.

The Least You Need to Know

- Being creative works best when your mind is open. Start by removing any limitations you've placed upon yourself, let go of judgment, and start thinking of all you can create if you knew the only outcome was success.

- It's important to develop a creative play space in your home and office that supports your mental, physical, and emotional well-being. Stock your space with the tools and materials you'll use regularly, ensure proper lighting, and select colors that enhance your creativity.

- While some research has shown that clutter can enhance your creativity, other studies have shown that a more orderly environment also can be advantageous. Only you know if being surrounded by a mess hampers or helps your creativity.

- In developing the ideal creative environment, consider how the five traditional senses and the sixth sense of intuition may help support you.

Jump-Starting Your Creativity

In reading this book, you have been building toward a more creative life. You've gotten a chance to test out different methods, attitudes, and beliefs and achieved a greater understanding of what it takes to be creative. Perhaps you've felt inspired along the way. But the most effective way to truly live a creative life is to experience it, not just read about it. This chapter is filled with a number of no-cost or low-cost creativity stimulators you can incorporate into your life to jump-start your creativity.

Read about the different techniques with an open mind. It's possible your first reaction will be one of resistance. You might think *That sounds silly* or *There's no way I could ever do that.* My advice to you is to give the different suggestions a chance. They may develop over time—or not—but at least allow yourself to experiment and explore. You also may play off of some of the ideas presented here and create some methods of your own. That's how creativity works!

In This Chapter

- Low- to no-cost ways to stimulate your creativity
- Opening up your creative spirit
- Forming creativity habits

Channeling Your Creative Side

I'm a creative being. You're a creative being. That has been well established up to this point. Perhaps you believe you're creative now but are still not really feeling it. You may be feeling like your engine has had a couple of false starts or has stalled out a lot. Just like a car, you have to take steps to keep things running.

In order to be productive, you need to find the spirit to create. The following are some fun, easy ways to invigorate yourself for the creative journey.

The Power of Play

One way to find motivation is to make sure you create enough fun in your life. Not only is building fun activities into your life stress-relieving, but you're also more apt to feel and be creative if you've built enough pleasure into your life.

You can see the power of play in action with children. If you go to your local playground and watch their gleeful spirits in action from a distance, you can learn some powerful lessons about the openness to creativity they have.

For starters, kids are naturally curious, innocent, and uninhibited. And, generally speaking, children are very focused on what's right in front of them. They're not wrapped up in thoughts of what may happen in the future or recalling painful memories of the past. Although kids may have to deal with some very challenging periods from time to time, most of them have a resilience that keeps them from dwelling incessantly on their troubles, unlike many adults.

Because kids are so curious, they naturally explore all of their surroundings. Hand them a box of crayons and paper and they'll begin drawing. They don't need to be told what to draw; they do whatever comes to them. They use their imaginations to make entire kingdoms out of sandboxes, make up their own versions of games, and become absorbed in so many other activities that require nothing more than their own ingenuity. They don't seem to care that their works aren't perfect—at least not until they start to grow older.

So be childlike (not childish) and be sure to include enough fun times in your life. Your only goal in being playful should be to have fun! Allow yourself to dream, be spontaneous, and pretend. By getting in touch with your lighthearted spirit, you'll be more likely to look at your challenges through a child's eyes. Like a suitcase filled with boulders, it's the heavy feelings that you carry with you that weigh you down and will keep you from this sense of play. Dump the suitcase and engage in recreation—or a re-creation from times gone by.

CREATIVITY COMPASS

One of the most touching experiences I've ever had was during a time I was feeling sad and my son, J. P., picked up on it. To cheer me up, he gave me a calendar as a Christmas present that featured beautiful sunrises and sunsets, the type of images he knew I liked to photograph but had gotten away from doing. He gave me a handwritten note along with the gift, which read, in part, "Get back to walking and photography; it's your savior!" At age 14, he was able to express his empathy without bringing himself down. I think he was able to do this because he knew his actions would inspire me to get back to what I loved doing—and in fact, it did!

Creative Play: Being Childlike, Not Childish

The purpose of this creative play is to get in touch with your playful nature by reflecting on those things that brought you joy as a child.

Tools Needed: An 8½ × 11-inch piece of paper, a writing instrument, and a timer

At the top of your paper, write "My favorite childhood things were …." Sometimes when you're working against a deadline, you're forced to think quickly and there's no time to analyze, so set a timer for three minutes. Start your timer and begin writing down all of your favorite childhood things as fast as they come to mind. Just write down anything you liked as a child, such as your favorite colors, teachers, school subjects, fruits, vegetables, activities, pets, games, and playmates. What brought you joy? What excited you? Did you have a favorite stuffed animal? Do you remember its name?

Once the three minutes are up, examine your list and see how many of those things are in your life today. Why or why not? Did this exercise help you remember things you had long forgotten? If they're no longer in your life, how can you recapture the feeling they gave you as a child and incorporate them into your life today?

You may not immediately have any big insights from doing this creative play, but be open to revisiting what you wrote to see how they might bring even a small pleasure to your life. For example, I was recently at a craft festival and there was an artist who made very detailed animal whistles out of clay. They only played three or four notes, but as a musician, I could still appreciate their sound and I selected the monkey because in my teens I had an extensive collection of monkeys, mostly stuffed animals. Now every time I look at this monkey or pick it up and play the whistle, it makes me smile.

Lightening Up with Laughter

Here's another cue to take from children—having a good laugh! Laughter keeps you in an upbeat emotional state, relieves tension, and keeps you loose, which provides an advantageous backdrop for activating creativity. Laughter also connects you with others, which can be good in the workplace, among volunteers, and with friends and family—anytime you want to create a stronger bond. As long as you avoid inappropriate humor, which is delivered at the expense of others or may not go over well because of bad timing, you get the benefit of putting both yourself and others in a better mood.

Studies also show humor can help spark ideas and solve problems. Researchers have found that fully grasping a joke involves a complex cognitive process involving both hemispheres of the brain; the left side processes the joke's words, and the right side helps your brain understand the joke. (So don't feel badly if you don't always get the joke!) Because the creative process involves whole-brain thinking, you can probably understand how that complexity of understanding can promote creativity. Learning to laugh at yourself also may help your creative process because it means you're letting go of your inner critic and allowing yourself to be imperfect.

Can you remember the last time you had a good laugh? It's hard to "make" yourself laugh, and when you really need to lighten up, that's usually when it's the hardest. So right now, write down those things you can do for a quick laugh. This will be your "Laugh List." An example of something you can put on your list would be to go online to YouTube to search for your favorite comedian's videos and then take five minutes to watch a couple. Just put anything on your list that may provide you with the mood shift you need. The next time you're stuck for a creative solution or simply having a bad day, you can then grab your "Laugh List" and see if you find that partaking in one of your items is funny enough to get you back on the right track.

Dating Yourself

In her book *The Artist's Way,* author Julia Cameron recommends a practice she calls "the artist date." This involves taking yourself on a date—no other passengers allowed!—and dedicating some time each week to tap into your creative self. On these dates, you should be spending some quality time alone engaging in activities that nurture you, inspire you, and feed you in positive ways. They are about letting your guiding light shine in—receiving insight, ideas, and revelations that help steer you in a creative direction.

Artist dates are also a way to indulge yourself. They do not have to be about art and they do not have to cost any money. For example, you might visit a park you've never been to before and explore the new surroundings. So think about things you've thought about doing but never did or engage in an activity in a different way. For example, I have gone to the movies plenty of times but never by myself. Therefore, I decided to see what that experience would be like to go alone, and I thoroughly enjoyed myself. And if you schedule these dates into your calendar the same way you do a business meeting, they will take on great importance.

> **CREATIVITY COMPASS**
>
> Shirell was a participant in one of my creativity courses that was based on *The Artist's Way*. When I explained to the class the concept of taking an artist's date, she immediately reacted negatively and stated aloud "This isn't what I signed up for!" Although her resistance was strong, I gently encouraged her to experiment with the practice at least once and told her that she had nothing to lose. The following week, she ended up being the "star" of the evening. That week, she took not only one artist date, but two, and her description of her dates was so amazing that she inspired everyone in the class! You may be surprised how good this activity feels once you get in the habit of "dating yourself."

In the creativity groups I facilitate, the participants begin the class by sharing how they spent their artist date. Some describe doing things like taking an hour to visit an art supply store to really examine all of the different aisles and their contents—where buying wasn't the focus—and coming away feeling refreshed with a handful of ideas. Some of the experiences sound like so much fun, they inspire others in the group to plan the same kind of artist date. Like these people, make your artist date an adventure you look forward to each week.

Getting Loose and Dancing

Do you love to dance, or are you intimidated by the thought because you don't consider yourself to be a good dancer? If you dance as a creativity warm-up, you have nothing to worry about because you will not have an audience. You'll be dancing in the confines of your own living room, bedroom, or whatever room works best in your own home. If nobody's watching, there's no judgment—unless your inner critic is speaking up. Here's the good news: That little voice can be quickly silenced. Cue up your favorite upbeat music, crank up the volume, hit play, and just begin dancing!

Dancing is a great way to loosen up and feel relaxed. There's no thinking involved. Pretend you're a ballet dancer, a break dancer, or even a rock star. Play air guitar. Sing into your hairbrush. Be silly. Start or end your day this way, and if you spend your days at home either working or not, you can do this in the middle of the day, too. Dancing helps to decrease your stress. When you're free from tension and anxiety, that's when creative insights are most likely to occur. One unknown source summed it up this way: "We're fools whether we dance or not, so we might as well dance."

Becoming a Conscious Observer

By now, you've probably gathered from the various suggestions in this book that increasing your awareness—becoming a conscious observer—can enhance your creativity. The following are three ways you can do this:

Take the "wrong" way. Going the same way every day has probably become so routine to you, there have been times when you missed your exit or drove right past your destination. You stop noticing what's around you unless it practically hits you in the head, such as seeing orange cones in a construction zone that make you slow down. So if you take the same way to work, the gym, the grocery store, or anywhere you drive or walk on a regular basis, deliberately take a different route, even if it means going out of your way. Occasionally taking the "wrong" way, even if it's the long way, is a good idea to include in your creative practices. Anything that can shake up your day in some way has the potential of inspiring you because it's new and different.

 INSPIRATIONAL INSIGHT

"The only person you are destined to become is the person you decide to be."

–Ralph Waldo Emerson

Put your head in the clouds—observantly. Another free way to boost your creativity is to look up and play a game you've probably engaged in before—finding creativity in the clouds. That's when a particular cloud configuration reminds you of an animal, an angel, a monster, or any number of things your imagination conjures up. Make it a practice to look to the skies on a regular basis to see if you can discern any interesting shapes. You can jot down your thoughts about what you see in your idea journal or dictate them into your recorder. You might even take it a step further and play around with writing a poem, short story, or song lyrics that describe your observations. The idea is to get your wheels turning on a continual basis.

Take a walk. Hiking may be a favorite pastime of yours, but whether you walk in nature or indoors, either practice may spark your creativity. In fact, a team of Stanford researchers found that walking amidst any surroundings significantly increased creativity levels compared to sitting. Even those who walked on a treadmill with nothing more than a blank wall before them produced twice the number of creative responses as those who were sitting down. So the walk itself and shortly afterward—not the environment—was the primary reason for this boost. The results also showed that while walking helped the participants with coming up with new ideas, focused thinking that required a single correct answer did not benefit from walking. When given a word-association task, the walking participants actually did a little worse than those who were seated. The researchers concluded that walking is useful for divergent thinking as opposed to convergent thinking (see Chapter 4 if you need a refresher on those two types of thinking), making walking especially beneficial in the beginning stages of creativity, when you are just coming up with ideas.

Seeing What's Not There

Throughout this book, I've suggested how important it is to be aware of your internal workings, as well as your surroundings. As you know, being a keen observer can lead you to insights that go unnoticed for those who walk through life unaware. Just as important as seeing what's around you is seeing what's *not* there.

So whether you're involved in a work project, creative activity, or just taking a walk with no particular thoughts in mind, pay attention to what's in front of you. Use your sight, your hearing, your touch, your sense of smell, and (if it makes sense) your taste to make observations and then think about what isn't there that might add value. Start asking questions such as "What's missing?" or "What could be added to make this more appealing for my customers/family/pets?" This is one way ideas are born. Doing this practice on a regular basis may not enlighten you every time, but it will get you in a habit that may prove useful when it's most needed.

Making Creativity a Habit

It takes a long time to form a habit—longer than the 21-day myth that has been perpetuated for years. According to James Clear in his article, "How Long Does it Actually Take to Form a New Habit? (Backed by Science)," the belief that a habit takes 21 days to form sprang forth from Dr. Maxwell Maltz, a plastic surgeon, who observed that it took a minimum of 21 days for his post-op patients to adjust to their new situation. Many people latched on to the doctor's observation, which also included noticing his own behavior and adaptation period. However, they failed to realize this was his opinion based on his own observations, not a scientific study. In reality, Clear found based on a study published in the *European Journal of Social Psychology* that it takes 66 days for a new behavior to become automatic and 18 to 254 days to form a new habit, depending on the person, situation, and their actions.

Given this information, what are you willing to commit to as you cultivate your creativity? While it might take you a little longer to form healthy habits than you thought, the good news is the study also showed that if you miss a day along the way, it's not like you have to start all over. As I said in Chapter 1, creativity is a commitment. You will find that your creative spirit is alive and well as long as you have a strong dedication and patience with the process. The following suggestions can help you slowly build toward making creativity a habit.

CREATIVITY COMPASS

A technique I use whenever I have a lot of writing to do that's on a tight deadline is to change my environment. I work out of a home office, meaning there are plenty of distractions to contend with every day. When I need to write my magazine articles, I usually go to an internet café to get away from my usual surroundings. I have done this practice so often that when I arrive at my destination, it's like a signal to my brain that it's time to write. I set the parameter that I'm not "allowed" to leave until I completely finish the articles on deadline. When I'm finished, I usually reward myself with a caramel latte! Like me, see how changing your environment can heighten your productivity and creativity.

Tabling Your Technology

How many times have you observed entire tables of people at a restaurant who have their heads buried in their mobile phones? Rather than actually conversing with each other, they're "checking in" via social media apps and seeing what others around the world are saying rather than enjoying the company of those right in front of them. It's becoming more prevalent in a society that seems to depend on its technological advances. Have you ever been guilty of paying more attention to technology than people? I certainly have, and my aim is to do less and less of that. Technology isn't really to blame as much as your own behavior with the devices. So it's not that you use them; it's more a matter of how and when.

Therefore, I am recommending that you set up a period of time where you go technology free in order to help you focus creatively. This means temporarily ditching your cell phone, tablet, computer, camera, video games, or anything electronic. While you may be resistant to this idea at first, take a moment to consider the benefits and how you might structure it. The following are some small changes you can make in your technology use that can yield big results:

- See if you can make it through working on a project without your cell phone. Let your voicemail handle the call when an interruption could cause you to lose focus.

- Keep your internet browser and email program closed for an hour or two when working on your computer. Just because your inbox notifies you when a new email arrives doesn't mean you have to stop what you were doing to respond to it.

- Set up a program within your own family with rules such as no mobile phones, laptops, or tablets at the dinner table.

- Declare one day a week—perhaps a Saturday or a Sunday—in which you don't turn on your computer.

- Set up a technology-free zone, such as in your bedroom, where no devices are allowed. For example, you can use a "real" alarm clock rather than an app on your smartphone to wake you up.

It's really about being conscious of how you use technology to your advantage. Playing a video game or making a fun post on a social media site every once in a while doesn't cause any harm if it's meant to give yourself a quick break; in fact, that kind of activity might actually serve to refresh you. It's when you engage in this type of behavior to numb out or avoid what's really important that it can become a problem.

By taking control of your technology, you may actually increase your productivity because you are at the helm rather than allowing the rings and dings to dictate your next action. And more productivity means you'll have more time to have fun in your life by yourself or with your friends and family, which is vital to your creativity!

Giving Yourself an A

In the book *The Art of Possibility,* author Benjamin Zander talks about a concept he used with his graduate students at the New England Conservatory, where they were studying the psychological and emotional factors involved in musical performance. To alleviate their anxiety and anticipation of failure, he decided to give every student an A right from the start. The only requirement was that the students had to write him a letter dated the following May that described their insights and accomplishments as if they had already happened. The idea was to use this grade of excellence to open them up to possibility. Zander was mostly interested in the attitudes, feelings, and views of the person they became during the course.

How can you incorporate this "giving an A" practice in your life to support you as a person overall and specifically your creativity? You could start by thinking about something you wish to create in the next year. Pretend you're getting graded and, like Zander's students, have been told you'll be getting an A. In keeping with his concept, put yourself into the future and write a detailed letter, looking back, that tells why you deserved to be given an A. Talk about your state of mind, your process, your perceptions, your gratitude—anything you realized along the way that supported you in your journey to an A. Talk about you as a person—*the* person—who pulled off precisely what you set out to do and how you feel about yourself as that person.

Don't limit yourself to this one time. This is an especially great exercise to practice over time if you frequently experience anxiety and fear of failure. Get in the mode of always giving yourself an A!

 INSPIRATIONAL INSIGHT

"To be creative means to be in love with life. You can be creative only if you love life enough that you want to enhance its beauty, you want to bring a little more music to it, a little more poetry to it, a little more dance to it."

—Osho

The Time Is "Write" to Capture Your Ideas

I can't say enough about what this next practice by Julia Cameron (author of *The Artist's Way*, which I discussed earlier) has meant to my life. In her book, she recommends writing three long-hand pages every day first thing in the morning, a practice she refers to as "morning pages." The idea behind this exercise is to write whatever comes to your mind—a "stream of consciousness." Its purpose is not to create art or meaningful writing (although it has been my own experience that the occasional flash of creativity hits me while writing and I just go with it). Sometimes those thoughts become songs, poems, ideas for blog posts, or business strategies, while other times they don't develop into anything. And that's okay! Again, the pages are really not meant to be anything other than a way to help you recover your creativity. Your writing may be filled with negativity, hope, optimism, and everything in between. There is no right or wrong way to write your pages.

You may feel like you couldn't possibly fill three pages each and every day. Make yourself, even if it means repeating yourself. This practice is for everyone—not just writers! If you're feeling resistance, dig deeply and ask yourself what's behind your opposition. For example, I have found that once I have written one and a half pages, the rest comes easily to me. Sometimes what I write is like a dumping ground, while other times I'm expressing my appreciation. If work is what's most prevalent on my mind, I've even used the pages as a kind of to-do list to help me prioritize my responsibilities. Having been dedicated to this practice for more than four years, I can't tell you how it has enhanced my creativity. Through writing my morning pages, I process and purge the thoughts I know aren't serving me or I gain a better understanding of new realizations. This opens me up to allow creative insights to flow freely through me.

Like me, think of all of the thoughts you would rather not have in your head as filling up a pitcher. You would like to add some pure, refreshing water to the pitcher, but it's already full—there's no room. Writing your morning pages every day allows you to dump the unwanted contents of your pitcher and fill it with more tasty contents. Some of the people I have coached have used the pages to write out their hopes and dreams and to express their gratitude. Again, you get to decide what you want to express, which happens in the moment of writing.

Beyond morning pages, I recommend you carry a notebook (or "idea journal") and a pen with you everywhere you go. It should be one that's small enough to carry with you at all times in a pocket or purse. That way, you can jot down your thoughts right away that may otherwise vanish like the wind. If you have a smartphone, another option is to download and use an app that's handy for typing notes as they occur to you.

Creating One Simile a Day

A *simile* is used to associate two different things by linking them together with the words *like* or *as.* This makes the description more visual, colorful, or detailed. Some familiar clichés are "She's as quiet as a mouse" and "He's like a bull in a china shop." In order to get into the habit of being creative, begin to think of your life poetically using similes. Perhaps writing one simile per week is a good start, but if you really want to challenge yourself, write one simile per day. This will get you in the habit of doing a "mini creation" daily.

You can use the different elements and people in your life for inspiration. For example, "My life is like a brook—always in flow" or "My kids are as different as snowflakes." Similes can be stated simply or be more involved, such as "Just as leaves fall to the ground in no particular pattern, my mind often has scattered thoughts."

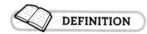 **DEFINITION**

> A **simile** is a figure of speech that links one thing to another using the words *like* or *as* to make the comparison more memorable.

Making Creativity a Game

When I was considering leaving the first job I had after graduating from college, I was at a real crossroad, unsure of what to do. I didn't just want to quit without having another job lined up yet, but I was pretty sure I wasn't in the right place. My father told me to pick up my favorite book, open it randomly to a page, and there would be my answer. I thought it sounded crazy at the time, but at around 2 in the morning when I couldn't sleep, I thought "What do I have to lose?" I picked up Richard Bach's *Illusions* book, opened it randomly as instructed, pointed to a section on the page with my eyes closed, and was absolutely amazed at what I saw. The text actually talked about leaving a job. I took it as a sure sign, quit that job, and never looked back.

This same fun technique can be applied whenever you're looking to generate more ideas or add to an existing idea. Or use it as I did to find a solution. It doesn't matter whether you select a book, dictionary, or other type of publication. The same concept applies. Open it randomly and see what you find. The wording that you point to may not give you as clear-cut an answer as my experience did, but you can look at it and determine whether there are any similarities or differences that may be applied to your concept. Or perhaps it will prompt new ideas altogether. You can boil it down to a single word on the page, a sentence fragment, or a paragraph. Usually shorter is better, but there is no specific rule about using this tool other than to use your imagination. The idea is that it helps you move forward in the creative process.

Another practice you can do on a regular basis is one called "What if?" I can recall as a child having endless fun with my best friend going through different scenarios and applying this question. Sometimes the questions were unrealistic, such as "What if the sun fell out of the sky?" and "What if we could fly?" Other times, they were more likely to happen, such as the time we asked "What if Duke (a mean-looking German Shepherd that was my family's watchdog) got loose?" and the dog actually got loose! If you play the "What if?" game, I think it's safe to assume you don't have to worry about any scary dogs coming after you, but you might come up with an unusual idea that leads you in a new, unanticipated creative direction.

Using the "What if?" question means you're expanding your thinking. Just like I did as a kid, get in the habit of asking absurd questions. When you make unlikely connections, it often leads to fresh insights. The results of this can be seen in everyday items, such as restaurant menus. Creative chefs may have asked "What if?" questions in developing and offering menu selections such as Caesar salad pizza, smoked beer, and arugula spaghetti. I'm sure you've participated in group discussions when someone has said "Well, we've always done it that way." Be the first to challenge that and respond by saying "What if we broke from that tradition and did it this way?" While you should be prepared for those members of the group who find their security in safety and convention to immediately discard such new ideas, there may be others who appreciate your new line of thinking.

CREATIVITY KEY

In reading about the various tools presented in this chapter, it's natural for you to feel more aligned with some more than others. I caution you to beware of your own resistance, as sometimes the thing that's causing you discomfort is the very practice that can lead to your greatest creative boost. Whatever that feeling is—anxiety, pride, fear, or some other emotion—allow yourself to feel into the sensation. Take enough time to get to a place of peacefulness and check in again. See if you are now willing to give the tool a fair shot. These practices, although simple, can lead you to breakthroughs you may not otherwise experience. You may even discover the benefits can be magical!

Letting Gratitude Fuel Your Inspiration

Even the most optimistic person has bad days and gets stuck creatively. One of the quickest ways to shift yourself from a negative emotion to a positive one is to come from a place of appreciation.

One way to feel appreciative of your own gifts, especially when you're feeling upset or disappointed due to criticism, is to keep a gratitude file. If you keep a gratitude file, you have somewhere to turn without having to depend on anyone else in moments like after your boss shoots down your idea or your friend doesn't embrace your latest painting. You can set up both a physical file and an electronic file. In the physical file, stash some of your favorite cards or letters you received from friends, family, your boss, or your co-workers. When you're feeling down, you can then take out your file, pick out one of the items, and read it to remind yourself how much you are loved.

For example, after my music partner, Mike, and I released our debut "Connected Souls" CD, I received many flattering emails from those who purchased it. I responded to each person and expressed my gratitude. When I went to discard the emails, they seemed too precious to trash; I so appreciated that they took the time to express their feelings. So I set up an electronic gratitude file that I simply named "Compliments" and saved their emails to this new file. Now anytime I receive a complimentary email from someone, I drag it into this file. I hardly ever look at the file, but I know it's there, ready to help me shift my outlook when needed.

Another way to become inspired and grateful is through other people. Surround yourself with people you admire, either in person or through the electronic magic of the internet. You can accomplish this by attending online workshops, listening to TED talks (short, influential talks presented by speakers through the nonprofit organization Technology, Entertainment, Design, which you can learn more about at ted.com) and audio presentations, and reading books. Some may be directly related to creativity, but choose any topic that makes your heart sing. Think about the people in your life whom you respect, bring you joy, light you up, and motivate you to be the best person you can be. What can you learn from them? Is it possible for you to emulate them and still reveal and display your own style? (In Chapter 12, you will have an opportunity to ponder this more deeply when creativity partnerships are discussed.)

The Least You Need to Know

- Stimulating your creativity does not have to be expensive. There are a number of free methods to kindle your creative juices.
- Your creativity depends on making enough time in your life to have fun. Creative insights happen when you least expect them and it's usually when you're feeling relaxed.
- It takes a long time to make something a habit. You will find that your creative spirit is alive and well as long as you have a strong dedication and patience with the process.

Priming Your Mind

By now, you probably realize that while there may be some mystique involved in creativity, much of the productivity and results come from your own commitment to draw upon and release your ingenuity. You may decide to create to simply have fun and enjoy the process; to improve the overall quality of your life; or to find solutions to a problem in the workplace, in your relationships, or within your own being. You get to decide what, when, why, where, and how you will create, and with whom. But what does it take to start your creative flow and stay there or revisit it often?

Like anything else, creativity requires practice. However, it doesn't have to be repetitive and dull! In this chapter, I provide some ways you can prime your mind to enhance your creative efforts.

In This Chapter

- The importance of letting go of assumptions
- Eight techniques for generating creative ideas
- How daydreaming can be productive
- The advantages of doodling

Confronting Your Assumptions Head On

One of the first actions you can take to prepare your mind for creative thinking is to let go of your assumptions—those things you *think* you know for certain but in actuality, there's no proof. It's the old way of thinking when you tell yourself "That'll never work." You say this because you think you already know the answer. You just assume it's a certain way. If you get in a roomful of people who also are thinking this way, dealing with their own assumptions and beliefs, the creative process will be over before it begins.

Check in with yourself on a regular basis whenever you are feeling resistance toward new ideas that either you generate yourself or someone else does. Write out your assumption, or your belief, and ask yourself "Can I be absolutely, 100 percent sure that this is really true?" The answer to that question will usually be "No." You can then ask yourself "How can I shift my thinking to open my mind so I am willing—maybe even enthused—to explore the ideas in front of me?" This, in combination with the techniques presented in this chapter, can help prime your mind for creativity.

Creative Thinking Practices

At some point in your life while driving or being transported, you've probably encountered a sign that reads in big, black letters "ONE WAY ONLY." On the road to creativity, you should never come across that sign because there is always more than one way on the creativity freeway. Finding your own way to express your individuality, whether working alone or as part of a group, is the basis of creativity.

The creative thinking practices that follow will prime your mind to start thinking differently— to break out of the linear, logical patterns to which you've become accustomed. Some are more geared for groups, while others may be used individually. All of them are designed to open your mind and to instill a sense of freedom, like traveling in a convertible with your hair blowing freely in every direction. So idle your engine as you learn about the creative thinking options presented here. When you're ready, you can then take them each of these for a test drive. (See Chapter 14 for techniques like these that are used in workplace situations.)

Combine Unlike Ideas

Most people are used to thinking in terms of association, not disassociation, so this technique gets you thinking in a way that may feel foreign to you. However, joining two or more unlike ideas can lead to some new and interesting ideas. In fact, it has led to some of the greatest inventions in history. For example, in the fifteenth century, Johannes Gutenberg combined a coin punch with a wine press to create a commercially viable printing press. You can find other examples of simpler but useful products created using the combination of unlike ideas all around you, such as mop slippers (I know from experience, they work well!) and tire swings. When it comes to those two products, unless you're using this thinking technique, it's unlikely you would think of a cleaning device when you first hear the word *slippers* or a swing when you hear the word *tire*. It's all about thinking beyond the normal boundaries and coming up with something unique but useful.

To begin, think of some everyday products that were combined into one, such as highlighters that have sticky notes on the other end or ink pens that also serve as a mini flashlight. Become aware of different places you go or products you use yourself and observe how they may have come together due to this type of thinking. Once you have some basis for this type of creation, try it out for yourself.

Think of a situation, goal, product, or service—anything you want to move in a creative or new direction—and go beyond the obvious. Look at different objects, methods, processes, and ideas that are unrelated to each other in their design, purpose, material, or packaging. The weirder the combination, the more likely you'll generate innovative ideas. Be gentle with yourself if you don't immediately make any connections; you can always come back to this method and explore again. This is simply about gaining a new perspective on things to drive your creativity.

 CREATIVITY COMPASS

I used the technique of combining unlike ideas in my public relations practice by bringing together two unrelated clients. I was representing a home show that was looking for a new entertainment attraction for its attendees. At the same time, I was working with a humane society that had organized a doggie wedding using its therapy dogs. Because a large percentage of homeowners own pets, the combination of the home show and doggie wedding worked. The fluffy matrimonial ceremony provided unexpected laughs for the guests and gave positive exposure to the shelter, which relies on public awareness and donations.

Think in Metaphors

Thinking metaphorically means you take two separate, unrelated things that are alike in some way but not literally. For example, a few commonly spoken metaphors are "The wheels of justice turn slowly," "Keep your nose to the grindstone," "The lights are on but nobody's home," "It's raining cats and dogs," and "You are the apple of my eye." It's similar to the simile but doesn't use the words *like* or *as* for comparison. Metaphors are used to make descriptions more striking, visual, and memorable. They work well when you're trying to communicate something complex because they prompt you to change your normal point of reference and connect two different things.

In the creative process, using metaphorical thinking opens your mind to new images rather than keeping you focused only on what's in front of you and what you've always known. For example, when I was working for a newspaper, the management's focus was on helping employees appreciate diversity and its importance in the workplace. In an employee seminar, the facilitators addressed the commonly heard metaphor "America is a melting pot"—which means many nationalities blending together to form the American culture—by offering a different metaphor: "America is a salad bowl." With this revised metaphor, they sought to drive home the point that while people of different ethnicities come together in America, they can still blend while maintaining their unique heritages. That was more than two decades ago, and I've never forgotten it. As you can see, using metaphors to spark new ideas is more about the imagery and deeper meaning you create than the phrasing. That's why I remember the salad bowl metaphor; it quickly brings to mind a visual, and the rationale made sense to me.

Here's an example for you to play with. Say your goal is to make more money, whether at home or at work. What words or phrases come to your mind when you think of making money? For example, one word that could pop into your mind when you think of the word *more* is the word *increase*. When first writing that word, I personally pictured someone blowing up a balloon. Maybe it's filled with cash. Put the book down for a few minutes and think of more ways to express the goal of making more money in terms of words, phrases, and pictures.

What ideas came to you during those few minutes of brainstorming? The two words and images that came to my mind when thinking about this exercise were *grow* and *blossom,* which made me think of nature. This then prompted me to recall the commonly known metaphor of "Money doesn't grow on trees." I then thought, *Well, what if money did grow on trees?* I pictured hundred-dollar bills hanging from the branches. In fact, the bills covered the branches and it just looked like a giant money tree to me. Did you come up with something similar, or was the metaphor vastly different?

So the next time you need some ideas beyond the logical, pick at least one of your own words and start making associations that are not meant to be literal. Once you have created a metaphor or imagined a strong visual for your situation, see what ideas come to mind that relate to the metaphorical description. After that, you can see if any of these ideas relate to the actual situation.

This can be a challenging process, but that's only because it's far easier to think the way you've always thought. When you're falling into your regular thought patterns, consider this saying: "If you think what you've always thought, you'll always get what you always got." So let go of any expectations and have fun with this process because there's no telling where this type of thinking may lead you!

Look to Others

This recommendation is more about getting accustomed to involving others in your creative process as opposed to a particular way of thinking. As the old adage says, "Sometimes two (or more) heads are better than one." It doesn't have to take away from your own ideas. In fact, the opposite is often true.

For example, Paul McCartney and John Lennon of The Beatles were one of the world's most imaginative and prolific songwriting teams ever. As very different individuals, their collaboration became one of the most successful in the music industry. And according to an Ultimate Classic Rock blog post by Jeff Giles, McCartney's creative process still involves his former writing partner. In the interview with *Rolling Stone* referenced in the blog post, McCartney stated that whenever his inspiration is blocked, he converses with the late Lennon and imagines what John would do. This exemplifies how two people can play off of each other's ideas and talents to produce a better product than had their approach been limited to their own creativity.

 INSPIRATIONAL INSIGHT

"A person who can create ideas worthy of note is a person who has learned much from others."

–Konosuke Matsushita

So consider approaching others who think differently than you do for creative input. Can you think of at least two people who always see things differently than you do? Perhaps they almost seem argumentative because their style is so different from yours. However, bear in mind that when you are really wanting to expand your creative thinking, it's best to seek the help of someone who complements you as opposed to someone who thinks just like you do.

When most people are looking for ideas or feedback, their tendency is to approach people with like minds. That's the egocentric part of people who are looking for reinforcement of their own ideas. Instead, take a chance on a complementary type of partnership and be careful of dismissing their ideas too hastily just because they're so different from your original vision. For instance, I have two friends who are my "go-to" people whenever I'm feeling stuck. Although we cherish the same values, we think differently. They are able to offer a fresh point of view, which is what I'm after during those times. Think about whom you will turn to when you're looking for help in developing creative ideas.

SCAMPER Away!

SCAMPER is a tool that was developed in 1991 by educational administrator Bob Eberle to improve children's imaginations and creativity. The acronym stands for the following: Substitute, Combine, Adapt, Modify, Put to another use, Eliminate, and Rearrange. The aim is to use these seven prompts when working with a challenge or looking for a solution to quickly generate a lot of different ideas that may be adapted and built upon, similar to brainstorming. The process is based on feelings of curiosity, risk-taking, complexity, and intuition. Although it was designed for kids, adults are effectively using the practice.

To illustrate how this process works, here's an example. Say you work for an art show that just celebrated its 25th anniversary. Despite this noteworthy achievement, you notice that attendance has been steadily dropping over the past three years. Your challenge is to find ways to boost the turnout. You could start by looking at what you currently do to attract people to your event and then launch into the SCAMPER process by asking and answering questions in each stage:

Substitute: What features, attractions, or incentives do you offer that you could substitute with something better or different? Focus on ideas you've never done before. They may seem silly or ridiculous at first. For example, if you're charging $10 for admission, what if you replace that with free admission? That might sound crazy because you've been charging for years and your knee-jerk reaction is "We could never afford to do that," but write it down anyway, as you might find a way to make it work later.

Combine: This technique was addressed earlier in this chapter as its own practice, although you're not limited to looking at combining unlike things. How can you combine what you're already doing with something else, related or not? Can you work with other organizations that can enhance what you're already doing, or can you bring a totally new feature to the table by uniting two new ideas? An example would be to combine art with music. Invite a mural artist and a band to combine their talents. The artist painting a large-scale canvas to the beat of live music could become a new attraction.

Adapt: Are others in your industry or an unrelated business offering features you could adapt to work for you? Can you take one of your existing attractions to make adjustments to make it more alluring? Most art shows also have food vendors. An example of adapting your food area would be to include an "artsy food area." Create a contest for your food vendors to see who can make the most artistic menu item.

Modify: Remember the belief that there's no such thing as an original idea? In this step, you can look at other ideas and change them in a way that becomes your own. Look at modifications you can make in all areas of your operation, from logistics and programming to marketing and sponsorships. An example would be to modify the craft section of your art show and include a "hands-on" space for attendees to make their own craft with guidance from instructors.

Put to another use: What parts of your art show can be used differently? For example, maybe you take the part of your event site you were using for artist demonstrations and turn it into a wine garden instead.

Erase: What can you remove, even if you believe it's essential? If your art festival has a kids' area and you don't have many kids who attend, maybe it's time to eliminate that area.

Rearrange: What can you reorganize? Perhaps rearranging your entire site layout or even moving to a different location will mix things up enough to prompt people's curiosity, which could boost attendance.

 INSPIRATIONAL INSIGHT

"Imaginative thought and expression require playing around with ideas, toying with responsibilities, and roaming around in the world of make-believe."

–Bob Eberle

This example is just a brief look at how the SCAMPER process works. When you actually use this tool for a work, volunteer, or personal situation, you will want to ask many more questions. With each phase of SCAMPER, pose as many questions as you can think of. A good technique is to frame your questions using the five Ws of journalism: who, what, when, where, and why. Also, questions that begin with "how" and "what if" work well in this process.

Use Free Word Associations

This tool can be used alone, in groups, in the workplace, at volunteer committee meetings, or even at parties just for fun. The idea is to freely associate one word or phrase with another. This is great for generating a lot of ideas quickly because you say the first word that comes to your mind. The words can have a similar or opposite meaning or be closely aligned to the subject. For example, if I say *peanut butter,* you might think of the word *jelly,* the next word might be *sandwich,* and so on.

You can find many creative applications of this tool in the real world. According to a Business Survival Toolkit online document, Campbell's Soup reportedly used word association that resulted in the creation of a new product. The initial word was *handle,* which spawned the word *utensil* and then *fork.* An idea arose about eating soup with a fork, and after pondering that thought, they came up with the idea that you can only eat soup with a fork if it contains large pieces of meat or vegetables. Can you guess what emerged from that? You got it—Campbell's Chunky Soups.

To try word association yourself, begin by selecting a word or phrase that relates to your circumstance. If you're alone, you can do this sitting down and writing on a piece of paper; or if you're working in a group, you could go big and do it on a flip chart. Writing one idea per Post-it note and sticking them on the wall also will do the job. Keep going until you think you're done—and then challenge yourself to continue. You might consider setting a timer, which will make you and any participants feel the pressure to blurt out whatever comes to mind. You won't have time to analyze—that's a good thing! Once you have finished, compile those words you see as most viable. Consider which words give you additional insight or evoke images that may be useful. You might even be able to connect some of them together just like the "combine unlike ideas" approach. While this technique may not produce an immediate result, it should ignite some useful ideas you can continue to pursue.

Not sure where to begin? Try this example to get a feel for the process. Pretend you are buying a birthday gift for your best friend, who seemingly has everything. First, grab a piece of paper and a pen or pencil to start making your list of words. What word would start the free word association? There's no rule to this. You could start with the person's name or a category of something you know she likes, such as shoes, cars, clothes, jewelry, electronics—you get the picture. Start writing as many words as you can generate. When you think you're done, press yourself to go a little longer. Sometimes the best ideas surface toward the end. Once you're finished, go through the words and see if you can put together any solid ideas. If you actually came up with a gift to give your friend, how cool would it be to have her say, upon opening it, "Wow, how did you ever think of this?"

Start with the End in Mind

If you're someone who often gets caught up in details and loses sight of the "big picture," consider this technique, which Stephen R. Covey addressed in his book, *The Seven Habits of Highly Effective People:* start with the end in mind. When you start your thinking with the end in mind, the "big picture" or your "grand vision" is the guiding force and will lead you in a more meaningful direction.

To illustrate this concept, I'll use an example from my own creative journey. I began with the end in mind when I decided I wanted to have a solo photography exhibit showing my latest work. I had no idea of when, where, or how I was going to achieve this. I just knew that if I could realize this big-picture goal, it would be a fulfilling accomplishment because it had been 20 years since my last solo photo exhibit. It also was important because my pursuing this would serve as a good role model to my creativity course participants. Once I created my vision, I then began to look at ideas of how to accomplish this.

Now contrast this big-picture approach with a step-by-step method in which I start at the beginning, which means setting an intention of more exposure for my photography without declaring the end creation up front. In other words, sometimes you can picture the end result and work backward and other times, you start small and work toward the end. Both methods require further ideas, exploration, analyzing, and executing—all stages in the creative process.

CREATIVITY COMPASS

Although Stephen R. Covey's book, *The Seven Habits of Highly Effective People,* was aimed at and embraced by the business market, the habit he describes as "Begin with the End in Mind" also gives you another approach to your creative thinking. You're looking first at your desired destination, what matters most—not the details of how you'll get there.

In this instance, once I decided that in the end my photography would be featured in an exhibit, I began selecting, printing, and framing my photos. Within a year, I learned about a nonprofit organization whose mission is to provide temporary lodging for the families of hospitalized loved ones. They had established a program for artists to display their work in the home as a way to add beauty and recognize local artists. I was selected to exhibit my photos for one month and enjoyed celebrating with many supporters at the opening. The opposite approach would have been to start at the beginning by generating ideas, exploring, and examining multiple options to feature my photography with no decisive end in mind.

Determining your specific goal up front and what it looks like may serve as the inspiration you need to start and keep going toward this creative vision. Otherwise, you can get lost in the details along the way, which may result in discouragement. When considering one of your creative undertakings, experiment with this practice by looking first at the big-picture results you envisioned and why this is meaningful to you. Once you have an idea of what you'd like to achieve, work backward from there, breaking the steps into doable action pieces.

Good Ol' Brainstorming

Brainstorming has been around for decades and is still a great tool for unleashing ideas. You can use it when you're getting ready to embark on a new project or creative direction, as well as when you want to improve on an existing one. This activity works best with groups, with everyone participating and every idea getting recorded. Usually, one person stands before the group and writes all of the ideas on a white board, chalkboard, or flip chart where all can see. This scribe should take notice of those who are not contributing and encourage them in a fun way to take part while putting limits on the folks who try to dominate the session.

The focus of a brainstorming session is on quantity, not quality. The quality part comes later during the "analyze and act" stage of the creative process (see Chapter 4 for a refresher on the creative process). Therefore, it makes no difference if the same idea is repeated with different wording; write it down anyway. Sometimes the same thought said another way can evoke other meanings and ideas. The process should also be done quickly. If a thought comes to your mind that you silently judge as being silly, say it anyway!

The key to an effective brainstorm is *no judgment!* Ah, but it's so tempting to blurt out, "We've tried that before. It'll never work." Resist that temptation! The scribe—or you could have another person who serves as a moderator—should remind the participants of the "no judgment" rule. This is especially crucial when and if someone shows any sign of criticism or disregard, which includes anything from outbursts to rolling eyeballs.

Now, all that said about judgment, there are some creativity experts who say this old style of brainstorming actually inhibits new ideas. They believe if there is no discussion as to why certain ideas won't work, there will be fewer creative ideas put out there because all of the ideas are already being seen as possibilities. No one is saying that ideas (and the people who say them) should be attacked in any way, but they propose if an idea is properly criticized, it may prompt other group members to improve upon others' ideas. I think this is a matter of trial and error to see what works better for your group. Personally, I believe you can still play off of someone else's idea without the need for judgment or why an idea won't work. See what works best for you and discuss all of the "rules" or guidelines before the session begins so everyone understands the process.

While taking part in this process, keep in mind that ideas also should not be discussed in depth during this process; you and other participants are simply throwing around ideas. When the time comes to select your best ideas, you can then potentially use the technique of combining unlike ideas. You may find that this combination provides a better solution than using only one idea.

 INSPIRATIONAL INSIGHT

"Creativity is a great motivator because it makes people interested in what they are doing. Creativity gives hope that there can be a worthwhile idea. Creativity gives the possibility of some sort of achievement to everyone. Creativity makes life more fun and more interesting."

—Edward de Bono

Create a Mind Map

Mind mapping is a process that uses a mix of images, colors, and thoughts that are visually organized with branches of keywords. This organization activates associations in the brain to further ignite ideas. You can draw the maps by hand or by the more modern version of software, such as iMindMap (app.imindmap.com). You do not have to be an artist to partake in this process!

I was first introduced to mind mapping in the late 1980s when I attended a seminar on time management. It was about 20 years before that when international speaker and author Tony Buzan developed the technique to help students take notes using key words and images. The visual aspect helps to make the material more memorable and conveys concepts that can otherwise be complicated in an easier fashion. Buzan believes that mind mapping increases creativity along with organization, productivity, and memory.

To make a mind map, start with a core idea that you wish to explore, teach, communicate, remember, organize, or study and write the word or phrase in the middle of the page, along with an image that ties into your topic. So if you were to do a mind map on "Things I Love," for example, you would write that phrase and draw some type of image, which serves as visual stimuli for your brain. Next, start adding branches with words that relate to their "mother" branches, which flow from your central image. So each branch contains one word, and the branches become your key themes. You can continue to add as many secondary branches as you wish that extend from the main branches. There are no restrictions! Your brain will naturally form new associations as you add more pieces.

To connect the visual and logical aspects of your mind map, Buzan recommends color coding your branches. This leads to whole-brain thinking and mental shortcuts. Adding color also enables you to identify even more links through highlighting, analyzing information, and categorizing. Plus, color makes it more pleasing to the eye!

Remember the old saying "A picture is worth a thousand words"? That concept applies to mind mapping, too. Add some images to your map to further express your topic. If you do an internet search for examples of mind maps, you will see a whole variety you can use for reference. They don't all follow the process I've outlined to the letter, but they follow the general principles.

To test-drive this tool, I suggest picking an easy topic, one with great familiarity to you, and playing around with it to get an idea of how it works.

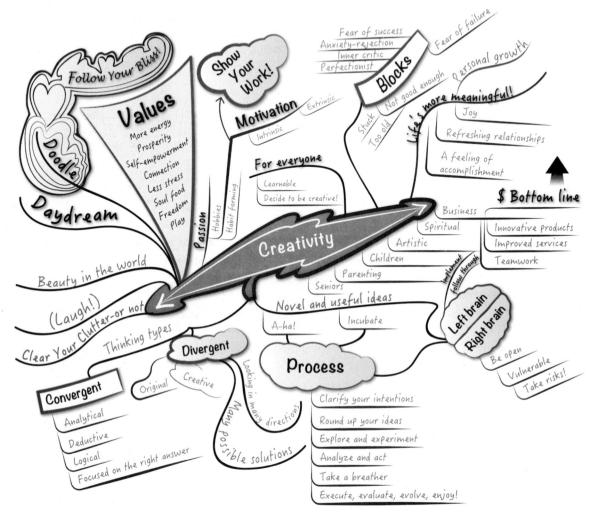

An example of a mind map on the topic of creativity.

How Daydreaming Can Be Fruitful

Have you ever listened to a friend talk and suddenly recognized you have no idea what she said? Or maybe you're in the middle of a business meeting and your boss calls on you unexpectedly for your opinion but you have no clue how to answer because you realized your mind was elsewhere.

The good news is you're not alone. Most people spend 30 to 47 percent of their waking hours daydreaming, according to scientific studies. Furthermore, daydreaming—or mind wandering— also has been found to play an important role in creativity. Studies show those who daydream score higher on creativity tests. There's also evidence of an association between daydreaming and creative problem-solving, memory improvement, and greater connections that are made when the mind is wandering. So if after engaging with some of the previous creative thinking techniques you feel you'd just like to let your mind wander for a while, don't worry—you may actually be supporting your creativity.

Daydreaming occurs when you lose sight of the present moment and begin thinking about things that don't relate to what's in front of you. That's why it's often viewed as a waste of time, just as doodling is often perceived (more on that in the next section). But neuroscientists have discovered that the mind is much more active when it is wandering than when it's wrapped up in reasoning with a thorny problem. Taking a break from the issue and allowing your mind to wander can actually help the creative process by giving your brain time, distance, and reflection space to naturally process and develop ideas while not focused on the problem. Connections—those out-of-the-blue, a-ha, profound moments—are often made between things that appear to be unrelated to the conscious mind during the daydreaming process.

 CREATIVITY KEY

> Some companies give employees time off for reflection before getting back to the problem at hand in order to encourage daydreaming. You can do the same for yourself when trying to figure out a work-related challenge or circumstance. Taking a walk without intentionally thinking of the concept or issue at hand is a great way to let your mind wander and possibly stumble upon a new and different perspective.

However, simply letting your mind wander aimlessly doesn't breed creativity. Unless you are conscious enough to acknowledge these insights, the value of daydreaming diminishes in the creative process. For example, mind wandering can disrupt comprehension when reading or trying to complete a task, according to Dr. Malia Mason, professor of management at Columbia University and former postdoctoral fellow in cognitive neuroscience at Harvard Medical School. She believes wandering thoughts are not random. Instead, they frequently occur due to things you have yet to finish, such as doing the laundry, returning a phone call, or completing a to-do list item. Therefore, she advises clearing the nonessential clutter from your mind so when it does wander, it latches on to more meaningful matters.

So while daydreaming offers benefits to your creativity, you may want to be more aware and selective when you choose to allow your mind to wander. If you're in a meeting and your mind starts to drift, you may have to lasso it and save the daydreaming for another time to spare getting in trouble—that is, unless you're with people who understand the benefits.

Why Doodling Isn't Dawdling

Doodling is another frequently misunderstood activity that carries creativity benefits with it. Some of the better-known folks who have been known to doodle include Bill Gates, Ralph Waldo Emerson, George Washington, Thomas Edison, John F. Kennedy, Lyndon Johnson, and Ronald Reagan. So as you can see, if you doodle, you're in good company. Yet much of society negatively perceives that doodling is for dawdlers. It's often frowned upon as a waste of time and a sign of disrespect when done in the classroom or in the workplace. Many a student and employee have been reprimanded when they and their doodles were "discovered."

While some may think doodling takes away the person's attention, the opposite effect has shown up in studies. A study by Jackie Andrade, a professor at the University of Plymouth, showed that doodlers retained 29 percent more information than their nondoodling equivalents. Engaging in these rough or sometimes not-so-rough drawings actually keeps doodlers from losing focus on matters that are boring or complicated, according to Andrade. Doodling provides just enough mental stimulation to support continued concentration and also prepares the mind for innovative and divergent thinking.

During a TED talk in 2011, Sunni Brown, co-author of *GameStorming: A Playbook for Rule-breakers, Innovators and Changemakers,* delivered a presentation in which she educated the audience about the benefits of doodling. She described doodling as a powerful tool that must be relearned by non-doodlers because it helps them think, creatively solve problems, and process information. Because people take in information in four ways—visual, auditory, reading/writing, and kinesthetic—to fully process information and act on it, she said at least two of those modes must be involved or individually combined with an emotional experience. Doodling captivates all four simultaneously with an emotional experience as a possibility. For example, while doodling at a personal improvement seminar, you may recall an experience from your past that makes you feel happy (emotional experience). However, while doodling is native to everyone, she feels most people deny that inherent tendency. Do you doodle, or have you avoided it due to pressure from others or yourself?

You can consciously decide to doodle in an effort to creatively resolve an issue, find solutions, or dream up new ideas. Or doodling may be done randomly in the spur of the moment. With the latter, you don't plan on doodling—you just do it. I've gotten to know myself well enough that I can almost guarantee that if I'm attending a conference that has one speaker after the next or one person who makes a long presentation, at some point I will begin to doodle—but it's not something I ever plan out. You could, however, try deliberately doodling as a technique to see if any illuminations come to you during the doodling process.

To get a feel for doodling if you're out of practice, experiment with doodling during idle time—for example, while discussing an issue or idea while talking with a friend on the phone or while listening to music. As much as possible, detach from your conscious mind and just allow yourself to draw whatever rises to the surface. Do not judge what you are drawing! No one ever has to see your scribbles or masterpiece (however you view it). Perhaps something in your doodle will stand out later as a helpful clue to your situation. The awesome thing about doodling is it's easy to do without expecting anything of yourself. Only the most intense perfectionist would expect flawless doodles. (Is there such a thing?)

 CREATIVITY COMPASS

Sunni Brown feels so strongly about the importance of doodling that she is literally leading a "Doodle Revolution." You can join her by signing up on her website, sunnibrown.com/doodlerevolution.

Creative Play: Doodle Instead of Dawdle

This doodle exercise will be one you do deliberately and with intention but with no pressure attached.

Tools Needed: Your choice of paper or a whiteboard and writing instrument(s)

Because this chapter presented a lot of ideas, your brain could probably use a break. Ergo, the theme of this doodle will revolve around any topic you choose. Make it fun and easy! If you're stuck, consider the topic of relaxation and draw whatever images come to you.

Now doodle away—and relax! Just let your subconscious mind lead your drawing hand. Scribble or draw circles, boxes, flowers, symbols, letters, or smiley faces—whatever moves you! Use different colors if you wish, or keep it simple and only use one. If you're new at this, create your own style. If you're a regular doodler, either enact your usual style or try something new.

Once you finish, reflect on this process. How did you feel going into it, while you were doodling, and afterward? Was it comforting, or did you feel any resistance? Did any new insights come to you during the process? Will you incorporate doodling more into your everyday life or use it only as a creative tool? To go beyond this exercise, try doodling in a real-life situation and see if you notice your mind reaping the benefits of mental stimulation.

The Least You Need to Know

- Letting go of old assumptions will further enhance your creativity by removing limitations to what you want to do.
- Being creative is less about mystique and more about being committed to exploring new ways to think.
- The more you practice your creative expression, the more it will flourish. It does not just happen magically.
- There are numerous creative thinking techniques that will help you make the shift from old to new thinking patterns. You just have to be open to shifting your mind-set.
- Daydreaming and doodling are often perceived by people in charge as a waste of time, yet research shows that they can actually enhance your creativity.

Pursuing Your Passions

Passion is a powerful driver of creativity. It is what makes your heart sing, your eyes light up, and your inner creator dance for joy. So in this delicious chapter, you will be tapping into your true, authentic self, as defined by you and your passions!

While you may already be aware of what you're passionate about, once you explore this chapter, you may find you've discovered some additional loves. Or if you're at a time in your life when you're not feeling enthusiastic about anything in particular, this chapter provides the perfect opportunity to give yourself permission to dream, notice what stirs your soul, and ultimately decide what is yours to do.

In This Chapter

- Seeing passion as "self-full" rather than "selfish"
- Getting in touch with your passions and hobbies
- How collecting can lead to creativity
- How achieving balance in your life makes room for creativity

What It Means to Be Passionate

In Chapter 1, I asked you to note the images, words, and phrases that came to your mind when hearing the word *creativity*. You may have listed things like painting, sculpting, photography, jewelry, woodworking, acting, screenwriting, filmmaking, writing, songwriting, playing music, or dancing. It may have even been something outside the arts that are typically associated with creativity. No matter the subject, they can be considered a passion.

What's your passion? Maybe it's an art form you've been practicing for years, or maybe it's a more recent pursuit. It could be something you do in the workplace or a hobby to which you dedicate your time and talents. Whatever the case, being passionate about something means you have a strong desire or interest in the subject.

Passions are often fueled by emotions that are tied into beliefs and social and moral issues, and the intensity of your feelings drives them. You're inspired, eager, and energized to learn more and take action to purse your passions. They feed your soul, make you feel happy, and help you live your life "on purpose."

Passions vs. Goals

Your passion doesn't have to be tied to a specific activity as much as a feeling that you're after. In the book *The Passion Test,* authors Janet Bray Attwood and Chris Attwood address this difference by defining passion as "how you choose to live your life" and a goal as "something you aim to achieve." So while a goal is focused on the outcome, a passion is about the process behind how you accomplish your goals.

For example, maybe you feel strongly about serving others, which can manifest in a number of ways, such as volunteering in a soup kitchen or visiting those without family in a nursing home. Decorating your home, walking on the beach, and staying physically fit are other examples of passions. For me, my passion of serving others comes in the form of supporting people on their creative paths. Recognizing that led me to become a certified creativity coach and made me feel strongly about writing this book. Simply put: your passions are things you love to be, do, or have. They hold value and meaning. They turn you on.

 CREATIVITY KEY

If you knew you couldn't fail, what would you do? If money were no obstacle, what would you pursue? If you didn't have to work, what would you take on? These are important questions for you to answer because they allow you to use your imagination without erecting walls and boundaries. Allow yourself to fully explore with no limitations whatsoever. This will help you tap into your passions.

Overcoming Common Blocks to Passion

I believe everyone is passionate about something. Passions are about what you love in life. However, there is a negative connotation to having passion that can keep some people—possibly even you—from fully embracing it.

For example, I once had a friend say to me "I'm not passionate about anything." In this case, the problem wasn't a lack of passion, but what my friend considered to be things people should be passionate about. This arises when you begin to compare yourself to other people, a block I identified for you in Chapter 6. You might think if you're not passionate about a cause that involves hundreds or thousands of people, your passions are not worthy. Yes, it feels great to help other people, but passion starts with one person—you. While it's true there may be varying levels of passion, that doesn't mean what you're passionate about is better or worse than anyone else's. In the end, passion should be something that is uplifting to your soul.

Another common issue in relation to passion is the "selfishness" associated with it. Sometimes people feel guilty because they think they're being selfish when they lock themselves in a room and spend a few hours painting or taking up some other solo activity. Pursuing your passions is what I call being "self-full"—filling yourself with the loves of your life—not "self-ish." Allowing yourself to become immersed in your passions is about filling up your tank. If you ignore what helps give you life, just like a vehicle, it won't be long before you're running on empty and unable to give to yourself or anyone else. Being self-full doesn't mean you shirk responsibilities to your family, friends, or co-workers; it just means taking the time to fill yourself up with goodness so you can function from your highest and best self possible. It is from this place of self that you are able to give back to others.

For example, one of my passions is having music in my life—learning and playing instruments, singing and songwriting, and listening to live and recorded music. For many years, I kept my songwriting and performing to myself, unable to share with others due to my own blocks. I derived a certain amount of satisfaction and pleasure by practicing this passion privately. Later, I learned how much more I nurtured myself and others by sharing my gifts. As you can see, what may be considered a "selfish" practice by some can nurture both you and others.

 INSPIRATIONAL INSIGHT

"I would rather die of passion than of boredom."

–Vincent van Gogh

So you're missing out on a big piece of your life if you don't allow yourself to pursue what you love. It makes no difference if you're a professional, a homemaker, retired, a full-time creative, or working in a field that has nothing to do with the arts. It's time to take a serious look at play! This is your time to dream with no limits; to really feel into your passions; and to discover, uncover, and recover what has either been missing or hiding from your life.

Creative Play: Seeing Your Passions Through Patterns

One way to help you identify and clarify your passions is by looking at different areas and interests of your life. What you're seeking to do with this exercise is to see whether there are any patterns that emerge that can give you a greater sense of awareness and direction that may help define your passions.

Tools Needed: Paper and a writing instrument

1. Write down activities that bring you the most joy or are meaningful to you. What do you derive from engaging in them?

2. What type of music moves your soul? List all of categories and how they make you feel. If it's easier, list the band names or names of songs.

3. Make a list of your top 6 to 10 favorite books. What stands out to you about each one?

4. List 6 to 10 of your most loved movies. What is their appeal?

5. Do you enjoy being in crowds, with small groups of people, or alone? You may enjoy all of these options depending on your mood. Do they rank equally or does one outweigh another? Provide a short explanation.

6. What type of people do you prefer to hang out with? Describe the personality types that inspire you.

7. Do you love the outdoors or prefer to be indoors? Write about your preference and the reason behind it.

8. Are you a morning person or a night owl? At what time do you feel the most creative?

Once you've answered all of the questions, see if there are any patterns. Can you identify any shared features or attributes? For example, you may see the movies, books, and songs you listed all involve love and relationships. Or perhaps most of your top movies are comedies and you like lighthearted, funny books. You don't need to come to any big conclusions with this exercise. The idea is simply to help you tune into your true, inner being and what stirs your emotions by examining whether there are commonalities that may point you to your passions.

Getting Lost in Time

One way you can determine what you love is by recalling those activities in which you lose all track of time. As long as this doesn't lead to you missing important appointments or obligations, this feeling can be wonderful because it means you're enjoying what you're doing in the moment. And without even noticing, those moments become minutes, which become hours. For example, as a night owl, I often stay up until 2 in the morning, especially if I'm engaged in a creative activity such as doing video postproduction. I am so engrossed with what I'm doing that time speeds by unnoticed. What causes you to get "lost in time"? What do you feel you could do "forever" and not grow tired of?

Start to observe when time seems to vanish into thin air. How often does it happen? When it occurs, do you seem to be more focused, more joyful, or more intense? While there are occasions when you get "stuck" in a situation that's beyond your control, for those times when you are in charge, notice how you spend your time, how fast or slow it seems to go, and the reasons behind these feelings. You'll know what constitutes good decisions on your part by how you're feeling both during and after your activity.

As you think of those occasions, are there any that feel like you're wasting your time? I'm not talking about taking a break every now and then. That's an essential part to providing balance in your life. See if you can get better at "catching" yourself spending time unproductively. One clue is when a guilty feeling comes over you while you're doing the activity. Once you become aware, you can either consciously decide to continue and enjoy it; stop in that moment; or set a reasonable time limit to continue and then stop. Making a conscious decision will turn a time waster into something more productive. You can also take a few moments now and write down three to five ways you waste time and then do the same for the activities in which it seems time flies. There's a reason for that saying "Time flies when you're having fun!"

If you recall in Chapter 6, I made the point that the amount of time doesn't change. The quality of how you spend your time does change though, depending on what activities you undertake. The great news is that, once again, you get to decide! Ruminating what keeps you in the moment and causes you to lose track of time will help you prepare for the next creative play.

 CREATIVITY KEY

One of the keys to uncovering and discovering your passions is to allow yourself to be vulnerable enough to fully examine what's in your heart. Think about what really matters to you and leave all judgment behind. Do not compare your interests to anyone else's. Only you can determine what truly nourishes your inner being.

Creative Play: Identifying Your Passions

In the first creative play in this chapter, you explored your passions by seeing common threads or patterns that emerged among your interests. Here, you will be pondering more questions to further hone in on your passions.

Tools Needed: Paper and a writing instrument

Start by carefully contemplating the following questions; however, do not write your answers yet:

- What do you absolutely love to do and why?
- What are you curious about?
- What can't you live without?
- What brings a smile to your face?
- What do you look forward to doing?
- Is there anything that has intrigued you that you have yet to explore?
- What kind of environment makes you feel the most alive?
- What do you observe others doing that makes you think "I wish I could do that"?

Now sit erect in a chair with your feet touching the ground and your arms at your side. Close your eyes and focus on your breath. Begin to inhale and exhale slowly, and then start to visualize your answer to the first question. When you have some clear pictures and thoughts, write your answer, and then go through this process again for each question and response. Be as detailed as possible to glean as much insight as you can. Finally, write down the passions that come to mind using the information you just gathered.

Identifying your passions is not a finite process. You may find what you are fascinated by today changes over time and you develop new passions, or you may have a lifelong passion to which you dedicate your life. It's possible to have both.

Connecting Creativity with Collections

Sometimes your passions are tied to things you collect—coins, comic books, butterflies, stamps, sports memorabilia, antiques, cars, autographs, shells, tools, recipes, books, political paraphernalia, artwork, records, and dolls, to name a few. Some collections hold financial value, while others only hold sentimental significance. Some may collect to associate themselves with a part of history, while others collect and share their treasures with people simply because it's fun. Some may even collect as a way to establish a unique identity, such as "the tie-dye queen" or "the king of pocket knives." Are you one of the many folks who enjoy collecting things? Collecting is a process that may be helpful in identifying your passions and inspiring your creativity.

For example, I grew up in a super-small Ohio town and there were very few stores. But there was one place within walking distance to my home that intrigued my siblings and me. I'm not sure if this was the actual name, but we called it "The Rock Shop." The man who ran the store had beautiful collections of rocks and I guess it's that memory that inspires me to collect rocks today. In recent years, a creative spark moved me to paint encouraging words on some old rocks I had gathered from a brook, which provided a pleasurable afternoon of creative activity.

Do you have collections that inspire your creativity in some way, either directly or indirectly? For instance, if you're into collecting butterflies, you might have them strewn throughout your house in the form of paintings, designs in mugs, or a stained-glass ornamental piece that hangs in front of your kitchen window. A direct creative connection could be that you paint pictures with butterflies in them or photograph them. An indirect connection might be that just having them around your house provides an atmosphere that makes you feel cheerful and light, which sets the mood for you to create. Whatever the case, your passion for collecting can turn into a creative outlet.

Committing to Personal Pleasure

Now that you're better attuned to your passions, you may have discovered they are associated with a particular hobby or perhaps more than one. However, this isn't the case for everyone. Some may feel like their lives are already too packed to add a hobby. If you are not actively engaged with a hobby, I strongly encourage you to begin one—if for no other reason than to see what kind of a difference this commitment may make in your life. You could be pleasantly surprised.

Benefits of Having a Hobby

There are many benefits to having a hobby that can enhance your creativity and then some. In a *New York Times* online article, Eilene Zimmerman referenced several medical experts on the benefits of hobbies. One said hobbies can help you think with more clarity and concentration and can elevate your creativity, while another stated that "lost in the moment" feeling of focus can release brain chemicals that ultimately help to energize you and make you feel more optimistic.

CREATIVITY COMPASS

From the time Diane was a young child, she enjoyed drawing and painting and went on to major in art in college. She worked briefly as a graphic designer before getting married and starting a family. Her artwork went by the wayside as she reared her family of four and homeschooled them. Once her youngest child began attending the public high school, however, Diane felt the urge to start painting again. She felt very unsure of herself after taking a 30-year hiatus from a hobby that she once loved. But with some coaching encouragement, she began painting every day. Within three months, she not only completed her first painting in decades, she also was accepted to show her work in a public art show!

Hobbies have also been known to help those involved with them to improve their mental and physical health with lower blood pressure, less depression, and reduced stress. For example, spending time focused on a specific leisure activity can provide a positive diversion from the workplace and routine responsibilities, which can lead to a more relaxed attitude.

Hobbies also help you tune in to your talents—gifts you may not have even realized that you had—and open up a whole new world for you. For example, one of my creativity students thought her primary creative interest was music until she started painting. Her life then took off in a new direction. So engaging in a hobby allows you to learn more about the chosen subject and develop new skills, which makes you a more interesting and creative person.

There's also a social element to hobbies that can foster creativity. Being involved with your hobby may lead you down a path of connecting with like-minded people and making new friends. Plus, breaking from your routine also gives you a chance to see things from a new perspective, which may translate to new ideas in the workplace, with your family, or insights about yourself.

How to Get Started

If you're feeling hesitant to make such a commitment, the following are some ways to get you started (check out the creative play for another option):

Begin with a short-term project and see how it makes you feel. That way, you can always decide later whether you wish to continue. For example, if you have an interest in making art, check to see if there are any classes available that are packaged in six-week courses in the medium of your choice, be it painting, sculpture, stained glass, woodworking, or something else. If you're interested in dance, different types of dance classes are usually offered for couples and groups on a short-term basis. Or you can attend a single daylong workshop on a topic you want to explore to see if you leave feeling inspired to take action.

Harness the power of the internet. Going online to YouTube provides a quick and cost-free way to learn many new things, from playing an instrument to making birdhouses. It also lets you explore hobbies on your own time, from the comfort of home.

Follow your friend's lead. If you have a friend or co-worker who is already involved with an activity that interests you, see if you can tag along to see how inspired you feel from observing or getting involved while having someone who has been at it for a while share information.

When exploring a hobby, do it with an open mind and a positive attitude. Otherwise, you'll defeat the purpose without giving it a fair chance. If you find a hobby that brings a sense of freedom and fun, you can keep going as long as you'd like. If your interest turns out to be different from what you had hoped, it's not permanent; you're free to seek another hobby at any time. Investing in yourself, even if it's for a limited period of time, may bring you more joy than you could have ever expected and leave you wanting more!

 CREATIVITY KEY

By engaging in a hobby, you may benefit from increased self-esteem and self-confidence, decreased anxiety, and improved job performance due to your boost in confidence. For example, you may be able to come up with new ideas for the workplace or another personal pursuit that you glean from your newfound hobby. Therefore, choosing to use your leisure time with hobbies helps you to branch out beyond your existing identity. You'll begin to see yourself in a brand-new way—and others will, too. Chances are, your new, inspired self will serve to make others look at you and say "I'd like to bottle some of that feeling myself!"

Creative Play: Rewarding Yourself with a Hobby

If you do not currently enjoy a hobby or are open to a getting involved with a new hobby, this exercise will help you get started.

Tools Needed: Paper and a writing instrument

Looking at the passions you identified and your collections, do any of them relate to a hobby that interests you? Are you considering something you've never done before, an activity you've longed to do for a long time, or revisiting a past interest you dropped a while back? List all of the hobbies that you are seriously considering.

Next, think about what interests you most about taking on a hobby. Are you looking for a stimulating challenge, more relaxation and less stress, an opportunity to feel more alive and childlike, a way to meet new people, or a sense of completion? Write down everything you can think of that would motivate you to take action to begin one of the hobbies you listed.

Now describe the level and length of time you are willing to commit to a hobby—at least what you are thinking right now. For example, you may think you only have time for a six-week commitment, but you may end up enjoying the time spent with your hobby so much that you continue. What will you either eliminate or cut back on to make room for a new hobby (such as spending less time on social media and watching TV)? Also, will your hobby be taken up strictly as a side interest or would you like to develop it into a professional undertaking?

Before selecting your new hobby, also consider your resources. Does the activity require tools, materials, or other things that require money and are you willing to make this investment? Beyond materials, do you feel you need personal support to get started? Is it possible you could interest a friend in participating in a hobby with you? Perhaps there are group sessions available. Or you may just need someone to serve as your cheerleader and encourage you along the way.

Once you've thought about the investment you want to make, be sure to schedule in "hobby time" on your calendar. Make it as important as a business meeting or another important responsibility.

Are you ready to take action? If not, what's holding you back? Are any of the same obstacles that were getting in the way of your creativity now interfering with this initiative? When you've dealt with those obstacles, you can select your hobby.

There are all kinds of creative possibilities that are built into hobbies. I truly hope you will take this leap of faith to add another opportunity for self-expression. It's just another way you can enrich your life. Enjoy the process!

Enhancing Your Creativity Through Bliss and Balance

Whether you're engaged in a new hobby or vigorously pursuing your passions, the idea is to "follow your bliss." That's a catchphrase coined by Joseph Campbell, who dedicated his personal and professional life to studying the human psyche along with past and modern-day myths. He practiced what he preached by completely immersing himself in studying and teaching how many cultures and myths manifested in individuals (including artists and philosophers) and in societies. Like Campbell, there is something sacred to be known and expressed inside you, and it is in this knowing and actualizing that you're following your bliss. This knowing is the ability to recognize what moves you for the greater good of both yourself and those whose lives you touch and may be accomplished through your passions or hobbies.

Continue to check in on a regular basis to see if you're doing what makes you truly happy. Another clue that you're on the right path of your passions is that you feel you just can't get enough of whatever it is you're doing. Also, continue exploring your passions and hobbies with an open and curious mind. Let go of judgment of yourself and others and perpetually focus on what brings you joy. This will help clear your mind of those things you don't want. Just as with affirmations, you want to tell yourself what you desire. In following your bliss, you are concentrating on positive aspects. If you fill your mind with radiant views, the light will outshine any darkness.

When it comes to working, you may love what you do. Still, it's important to be sure you're making room in your life for your personal passions to provide a healthy balance. Those who deal with the dying don't hear many (if any) people say their only regret is that they wish they would have worked more or been more serious. The opposite of that is true; they wish they would have spent more time with the people and activities they love. When it comes to me, if I have one addiction, it's that I'm a workaholic. However, through the years, I've gotten better at balancing my life by making time to pursue and enjoy my passions and hobbies, spending more time with loved ones, planning fun activities, and being there for others when they most need me.

So like me, take an honest, hard look at yourself and determine how balanced your life feels. If you're feeling out of whack, ultimately your creativity will suffer. Look beyond the workplace and financial security and into all areas that are important to you. This may include relationships, friendships, spirituality, leisure time, continuing education, physical fitness, emotional health, rest, hobbies, and your passions (which could be anything from a noble cause such as feeding the hungry to an activity as simple as hiking). Once you are aware of how you spend your time, you can begin to create a better balance. This greater balance then makes it easier to create because you're coming from a more stable position.

 CREATIVITY KEY

To take a critical look at how you spend your time, write out all of the areas that are important to you and assign a percentage to each until they add up to 100 percent. Next, close your eyes and come from your heart space to see if the areas with the highest percentages are in alignment with the parts of your life you feel are the most significant. This will provide a roadmap of where your imbalances are, which starts the process of achieving a more balanced life. Begin to work toward making any necessary adjustments and repeat this process at least once a year because your priorities may change.

The Least You Need to Know

- When you tap into the core of your essence—that is, what truly makes you happy—and you heed the call, you'll not only feel the joy within your own being, others also will benefit from your unique self-expression.
- Being passionate encompasses all of the things in life you feel strongly about. Consider your passions to be the "loves of your life."
- You know you're in a state of positive flow when you get lost in what you're doing, not to the exclusion of your responsibilities, but in addition to all you accomplish and enjoy. Time becomes timeless!
- There are numerous benefits to starting and maintaining a hobby. You owe it to yourself to turn an interest of yours into a hobby, one that can potentially feed you emotionally, mentally, physically, and spiritually.
- You will be more creative if your life is balanced in all of the areas you deem important.

Enhancing Your Creativity with Partnerships

Creating on a regular basis is much easier when you have the proper support. This support may come from friends, family, mentors, instructors, counselors, or community members. What is most important is to get the encouragement and assistance you need to get started and keep going.

While creating in a vacuum is possible, in this chapter you learn the value of ensuring you have a support system. I also talk about being open to how your talents can make a difference in your community, even if that is not your main motivation to create. After all, many lives have been changed when people decide to reach out and share their gifts, which is a powerful part of creativity that awaits your participation.

In This Chapter

- Prepping yourself to collaborate
- The benefits of partnering
- Growing creatively with a support group
- Using your talents to give back
- Working with a creativity coach

Making Connections

Some creative projects are a solo act, while others excel as a duo or with an entire chorus of people. This is not a literal translation (although it could be, if you're talking about music). What I'm referring to are your preferences to create. Do you prefer to engage in creative pursuits on your own, with a partner or group, or involve the community at large in some way? Perhaps you have experienced all of those situations depending on the project. There also may be times you are asked to partner with a person or group of people in a classroom setup, with a volunteer opportunity, or in the workplace. Sometimes working with others can be inspirational as you see how each person contributes to the whole, uniquely contributing her part. When the creative endeavor is completed, you can see how much better the outcome was because of the different ideas that came together. That's called *teamwork*.

However, in order to be a good teammate, the first connection you need to make is with you. It's a good idea to check in with yourself daily to sift through your thoughts and feelings and determine if any adjustments are needed. You may notice doubts that are continuing to pop up now and then or maybe they're swirling about on a regular basis. Just as being comfortable with yourself helps your creativity when you work independently, feeling free and easy also makes you a better creativity partner.

Also, before approaching a potential partner, notice if there are any voices that pop up in protest saying things like "No, you're not ready for that" or "Remember the last time you tried that? Look how disappointed you were." These are among the blocks that were discussed in Chapter 6. You have now been given many tools to use to work through negative thoughts that block you. It might help to realize that collaborating with another person or a group of people relieves the pressure of coming up with all of the answers on your own. Plus, partnering with others can create a synergy that can be fun!

Engaging a Partner

As discussed in Chapter 4, some people feel they're great at coming up with innovative ideas, while others feel stronger at putting them into practice. Where do your strengths lie? Do you feel you would benefit from working with a partner? While it's not necessary for every creative quest, there may be times when having another person involved would benefit you. The advantage is that the attributes of you and your partner could complement each other, especially if you each have different strengths.

Partnerships work best if you are equally interested in the activity itself and share a common goal. For example, one of the best collaborations in music history is Bernie Taupin and Elton John. Taupin has written most of the lyrics for the songs that have made the pop star famous; it is a duo that has the shared goal of musical creativity. Other examples of successful partnerships with shared creative dreams are Steve Jobs and Steve Wozniak of Apple fame; dancing partners Fred Astaire and Ginger Rogers; Ben Cohen and Jerry Greenfield, who co-founded Ben & Jerry's ice cream company; and Nathaniel Currier and James Merritt Ives, better known as the print-making duo of Currier & Ives.

CREATIVITY COMPASS

Don't be afraid to reach out to others. They may be willing to be a mentor to you. If they can't help you personally, they can probably point you in the right direction. For example, I have a friend, Nancy, who is a professional painter. I not only admire her work, but I also enjoy her pleasant personality. In short, she's easy to be around. I became interested in printing some of my photos on canvas and when I mentioned it to her, she offered to show me how to stretch my own canvases. She told me what tools I would need and then showed me her technique. This was a generous offer, as it saved me money and helped me grow as an artist.

Learning and Mentoring in a Partnership

Partnerships don't necessarily have to be on equal footing in terms of knowledge and experience. Some partnerships come in the form of learning from an instructor, whom you seek for more formal training on a regular basis, or taking a short-term course or workshop. The best teacher-student relationships are those that are viewed as a true collaboration. If you're interested in learning more about your craft, seek teachers who still have that creative spark in their eyes; just being in their presence can inspire and motivate you to learn and grow as much as possible. Another way to support your creativity is to find a mentor. This is usually a person with skills and talents you admire who is willing to help you. This may be in the form of hands-on support or advice—someone you can call when you have questions or need an emotional boost.

There are different ways you can find a mentor or teacher. See if one or more of these options resonates with you:

- Seek recommendations from people you know who have some knowledge or association in your area of interest. They may not know someone directly but may be able to lead you to someone who does.

- Reach out on social media sites such as Facebook, LinkedIn, and Twitter. In your post, be clear whether you're looking for a teacher or someone who is willing to offer you suggestions or advice, which can lead to a mentoring relationship.

- Search the internet with a phrase that addresses your interest. If you're specifically looking for a teacher, include that in your search terms.

- Find out if there are professional associations or clubs that have local meetings and plan to attend one so you can meet people who share your interest. Meetup.com is an excellent resource where you can start or find the group of your choice.

Once you do make a connection, be informal. Tell her why you're attracted to the subject at hand and why you would love to learn more. Your enthusiasm may be enough to inspire her to mentor you.

Another way to help your creativity prosper is by you becoming the teacher or the mentor. While you may not feel like you've been properly trained or educated, teach or share what you know anyway! Chances are you have something of value you can offer to another. In the process, you may have some a-ha moments that you didn't realize until you took the time to explain or demonstrate to another person. If you wait until you feel "ready," you may never do it. Remember, you don't have to do it perfectly! I am guilty of taking my own knowledge for granted. I think everyone already knows what I know because it seems to be common sense. I then think about accountants and how numbers are a matter of common sense, yet I would probably make a very lousy accountant!

So do not take your knowledge, skills, and talents for granted and share that expertise with others. The following are a few ways that you can become a mentor to another person:

- Consistently show a genuine willingness to help others. That makes you approachable to others.

- Offer to be a guest speaker at different clubs, schools, or professional gatherings to share your knowledge. It's possible a mentoring relationship could develop from that opportunity.

- Volunteer with organizations that seek mentors, such as your local Big Brothers Big Sisters charity or the Boys & Girls Clubs of America.

Mentoring an individual doesn't have to be a full-time commitment. It may be a matter of answering questions from time to time or making recommendations. For example, just recently, while shopping at a clothing store, the young man who assisted me overheard me say I was on my way to meet a television crew. That led to a discussion of him telling me how he'd like to learn more about getting into the public relations field. I gave him a few starter tips and he asked if he could contact me later with more questions. I gladly said yes because I am always willing to help, especially young people who display a passion and eagerness to learn. As you can see, sharing your knowledge could make a tremendous difference in the life of another person.

When Problems Arise

Creative relationships are really no different than romantic relationships in that not all of them will last a lifetime. Sometimes the very qualities that attract you to another person are the very things that can cause dissension and separate you later on. It's important to recognize if the setbacks are temporary and can be overcome or if the collaboration has outgrown its usefulness.

If you've enjoyed working with your partner and tensions begin to grow, before throwing in the towel, carefully analyze the situation using the following questions:

- How long has the relationship been stressful? Has it become a pattern, a way of being that's not likely to improve?

- Do you still share the same vision but are seeing different roadways that will take you there, or have your egos stopped you from supporting each other because you're both stuck in your "rightness"?

- Have you accomplished what you set out to do together, or do you feel there is more that can be done in the partnership?

While the partnership doesn't necessarily have to return to the days of old when it first began, it should be something that feels fulfilling for both you and your partner. If you've accomplished what you set out to do or realize your differences are too great, it's probably time to end things. Hopefully, you'll be able to appreciate what you did together and will leave on good terms.

 CREATIVITY COMPASS

> I once ran a small poetry circle in my home. Once a month, about 10 of us would gather, and we would start by sharing a poem that we had written. They didn't have to be recent poems; in fact, I pulled some from my childhood just for fun. Someone later suggested we begin writing to a theme, so we spent the next month writing fresh poetry based on that theme. At the next meeting, we shared our poems. This suggestion prompted us to write new poems to spur our creativity. Listening to the others' poetry also inspired us to write even more.

Forming Support and Interest Groups

If you've ever been a part of a support group of any kind, you already know the power of sharing with others. A great way to massage your creativity is to launch a group for individuals who also want to develop their creative potential. This can be done with or without a facilitator or the use of a how-to book or curriculum, although they can be helpful. You can pick a particular niche you're interested in—such as writing, painting, or photography—or keep it more generic with a revolving creative theme. Just know you can fashion your support group however you want. Be creative!

The following are some general tips to help you best establish a functioning and beneficial group:

Decide how many people you think will work best for your group. Usually, you'll be able to think of a couple people right away who will be interested in participating. Get their feedback on what they think will work. I would caution you from starting out with a large group. The more people you have, the harder it can be to manage. However, if you start out with too small of a group, it may not be long before you find yourself with just a couple other people. That may be all you want anyway, but people often drop out of groups without warning. To keep the flow going, concentrate on inviting people who are truly committed. At the same time, don't organize it so it starts to feel like another obligation. You can play around with the numbers until the group settles into a comfortable mode.

Consider an ideal time and location. Your group can decide to meet weekly, every other week, or once a month. When it comes to how long the meetings should run, give yourself enough time to make the time meaningful; I recommend two to three hours. As for location, select one person's home, rotate homes, or perhaps use a free community center with an available room.

Set some ground rules—mostly common courtesy guidelines—for the group. While you don't want the group to be too structured (as that in and of itself inhibits creativity), everyone should find benefit from being in the group. Make sure every member of the group has a chance to speak and that everyone listens—no interrupting and talking while another already has the floor. For example, some groups use a *talking stick*—commonly used by indigenous populations and Native American tribes to command respect and quiet attention while voicing their views— to combat this issue. The stick is passed around the group and the person holding the stick is the only one who is allowed to talk.

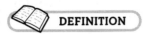 **DEFINITION**

> A **talking stick** is an effective visual tool used by Native American tribes and groups to control who is speaking. Only the person holding the stick may talk, while others listen and wait their turn to hold the stick and speak.

Avoid offering advice. The main purpose of a support group is to encourage each other without the need to tell the members what they "should" be doing. It's more important to show compassion and to listen respectfully to allow the person to share what she is prepared to reveal. You can structure your group to be more of a "talking" group in which you share your challenges and successes. Or you can include an activity that doesn't have to be involved or even related specifically to your group's focus. For example, you could use one of the techniques in this book to develop a creative brain game or have one of your members submit a real-life challenge and use one of the creative thinking tools to generate ideas.

Reaching Out to Your Community

There are many ways to reach out to your local community to share your creativity while inspiring others in the process. Depending on your energy and inspiration level, this may be done occasionally or regularly and on a small scale or on a larger, more encompassing scale. It's really a matter of how you wish to reach out.

For example, one man's creative vision has fostered connection and caring and connected people of all ages and backgrounds. After observing how rarely people make eye contact with one another and actually speak to each other in public places such as on buses, at parks, or in cafés, artist Hunter Frank decided to take matters into his own hands and developed and launched entire creativity programs to change that. Frank's premise was that people really want to connect with each other but they don't know how. Through the Neighborhood Postcard Project, he brought together people from diverse ethnicities and lifestyles through the sharing of postcards that contained positive personal stories.

He also founded the League of Creative Interventionists, a network that involves folks worldwide building community through creative efforts. He organizes monthly interventions that focus on using public spaces to encourage strangers from various social and economic backgrounds to speak with each other. Using the prompt "My first love was …," people share their sentiments on vacant walls and other spaces in San Francisco; Minneapolis; and Cologne, Germany; by completing the sentence on sticky notes and postcards and posting them on the "Love Wall."

He recently gained the support of the Knight Foundation, which has enabled him to start a Creative Interventions Tour in which he is implementing and evaluating how these activities can create more engagement. With what he calls *creative placemaking activities,* he hopes to help people create more spontaneity, playfulness, and connection within their communities that will result in long-term positive change. One activity is called "Vacant Love"; for this, residents write love letters to their neighborhood, which are tacked onto a vacant building. A fundraising event is then held to help renovate the building. He also is conducting workshops and devising interactive activities that are specific to each community.

 INSPIRATIONAL INSIGHT

"Art is essentially communication. It doesn't exist in a vacuum. That's why people make art, so other people can relate to it."

—Conor Oberst

Another wonderful example of using creativity to help mankind is illustrated by Mark Bustos, a New York City hairstylist who works at an upscale salon. He spends the one day he doesn't work giving free haircuts to the homeless, as well as offering food. In a *Huffington Post* online article by

Robbie Couch, Bustos was quoted as saying "I want to do something nice for you today," which is the line he uses with every person he approaches. Why does he use his creative haircutting skills to help? One reason: Because of the rewarding feeling it gives him. He's hoping his generosity inspires others who watch him to also offer their kindness.

Just reading and writing about these creative community outreach projects inspires me. What about you? Did it get your wheels spinning? Hopefully these projects gave you ideas for potential outreach programs you could start in your own community.

However, does the thought of doing such large-scale things fill you with fear? Don't worry! You don't have to take on such ambitious projects. It's about what's in your heart. For example, I once participated in a program that was organized through the local arts council. The other volunteers and I would visit elementary schools and present prints of famous artists to educate and inspire the kids to do art of their own. All that took was a willingness to give my time and to learn about the artists myself.

Like me, speaking to schoolchildren about the importance of creativity is something you can do fairly easily and is a way to give back in a more low-pressure setting. You can do it as a kind of "show and tell" if you have artwork of your own or play an instrument, or you can plan a hands-on activity for the kids in which you guide them. Retirement communities also are prime spots to share your creative work, ideas, and passions. There are organizations—such as AFTA (aftaarts.org) and Generations United (gu.org)—that look to connect people who can participate in programs for older adults.

You don't even have to leave home to reach out to others. There are many other online communities that have formed as a way to connect with one another. One such online community is creativ.com, where members worldwide are sharing samples of their own creativity, inspiration, and ideas. On another, creativity-portal.com, you'll find exercises, articles, and other free stuff all having to do with creativity. So even if you're not meeting with people face to face, you still have a way to impact someone else's life by sharing online.

Whether you spend the rest of your life helping one person or interacting with the world, using your creative expression to make the community in which you live a better place is a worthy and achievable goal. I encourage you to use your imagination to do just that!

Creative Play: The Gift of Giving

For this exercise, you will explore how you can use your creativity for the betterment of your community.

Tools Needed: Paper and a writing instrument

To start, think about your local community. What's missing? What could be improved? What would you like more of? Is there anything that should be dismantled, such as an eyesore? You also can think in terms of a segment of your community—such as nursing home residents, troubled teens, or single parents—and how they may be helped.

Based on your answers to the questions I gave you and any others you asked yourself, make a list of two to five community needs or a particular population you wish to help. Select one of the areas you identified, and use your imagination to generate ideas for how that need can be addressed. You can use your own skills and talents and also involve others, too, especially because your idea is meant to improve your community.

If your idea is bigger than what you can handle right now or requires resources you don't yet have, think of how you can break down your idea into manageable pieces. An example to illustrate this is cities and towns that have transformed their vacant storefronts into a positive experience. In some cases, emerging artists painted the windows to showcase their artwork and art contests were held among students. In other cases, volunteers decorated the windows with holiday trimmings, and the space was then offered to charities to do gift wrapping for customers shopping at nearby stores.

Your idea can be a one-time event or an ongoing activity and on a small or large scale, depending on your resources and volunteer participation. As an option, do this creative play with friends, co-workers, or key members of your community to include partnership in your creative work. Now make a plan and go do it!

CREATIVITY KEY

Creative partnerships that are based on trust, respect, and a sincere desire to co-create can produce results that surpass what you may have accomplished on your own. Play off of each other's energy and ideas and have some fun!

Is Creativity Coaching for You?

Creativity coaching is a fairly new profession that came about in the early 1990s. Eric Maisel, a licensed family therapist and author of more than 40 books (many of which are about creativity), founded this new profession as a way to help his clients overcome their blocks, effectively deal with the marketplace, produce more meaningful work, and deal with other issues relating to their creative process. You may have not even heard of this practice until now and you may be wondering, what exactly is a creativity coach, and what can one do for me?

Creativity coaches can assist you in understanding and getting past your creative blocks and barriers that prevent you from starting or completing your projects. They can serve as an impartial sounding board and guide you toward solutions. The operative word here is *guide,* for a good coach doesn't *tell* you what to do; rather, you are led in such a way that you realize on your own what direction you should go. Coaches are there to empower you, not make you depend on them for a long period of time. An effective coach motivates you to pursue your creative goals and dreams. In short, creativity coaches support you on your creative journey. There are some coaches who specialize in certain areas. For example, some only work with writers, visual artists, or actors. Others, including myself, have a more open clientele and work with creative and business professionals, hobbyists, emerging artists, retirees, and homemakers—anyone who wishes to create something new or different in their lives.

Reasons to Work with a Coach

Individuals seek coaching for different reasons. See if any of the following resonate with you; if so, you might benefit from working with a creativity coach.

- You have one or more specific creative projects in mind but don't know where to start.

- You want to create new opportunities in your life but need help honing in on what's really important.

- You want to make changes in your life but fear keeps getting in the way.

- You're feeling stuck and need help working through your blocks.

- You're in the process of a major transition and you're feeling overwhelmed and uncertain about what lies ahead.

- You could use support in establishing, focusing, and organizing your priorities.

- You need help with accountability and believe checking in with a coach will motivate you to follow through.

How Do Sessions Work?

Some creativity coaches will give you the option of working together in person, by phone or video conferencing, via email, or a combination of these methods. Regardless of the communication system you choose, most sessions are conducted informally, like a conversation. Every coach has her own style, but the whole idea is that you feel supported by your coach. Your coach should be your biggest cheerleader while at the same time pointing you in a direction that serves you. As the client, you set the agenda for each session.

Expect your coach to ask you powerful questions that will make you think more deeply than you might on your own. Working with a coach also might save you time, as you may achieve a breakthrough more quickly compared to figuring it out yourself. She may even suggest exercises that you do in between sessions to further enlighten you. The goal is to help you achieve clarity and follow through on your intentions.

Where You Can Find a Creativity Coach

One of the best resources is the Creativity Coaching Association (creativitycoachingassociation. com), which trains individuals to become certified as a creativity coach and provides information to those looking to work with one. Founded in 2005, the CCA is a free forum that offers a database of creativity coaches to artists and creative thinkers of all types. You can use the CCA as a resource or sign up to take creativity classes with or without the intention of becoming a creativity coach yourself.

Kaizen-Muse Creativity Coaching (kaizenmuse.com) also lists a number of creativity coaches on its website. Many creativity coaches offer a free consultation. You can take advantage of an introductory session to see if you feel there is a match between you and the coach.

The Least You Need to Know

- Before you can successfully co-create with anyone else, you first have to make sure you're connected with yourself. If you find your inner child is expressing concerns, soothe that small voice within by offering words of comfort. Be both gentle and reassuring with yourself.

- If you choose to work with a partner, recognize that some of the best creative partnerships are those in which your skills and talents complement each other. Expect there to be creative differences on occasion.

- You can support and expand your creativity by finding a mentor or an instructor who values you. You also can take on this role for others.

- Support groups are another way to further your creative passion. Getting together with those who share a passion for creativity is often inspiration in and of itself.

- Creating for the betterment of your community can offer rewards that money can't buy. Start noticing what you can do to creatively enhance your community.

- Consider working with a creativity coach to move through your blocks more swiftly, focus on what really matters to you, help you to be more accountable and follow through, or any number of areas in which a coach can support you.

Creativity and Innovation in the Workplace

Creativity in the workplace is becoming more of an expectation than an option. Perhaps you've already experienced this call to action and you're not quite sure how to respond, especially if you've been doing your job the same way for years. In this part, you learn that creativity isn't just for the folks in the art department; there are opportunities for everyone. Even if you work from your home or don't work at all, you will still be able to glean some tips.

This part starts by giving you ideas on how you can be more creative at work and why that's important. You also take a look at your own mind-set and if your office space is helping to maximize your creativity. I then provide more creative thinking techniques that are designed to help you find innovative solutions to problems, as well as information on why it's important to accept failure as part of the process. This part also addresses creative teamwork. Whether you're the leader or one of the players, you play an important role. Finally, I demonstrate how it really is possible to create when there appears to be no opportunity, honing in on creative burnout and possible causes and solutions.

Developing a Creative Culture in Your Organization

The blog posts and articles are all over the internet. Many corporations, nonprofit organizations, governmental agencies, and small businesses are now asking employees to do more with less—and to do it creatively. Some companies are just jumping on the creativity bandwagon now, while others recognized the need long ago. But just what does being creative in the workplace mean? What does it entail? How do you go about developing a creative culture within your organization?

These are just a few of the questions that will be addressed in this chapter. Even if you are not in the workplace—perhaps you work out of your home or you're retired—you may be able to glean some useful tips from this chapter.

In This Chapter

- How creativity affects the bottom line
- The importance of including everyone in the creative process
- What it takes to be creative at work
- Surrounding yourself with inspiration

Creativity and the Bottom Line

The internet has changed the way just about everybody conducts business, as the world is literally at people's fingertips. As a result, business is conducted much more quickly for many companies and has led to increased competition, which demands generating and implementing new ideas to stay ahead of the pack. However, companies of any size, nonprofit organizations, various agencies, and entrepreneurs can use the entire process of creativity—from ideas and experimentation to innovation and completion—to positively affect the bottom line. Beyond contributing to profitability, other benefits of establishing a creative culture include a more motivated and enthused workforce, improved morale and teamwork, a reputation for attracting quality new hires and retaining happy employees, creative problem solving, and increased customer satisfaction.

For example, the Frito-Lay Corporation looked for innovative solutions to remain profitable while dealing with inflationary costs and keeping prices steady. Frito-Lay's goal was to attain savings of $500 million over a five-year period, so they turned to a consulting company that specializes in creative problem solving. During this process, employees were trained in a creative problem-solving process that consisted of identifying opportunities, clarifying their challenges, and finding and executing solutions. The focus was on "big-dollar opportunities," where savings could be made to offset the money being spent. The commonly asked question among employees became, "How might we …?"

In the end, Frito-Lay exceeded its savings goal time frame by one year—from five years to four years. Additionally, employees learned creative problem-solving skills they continue to use today. According to the consulting company, staff members' motivation and enthusiasm rose significantly, as the entire company culture changed to a positive outlook of possibilities.

As you can see, there's a need for more innovation in the workplace for everything from structuring organizations and involving employees to setting strategy and meeting financial challenges. In fact, according to an IBM survey, more than 1,500 CEOs from 60 countries and 33 industries worldwide identified creativity as the number-one leadership requirement to effectively work through the escalating business complexities involving major shifts, uncertainties, changes, and new regulations. They ranked creativity above "rigor, management discipline, integrity, and even vision."

What has your company or organization experienced? Have you experienced how creativity has helped you in a positive way?

CREATIVITY KEY

Being an inquisitive employee can help develop your creativity and save your boss time. For example, if you have questions about how to proceed with a project, don't automatically seek an answer from others right away. Use your creative thinking skills to come up with your own solutions before getting clarity from your manager. You may just hit upon an innovative idea that may have gone by the wayside had you looked outside of yourself first.

Creativity That Involves Everyone

Developing a creative environment works most effectively if every staff member feels included, from the janitor to the CEO. The traditional viewpoint is that creativity is limited to positions such as graphic designers, illustrators, marketers, PR pros, photographers, writers, production specialists, and editors. But for everyone to get on board and feel a part of a creative culture, ideas from all should be welcomed. If you are charged with instituting more creativity into your workplace or wish to be a part of that, what can you do to help bring this about? You may already have ideas of your own. If not, you could take a page from Michael Eisner, the former chairman and CEO of The Walt Disney Company. In an interview with Suzy Welaufer in the *Harvard Business Review,* he discussed how ideas come from "an environment of supportive conflict." This means employees should feel free to speak up—unlike some working conditions in which they don't dare risk speaking out of turn. The environment should also encourage employees to laugh and have fun.

One of the ways Eisner accomplished that was by launching his company's version of the humorous NBC *Gong Show* from the 1970s, which presented acts that ranged from the absurd to the truly talented. The idea was to perform long enough to survive the gong. The Disney version involved weekly sessions in which all "cast members" (in other words, employees) were invited to attend and offer their ideas. Many were gonged, but some great ideas emerged, including ones that resulted in the movies *The Little Mermaid* and *Pocahontas.*

Another technique employed was discussing ideas in the same room for up to two days and treating all who participated equally—"no pecking order," Eisner said. Eisner spoke about the importance of diversity—including ethnicity and differing viewpoints—and how it aided creativity in those situations. Contrasting opinions got shared and often led to dissension, slowing the process and in turn causing creative ideas may light up. He also described how the best ideas emerged toward the end of the process and how eventually someone said something to bring it all together (see Chapter 14 for how being tired can lead to the discovery of creative ideas).

Like Eisner, you could organize or suggest innovation teams that then feed the ideas to an executive committee. This may work for your company; if not, organize or suggest a structure that does. Even more important than structure is the business sending a message that all employees' ideas and opinions are valued.

 INSPIRATIONAL INSIGHT

"Innovation—any new idea—by definition will not be accepted at first. It takes repeated attempts, endless demonstrations, monotonous rehearsals before innovation can be accepted and internalized by an organization. This requires courageous patience."

—Warren Bennis

Building a Creative Environment

In addition to making sure everyone has the opportunity to be heard, how do you go about establishing a creative culture in your organization? If you're the boss and get to call the shots, it's important to recognize it starts at the top. You set the example (more on this in Chapter 15), and if you're not willing to do what it takes to demonstrate your own creativity and encourage your employees' efforts, your staff isn't going to buy into it. Your creativity quest must be believable through your actions. In other words, that old adage applies—you must talk the talk and walk the walk. If you are an employee who is not charged with making overall organizational decisions, your input still matters—at least in a truly creative work environment. Whether you're a manager or employee, the following are other considerations in setting the tone for a more creative environment.

Rewarding Employees

Recognition goes a long way. If you have employees who report to you, consider setting up a formal rewards program. To do this, think about ways you can reward them for creative thinking, even if the ideas don't pan out. Determine if you want to acknowledge individuals or if there's a way to have staff members work as teams to be recognized together. Monetary rewards may be used but remember, the best ideas often emerge more from an intrinsic motivation rather than extrinsically. Ask your staffers what would be meaningful to them. Obtaining that feedback could be structured as a creative activity in which your employees make suggestions on what would excite and motivate them. If you're not in a position with anyone reporting to you, you can always contribute by letting your boss know what would motivate you to be more creative at work.

Employee flextime is another workplace benefit to consider. As a manager or owner of a company, this can work wonders for your employees' creativity because it gives them a sense of freedom and allows them to play with ideas. For example, many articles have been written referencing Google's 20 percent program, in which Google's employees may use up to 20 percent of their workweek to spend time on projects that have nothing to do with their normal job responsibilities. Some of these pursuits have resulted in actual Google products. However, if you're going to do this, you have to come from a place of trust that they won't take advantage of this opportunity.

If you're an employee who is not in a managerial role, you can always request flextime. First, find out if your company has a flextime policy. If nothing formal is in place, be specific when you approach your boss about being given some flextime. Is this a one-time request or something you wish to do on a regular basis? Are you looking for flextime within the office, or does it involve a different location? For example, are you looking to work a certain number of days or hours at home? Be ready to talk about how the company will benefit, which could be due to improved morale, efficiency, and productivity. Flextime also can mean the difference between an employee staying with the company or leaving. If that's the case for you (perhaps it has to do with child care or a situation that's critical for you to work out), be sure to voice your concern without sounding threatening.

Being Tolerant of Mistakes

Creating a culture in which failure is accepted will help employees to assume risks they might not otherwise take and keep them from playing the "blame game." There's no need for blame if mistakes are viewed as a way to learn and grow.

Remember the discussion on mistakes in Chapter 7 and the response of saying "How fascinating" after making a mistake? Have you adopted a phrase yet that works for you? If you knew your boss would be accepting of mistakes, would this encourage you to explore outside the box more? Chances are, an attitude that is indulgent of mistakes will make you more apt to take responsibility for your own actions as you generate and pursue new ideas.

Having a workplace that's tolerant of mistakes and encourages employees to try new approaches doesn't mean you should throw good judgment out the window. Taking balanced risks is the key, which means you or your co-workers are exploring ideas outside of the norm without putting the organization at serious risk—financial or otherwise. You'll have to find that balance, and hopefully with the help of the overall creative culture, you and your co-workers can reach an understanding that works for everyone.

If you're in the role of manager, there are many different ways to promote "out of the box" thinking. One way is to set up an actual box on a table with colorful sticky notes and announce to your employees that whenever they think of an idea—however large or small—to grab a note, write it down, and stick it on the outside of the box. Their thoughts will literally be "outside of the box" for all to see. Okay, you don't have to set it up exactly that way; that was just my thought of making a fun suggestion box. But you get the idea. It's about letting staff members know they have a place where they can submit ideas either openly or confidentially if they prefer to be anonymous. It's a good practice to give employees opportunities for both private and open sharing to make them feel comfortable with taking risks.

CREATIVITY KEY

Having an environment in which you and any other employees don't feel like you're being watched is vital. How exploratory would you be if you felt like someone's eyes were monitoring your every move?

Promoting a Fun, Casual Environment

While being too casual should be avoided, an environment in which employees can have fun and feel relaxed can help encourage creativity. Remember the benefits of humor that I discussed in Chapter 9? They also apply to a business setting. Research has shown that joking around, especially as it relates to the job itself, can improve the workplace in terms of increased creativity, bonding with co-workers, and accomplishments. Jokes depend on a punch line you don't see coming, just as creativity often depends on linking two unrelated things together, which can lead to innovations. People who can make others laugh easily are often perceived as creative as well. So lighten up and laugh a little more at work—and encourage others to do the same!

Dress-down days are another way to encourage creativity. This enables employees to show their personalities through their clothing, as opposed to a uniform, a dress, or a suit. For example, many companies adopted "dress-down Fridays" a while back to give people a chance to be casual at the end of the week. Of course, all of this depends on your line of work and what's appropriate and what isn't. Still, don't assume you or your co-workers must dress a certain way. "We've always done it this way" isn't acceptable in a workplace that is striving for a more creative climate. Whether you're a manager or employee, closely examine the dress code to see if you think it's time to throw out the old rules and create new policies.

Balancing Deadlines with Flexibility

There's a fine line that separates the need for flexibility and no or low time pressure and the need for constraints or deadlines. On one hand, giving employees flexibility creates more freedom for them, which can be conducive to creativity, because it gives them time to explore and play with ideas. They can examine possibilities to questions such as "How might this work?" On the other hand, too much leeway may take some of the motivation away and lead to procrastination and being unproductive.

A deadline requires you to discipline yourself to create against the clock. Studies show that working under time constraints often results in more productivity but less creative thinking and innovative ideas. In an online *Harvard Business Review* article, "Creativity Under the Gun," the authors suggested that managers should avoid putting employees under extreme time pressure, especially where creative ideas and experimenting with new concepts are involved. There are cases when this can't be avoided, and when that happens, the authors say to develop a mentality of being on a mission in which the employees understand the work is genuinely urgent and critical. In such cases, interruptions and other distractions should be minimized to offset the time pressure and still allow for creativity.

If you're not the decision maker and you feel more time on a particular initiative will lead to a better decision or a more creative process and outcome, take the initiative to ask your supervisor for more time. In the meantime, start to observe your own tendencies when you're working against a deadline and when you are able to function in a more lax atmosphere. Notice if your creativity really thrives when you're on a deadline or if you're being prolific but without the creative insights. You can then do the same when you're working without any kind of time constraints. This kind of observation will help you understand your own needs better.

Designing an Office Space That Speaks Creativity

Whether you work in a home office, a large corporate space, or something in between, how would you assess the design of your workplace environment? Does it inspire you to pursue new ideas, take risks by venturing into the unknown, and energize you? Or are you surrounded by plain, boring beige walls with poor lighting, no windows, and cramped quarters? Are you in an open office space; a cubicle; or a private office with four walls, a ceiling, and a door? If you are serious about establishing a creative climate within your organization, it may be time to take a fresh look at your office space.

The look and atmosphere of your workspace should match your company's mission. Still, even if your business is conservative in nature, that doesn't mean you can't have designated "creative think tank" areas. Of course, it depends how far you're willing to go. One thing's certain: gone are the days where all offices have a traditional layout.

As you read about the possibilities, notice if you are allowing possibilities to swirl about or if you are automatically shutting them down. You know you're keeping an open mind if you're having more positive thoughts, such as "How interesting" or "I'm wondering how that might work in our organization." The negative, closed-minded thinking is what so often gets in the way of creativity. Having more promising thoughts, even if it's something that isn't feasible for your workplace, can lead to new ideas on how to set things up.

Allowing Play in Your Office

What does allowing play in your office mean? No, it isn't intended to encourage goofing off. It just means you recognize the importance of allowing yourself and/or your employees to take breaks and be inspired by their surroundings. Some people spend more time in their workspace than at home yet oftentimes so little thought is put into how an office looks and feels. Challenge yourself to design your office space in a way that beats the typical uninspiring, white walls and lifeless cubicles. Granted, some of the aforementioned items may not be appropriate for your workspace, not to mention the hefty price tag they carry. But what can you do to begin to spruce up your space to encourage more creativity?

CREATIVITY KEY

As you modify your workspace, pay careful attention to how you're affected. See if even the slightest change brings about positive or negative feelings or impacts your inspiration and productivity levels. Keep making changes until you feel you've arrived at the ideal workspace. You can then check in at regular intervals to see if it's still working for you.

Google is one company that is leading the pack when it comes to unconventional office design. A quick internet search of Google's office space reveals photos that show a very colorful, fun, funky, yet functional office space. The colors they use are limited to those in their logo: blue, red, yellow, and green, which reinforce their brand. These colors are featured in signage, lounge furniture, wall accents, and seating. Employees can literally slide from one floor to the next. Wouldn't you love to slide into your workspace? And how about a free haircut on your work premises? That's yet another Google benefit.

Want more unusual examples? How about installing wooden swings, hammocks, billiard tables, full-size basketball courts, video game rooms, beanbag chairs, and a bowling alley—yes, you read that right. You'll find this pastime in one of the Infosys offices. St-rike! These things and more can be found in the comfort of office spaces around the world. If you worked in one of them, you might never want to go home. And that's part of the idea. If employees are surrounded with objects and activities that send a message the organization is serious about play, the results can pay for themselves.

Behind Closed Doors or Open Spaces?

When is the last time you really thought about how your space supports—or doesn't support—you? Look at how your space is currently structured. Whether your setup contains traditional closed offices, open or closed cubicles, or is a wide-open space, ask yourself if the organization would benefit from changing how it's organized.

Open workspaces are becoming more commonplace these days. A more open design encourages more spontaneity and connection among employees and can reduce the amount of internal emails, texts, and instant messages. For example, GlaxoSmithKline reportedly stated that its email traffic decreased by more than 50 percent after its employees moved from cubicles to unassigned worktables. Decision making also was expedited by 25 percent because workers readily met informally rather than turning to emails, according to the *Wall Street Journal*.

The downside to open workspaces is there isn't much privacy, making you possibly feel like Big Brother is watching you—either a co-worker who's tracking your comings and goings or your boss. Being in the open also can mean having to deal with more distractions, including noise and loud conversations.

A way to give more of an open feeling while still maintaining some privacy is to consider the use of glass walls or offices with lots of windows. This is aesthetically pleasing and provides a degree of privacy in that conversations are not out in the open yet happen in a welcoming environment. Glass walls also provide the perfect backdrop to post sticky notes or even use removable paint markers (colorful, of course) to add your points or encourage doodling. Along those same lines, erecting a giant white board in a common area is another way to record ideas, inspirational thoughts, or encourage employees to take a break and doodle. If there's room, put up several white boards in different locations throughout the workspace.

Another common layout that falls somewhere between the totally open-space concept and the conventional office space is cubicles. There are many ways you can spruce up your cube to encourage creativity. For example, Cartoon Network employees deck out their cubicles with cartoon characters, brightly colored furniture, stickers, toys, and stuffed animals, sometimes with themes. Perhaps you can theme your office in a way that supports your creativity day in and day out.

Hot Desking

Remember the game musical chairs? That's where you would set up one chair less than the number of players. Music would play in the background, and when the music stopped, everyone would quickly sit down in a chair—except the one who wasn't quick enough. That game came to my mind when I learned about an up-and-coming practice known as *hot desking*, also known as *activity-based workplaces*. There's no music involved and everyone gets a seat, but it's similar in that employees choose from among the different desks, tables, and work stations at will because no one has an assigned desk. You're guaranteed a spot, but you might not always get the location you were after. As for storage, sometimes employees are given a storage locker to hold their office supplies and other belongings. Described as the "workplace of the future," the idea is to prompt more employee cooperation, teamwork, and innovation.

Some companies are taking this approach as a cost-cutting measure (mostly with regard to real estate) and to address the fact that more of their employees are mobile or spend part of their time working from home and therefore spend less time in the office. Other organizations use this more "free for all" setup to encourage more unusual connections. Each hot desking system can be set up with its own set of rules, including allowing certain spaces to be reserved in advance and dividing the space into sections so employees in certain departments who work together often can be near each other.

DEFINITION

> **Hot desking** is a way of organizing the overall workspace so employees do not have a designated desk of their own. They are free to choose a different desk, table, sofa, or station each day.

Like the other workspaces, hot desking has pros and cons. As for pros, some workers speak of having a higher degree of connection and contact with their fellow employees. Particularly in small offices of less than 20 people on staff, this method makes it feel like they're more of a family. Others report greater collaboration between teams and opportunities. They often lunch together and sometimes enjoy dinner with one another on long days.

Being in close contact also encourages more impromptu conversations and learning opportunities by observing more closely what co-workers from a different division are doing. Also, shared positive energy can lead to even more passion on the job. Some employees also said they like the simplicity of an "instant office"—just grab a table, remove their backpack, fire up their laptop, and they're ready to go. And with more documents being organized electronically due to people not having a standard desk at which to leave materials, there is less paper to file, which allows for a more streamlined operation overall.

The negative aspects to hot desking are a lack of privacy, especially where sensitive information is involved; arguments that can arise and cause disruption; dealing with those who "park" themselves at a workstation; the amount of time it takes to set up each day at a new station; not feeling organized; and the potential spread of germs. As one employee put it, sometimes you just want your own space. Others complained of a lack of identity by not having the opportunity for a personalized space, although in some situations, employees dress up a certain space with photos of their families and personal items that then give those who sit in that space a closer glimpse of what that person is about.

There's no question there are a lot of variables when it comes to this technique, and it won't make sense for every company and every situation. In fact, some companies have found that hot desking works for certain departments, while other divisions work better with a more traditional office setup.

In reading about hot desking, what are your thoughts and feelings? Was your immediate reaction one of negativity, such as "That would never work in our company" or "I would hate that"? Make sure you keep an open mind. Even if hot desking may not be ideal for your workplace, it may serve as a springboard to a whole new pool of possibilities.

Creative Play: My Space Is My Kingdom

In this exercise, you will be looking at what you can do to start creating your ideal office space.

Tools Needed: Paper and a writing instrument

Begin by looking at your current office space. Consider the size of your space, the layout, all of the furniture, knickknacks, what's covering your walls, desk items, drawer and file space, organization, whether it's tidy or messy, colors, smells, and whatever else you notice. Once you've done that, at the top of the page of your piece of paper, write "What I Love About My Office Space." Make a list of what you like on the front of the page, leaving a space next to each thing you like.

Next, turn your paper over and at the top of this side, write "Things That Bother Me in My Office Space." Now list everything that bugs you or you would like to change. Write it down, even if it's something you perceive is beyond your control. Once your list is complete, write down how you would like to change the items that bother you. For example, if you identified the color of your walls as bothersome because they are plain white, you might write "Paint walls green and add decals with inspirational sayings." Write down your ideal solution, even if you don't think you'll be permitted to take this action. Do that for everything you wrote on the backside of the paper. Turn over the page again and, if there are any items you think can be further enhanced, note that next to them.

Now prioritize your lists on both sides of the paper. Pick the top three things you would like to address. Don't assume your ideal solution can't be done; it doesn't hurt to ask your employer, if you have one. If, indeed, the answer is no, think of what you can do to make an improvement that is acceptable to management.

Finally, think through what it's going to take to move on your ideas and then create a timeline that outlines when you will take action.

Because it's important to be in a space that supports you creatively, beware of limited thinking, which places restrictions on you before fully examining the situation. When you're writing your ideal solutions, allow yourself to get excited about what you're thinking!

How You Can Be More Creative at Work

Now that you have read the different considerations in developing a creative culture within your organization, it's time to look at what you can do personally to contribute and develop your own creativity. Whether you are a supervisor who manages people or are only responsible for yourself, if you do your part toward generating a creative climate, it will happen that much more efficiently and quickly and you'll start to see noticeable results. The following suggestions, in combination with what you've learned in previous chapters, can help you contribute creativity to the workplace.

Being Proactive

As you are now well aware, there are plenty of benefits to creativity, such as a feeling of accomplishment and a sense of renewal, as well as increased motivation and more meaning in life overall. In the workplace, more creativity can mean greater teamwork and bonding among co-workers, more commitment, improved morale, better problem solving, and more fun! So don't wait for management to declare a creative revolution. If nothing is being done toward this end, you can take charge by sharing what you know with the "powers that be."

The following are some steps you can take when discussing the creative changes you'd like to see in the workplace:

- Be clear with your intentions and be prepared to offer your ideas on how achieving them might work.

- Use an approach you feel confident will get management's attention without putting them on the defense. You're looking for buy-in.

- Acknowledge your gratitude for any steps that have already been taken (if any) and enthusiastically discuss your willingness to fulfill your role, perhaps as a leader.

CREATIVITY KEY

Before approaching anyone in management, you could see how many of your co-workers are on board. Or if you lead a group of people, you might consider asking for a meeting. That way, you can have a consensus on what everyone wants and can use that to back up your case for more creativity in the workplace.

Keeping an Open Mind

But what if you're not responsible for the creative changes? It's natural to resist change. Why? Because you're used to a certain routine and the changes mean you'll be venturing into unknown territory.

If you're the employee wondering how the creative changes will really make a difference or are skeptical because "we tried that once," do your best to keep an open mind and reserve judgment until you give any new ideas a chance. Be willing to listen, especially if a level of trust has already been established. When you think you already have all of the answers, that's a danger sign. Can you recall any times when you thought you knew how something was going to turn out and then, much to your surprise, the outcome was far better than you expected? If you keep your mind open, at the very least, you'll be willing to be on board and in the best-case scenario, you will be enthusiastic about the new creative direction!

This doesn't mean that you can't ask questions and express concerns. It just means you don't automatically reject the forthcoming changes because they make you feel uncomfortable. If you really think something isn't going to work, rather than being quick to criticize the idea, think about how you would do it differently. Spoken with a positive attitude, you could always offer it as an alternative for others to consider. Having an attitude in which you are willing to adapt will serve both yourself and your organization well.

If you're a manager and have been given the responsibility of leading your department (or perhaps the whole company) in developing a new creative culture, make sure to have the proper groundwork put into place to make everyone feel more comfortable. This means carefully considering the ramifications of the changes and being clear about your expectations based on those changes. Take into consideration the impact of how it affects employees ahead of time and acknowledge how they may feel and react. Also, be willing to listen to feedback. If this new creative directive is handled properly on your end, employees will back the effort from the beginning. They will see what's in it for them and for the organization.

Taking Risks Even When You're Uncertain

Not being sure of what's to come can surface anytime in the workplace, especially in times of economic challenges. While it's much easier to be in an organization that has already established a creative culture, creativity can still breed uncertainty, making you feel uncomfortable and hesitant to move forward with something new in uncertain times. If you can learn how to accept this as part of the creative process, however, you're more likely to move forward.

Being okay with taking risks when the situation is unpredictable ultimately means being okay with making mistakes. While there are known risks, there are also those that are unforeseen. Failures are going to happen—and so are successes. All you can do is examine the potential pitfalls and payoffs and determine if you're willing to take the risk. Developing your creativity involves taking more chances and relying on instincts.

Keep in mind, sometimes mistakes lead to something even better than you originally anticipated, as I discussed in the section on creating by accident in Chapter 4. You may even get to a place where you embrace taking risks because trying out new ideas keeps your job more interesting!

The Least You Need to Know

- Using creativity in the workplace can result in innovative solutions that save money and boost revenues.
- To develop a creative environment within your company or organization, it's crucial you develop it in a way that includes all employees.
- Consider establishing some type of reward system that encourages creative thinking among staff members.
- It's important to accept failure as part of the creative process. Otherwise, employees will be hesitant to pursue innovative ideas for fear of making mistakes.
- Assess your current office space to determine if it's working as efficiently as possible. Be open to making changes, if necessary, and involve your staff to get their buy-in before making any drastic changes.
- It's up to each individual to help establish a creative culture. Contribute your part by being proactive, keeping an open mind, and taking risks.

Solving Problems and Finding Solutions

The one thing that's predictable about the workplace is that it's unpredictable. You may come into work one day with a set plan, only to be greeted with an unexpected issue. Maybe your boss emails you a document that shows a significant drop in revenue for third quarter in a row and says it's mandatory for you and your team to develop a new strategy that will turn things around—and not one that the company has tried before. If she is looking for innovative ideas at a time when you're already feeling overwhelmed, being creative may seem impossible. Where do you start? How do you start?

By building on some of the creative thinking techniques that were presented in previous chapters, this chapter helps you find solutions whenever you're feeling challenged in the workplace.

In This Chapter

- Six innovative thinking techniques
- How changing your routine can have positive results
- Being willing to create change before it's necessary
- How finding the positive in mishaps makes failure more acceptable

Innovative Thinking Techniques

Getting in the habit of shifting your point of view in different ways will help you develop your character, courage, and creativity in the workplace (and in all areas of your life). This means being willing to get away from the way you're used to doing things, seeing with a fresh set of eyes, and thinking in ways to which you're not accustomed. Thinking differently is what can lead to ideas that might not come to you otherwise. In reading about these different techniques, think about problems you've experienced on the job that called for an innovative solution or a situation you might be facing right now where one of these methods will be useful.

Looking Beyond Logic

Your brain naturally wants to think logically because it provides safety and comfort. Logic helps you understand things. But how do you generate off-the-wall ideas or think in ways that fall outside of the norm? As I discussed in Chapter 4, sometimes lightning strikes and you exclaim "That's it!" But that is more the exception than the rule. If you can incorporate some different ways to think when looking for innovative solutions, you won't feel stuck within the confines of that well-known box—the one you're supposed to think outside of.

To move your brain into a different mode, throw logic out the window the next time you're in the idea generation mode. This means using your imagination 100 percent by discarding your assumptions, looking at the opposite of what makes sense, breaking rules, and asking "Why not?" and "What if?" questions. For example, the Pet Rock and its accompanying *Pet Rock Training Manual,* a product developed by ad man Gary Dahl in the 1970s, may not have seemed conceptually logical. However, he sold more than a million of them and became a millionaire. This is something that might have been considered a "crazy notion" for people thinking logically, but in a different thinking mode, it delivered something that was financially successful.

Now stop for a minute to consider your own workplace. What's one aspect of your job that could be improved? Look beyond logic to consider how you might accomplish that. Maybe you don't like the way meetings are conducted and consider them to be a waste of time. How do you move your mind beyond logic and into more imaginative thinking? One way is to think in terms of opposites. Using the meeting example, what would be the opposite of holding a meeting? Never holding a meeting. Does that make sense to your organization? Perhaps, but probably not. But just the thought of that could lead you to think of ways to conduct meetings in which time could be better managed.

You may run in to some resistance from co-workers or management when using this new perspective. Beware of the age-old statement, "That's how we've always done it." The only positive aspect of that statement is that it's an opportunity to respond by saying to the co-worker who said it, "Well then, it's about time we look for more innovative ways to do it." Oftentimes, when a certain business practice is traced to its origin, the reason for it no longer applies, yet the procedure continues because no one ever stopped long enough to question it to see if there's a better way.

 INSPIRATIONAL INSIGHT

"If you have always done it that way, it is probably wrong."

—Charles Kettering

While everyone's situation is different, if you think of an idea that prompts you to think "That doesn't make sense," stay with it. Break the problem down further. Keep asking questions and proposing answers until you find at least one idea that will work. It's about digging deeper and looking at problems from a new perspective. You never know what may come of it!

Creative Play: What If?

The technique of asking the question "What if?" to spur creativity is useful in both business and personal situations, as you learned here and in Chapter 9. Now is your opportunity to test it out.

Tools Needed: Paper and a writing instrument

Think of an existing work situation that you would like to improve or that poses some kind of challenge to you or your team. Write that scenario down at the top of your page in the form of a goal. For example, your scenario could be "Our goal is to modify our workspace into one that increases our efficiency."

Now begin writing "What if?" questions that are playful, irrational, or seemingly impossible. Let your unlimited imagination be your guide. Follow each question with other questions, such as "If we did that, would it mean that …?" or "Could that situation lead us to …?" Using the example I've given here, you might ask "What if, like one of the Google offices, we put a slide between our floors?" That may be totally unrealistic, but allow your imagination to go with it and build upon it. The thought of a slide might lead you to think of a sliding cubicle wall, which could lead you to ask "What if our cubicles had sliding walls that allowed us to slide them shut when we wanted privacy and slide them open when we wanted a more open feeling?"

Keep writing "What if?" questions and following up with more questions to see how many ideas you can generate that, in the end, are actually possibilities. An option for this creative play would be to involve fellow employees. You could appoint someone to be the scribe and use a white board to record the questions.

Playing the "What if?" game can be done on the job as a regular exercise. Get in the habit of looking at challenges with this question in mind. When you start this process, the more outrageous your questions are, the more likely you will arrive at creative ideas and innovative solutions.

Putting Yourself in Their Shoes

Sometimes in an idea-generating session, you may hold back from saying what you're thinking because you fear how you may be perceived. Do you think you would be more likely to share a new idea if you were acting as if you were actor Jack Nicolson or actor/comedian Tina Fey? Enter the creative thinking technique of *role storming*, where you produce ideas from another person's point of view. Rick Griggs developed role storming in the 1980s as a way for people participating in brainstorming sessions to get past their inhibitions. The supposition is you'll be more comfortable with putting yourself "out there" if you're assuming someone else's identity. After all, that's not you speaking, so you (or whoever you decide to be) can have fun with this!

The way the process works best is to first participate in a regular brainstorming gathering with co-workers to produce the initial ideas. You can then determine as a group what roles you'll use. Each person can play a different role, or the role may be played collectively as a group. The person doesn't have to be famous. You may choose a co-worker, your boss, a friend, a competitor, or anyone you know, as long as the person isn't in the room. You should know the person well enough to assume her identity or mimic her perspective, being mindful of keeping the characterization respectful. The better you understand the person, the more this technique will work in spawning new ideas.

Next, the fun part begins. You assume your character and start throwing out ideas using the character's perspectives. You can start your sentence by saying "My character or person thinks we should do it this way." As with brainstorming, everyone should be encouraged to speak. The process may be repeated as often as necessary, and new roles can be assigned.

Think about what character you would like to play during a role storming session. Would you assume the role of someone famous? If so, would it be an actor, musician, business executive, inventor, a professional athlete, or some other profession? Or would you opt for someone you know—a colleague, a mentor, a friend, your mother or father, or your boss? Pick a work situation and select an individual to role-play. Now imagine yourself presenting that person's point of view. Do you feel differently? Do you think this technique could work for you in a real work session? Would you feel less intimidated and more confident to share what others may feel is an off-the-wall idea? If so, perhaps you can be the one to suggest this technique the next time you and your co-workers engage in a brainstorm gathering. You can even play around with this technique in your own mind as you look at different situations as they arise. For example, you can ask yourself "How would Facebook founder Mark Zuckerberg see this?," inserting different names as needed.

CREATIVITY KEY

Aside from role storming, another way to change your perspective is to change the time period. Take yourself out of the present time period and look backward. Think about how the situation might have been solved in the 1800s. Are you familiar with the saying "Everything old is new again"? That idiom pertains to trends that were once popular becoming in vogue again. Taking a page from history may prompt new ideas. Or you can look ahead and imagine how a problem might be handled 50 years from now. Imagine new inventions or how popular tools, such as the internet, might evolve in the future and how different answers could materialize with these new innovations.

Brainwriting Your Way to an Answer

Brainwriting, originally developed by Professor Bernd Rohrbach in 1968, provides an alternative to brainstorming. Like role storming, it works especially well when you have individuals in your group who may be more reserved and hesitant about speaking up in a brainstorming session. Its goal is to produce 108 new ideas in 30 minutes. Unlike brainstorming, in which ideas are recorded one at a time, brainwriting produces many ideas simultaneously.

There are two different variations of the process. The first, the 6-3-5 technique, refers to "6 people who write 3 ideas in 5 minutes." The process begins with the six people who are supervised by a moderator. The participants are given a sheet of paper with a statement describing the situation or are asked to write the statement at the top of the paper themselves. Each person is then asked to write up to three ideas in five minutes that address the situation statement. An example statement would be "How to increase our sales in 60 days." At the end of five minutes, they pass their sheet on to the next person. The participants silently read and play off of the ideas before them and write three more ideas. The method is designed so the players can draw inspiration from each other. After 30 minutes of six rounds, the group will have generated 108 ideas.

Another variation of brainwriting is conducted using index cards (sticky notes also work). After the participants write down one idea per card, they put the card in the center of the table or another conveniently designated spot. Group members have the choice of selecting one of the cards to trigger another idea, which they write on another card, or they can take a blank card and write another idea without referencing the other cards. This process can even be done with hundreds of people, for example, at a conference. Each attendee could be given one or more index cards as they enter the room, or the cards could be placed in advance at each person's seat. The prompt could then be projected onto a screen in the front of the auditorium. Each person could be instructed to write one idea per card in one minute and, at the end of 60 seconds, directed to pass their card to the person on their right. The particulars of this activity can vary. It's only limited by your imagination!

If you're the one setting up the brainwriting session, you can decide whether to use preprinted numbered sheets of paper, blank pages, index cards, or sticky notes; which direction to pass the ideas around; and how much time to allot. When it comes to the 6-3-5 version, you can also consider whether it's best to divide the participants into groups of six. One thing I would recommend for both versions of brainwriting is that you ask the participants to print neatly so time is not lost in trying to decipher sloppy handwriting.

As with brainstorming, the ideas for brainwriting should be generated quickly and without judgment. Do not worry about spelling or grammar or using complete sentences. As with many of the other techniques already discussed, writing down thoughts that seem to elude the subject is perfectly okay. Remember, sometimes it's those paradoxical or unlikely combinations that work. Some of them can and should be quirky, silly, and seemingly illogical. If you really want to encourage unusual thoughts, you could set up the brainwriting session as a competition. Normally, competition can deflate creativity, but if it's set up properly as a fun gathering, you could announce that the winner is the person who comes up with the most far-fetched solution. It's yet another opportunity for you and your co-workers to use imagination in the workplace!

Changing Your Wording

Sometimes creative thinking stalls because you can't get away from the way you're looking at your challenge. Hard as you try, you keep asking the same questions … and keep getting the same answers. Edward Glassman, PhD, former president of the Creativity College (a division of Leadership Consulting Services, Inc.), recommends a process he calls *reversal-dereversal* in which you turn your problem upside-down to help point you in a new direction. The way it works is as follows:

1. State the opposite of the key verb of your problem statement. For example, *attract* becomes *detract, entertain* becomes *bore,* or *increase* becomes *decrease.*

2. Without judgment, write solutions to the reversed problem statement.

3. Dereverse each reversed statement by adding the words "How to" in front of each solution. Rework the wording of the new problem statement until it makes sense.

4. Select a suitable new problem statement to use while generating ideas.

The following demonstrates this technique. I use only one possible solution in the example that follows. However, when you use this method, you'll want to generate as many ideas as possible.

Problem statement: We want to increase our ticket sales.

1. Change the verb *increase* to *decrease*. The reverse problem statement becomes "We want to decrease our ticket sales."

2. A possible solution to decrease ticket sales is to double ticket prices.

3. Dereverse the reversed statement by adding "How to" before the proposed solution. It now reads "How to increase our ticket sales by doubling our prices."

4. The new problem statement becomes "We want to increase our ticket sales by doubling our prices."

It is from this new problem statement you start to generate more ideas—insights that may not have come to you when only looking at the original statement. In the preceding example, the initial belief might be that ticket sales would plummet if you doubled their cost. By reversing that thought to how to increase sales by doubling prices, it might lead you to think of reasons people would pay that much more money. That could lead you to thinking about the value you're offering.

The scenario used in the example happened in the 1990s, when a local music festival's admission increased from $5 to $10. Although I do not know what creative strategy or tool was used by the people who made that decision, I do know that many people protested the increase, yet in the end, the festival attracted the largest crowd in its history. This was a risk the organization took that paid off. Organizers justified the more expensive admission fee by changing their entertainment focus from booking lesser-known jazz groups to well-known rock and pop music bands.

The point is to keep your mind open to ideas that may seem to be the opposite of what you want. With this technique, you are using a reversal process to flip the problem on its head before turning it back around as a means to help you think in a new direction. Think of a workplace situation in which you could use this technique, and go through the steps as outlined to see how it feels to use this tool. Expect it to feel unnatural. It's not unusual for something you're doing for the first time to feel that way. If it doesn't work for you this time, you can come back to it on another day. It's all about challenging your mind to think in ways that take your thinking in new directions.

 INSPIRATIONAL INSIGHT

"There's no good idea that cannot be improved on."

-Michael Eisner

Maximizing or Miniaturizing

Think big and think small—literally. When you apply this creative thinking practice, you are going to take your concept or physical product and look at it from these two perspectives. You don't need to keep your thoughts realistic. In fact, using exaggeration can really open you up creatively. Remember, at this stage, you're not trying to come up with a final answer; you're simply trying to think of different possibilities.

What are examples of enlargements? Have you ever had the experience of going into a fast-food restaurant and being asked "Would you like to supersize that?" Some things may even start off large, get smaller, and then increase in size again, such as mobile phones, which were once bigger than soda pop cans. I can remember what a status symbol it was to later have the much smaller, compact flip phone. Now smartphones in larger sizes are becoming commonplace.

The flip side of this is products that have been miniaturized, decreased, or reduced. For example, one of the first products that came to my mind as I thought about this process is when Ty, Inc. introduced the world to Beanie Babies in the mid-1990s. These inexpensive, small plush animals took on a life of their own as the values on certain critters began to escalate among collectors due to limited quantities, availability, and retiring designs. To add to the craze, Ty began offering Teenie Beanies—smaller versions of the original Beanies—as part of McDonald's Happy Meals. Some people were so enthusiastic about getting the Teenie Beanies that I actually witnessed them completely discarding the meals and keeping just the toys.

There are numerous other examples of going small: mini iPads, minipads, miniskirts, and Mini Coopers. Music has shrunken from 12-inch vinyl albums, to eight-track and cassette tapes, to compact discs, to the smallest yet—MP3s. They're not even physical objects! Mini guitars have become even more compact travel guitars. Even dogs have gotten smaller. It wasn't enough for a Chihuahua to be miniature; now there are teacup sizes.

So how do you come up with ideas for products like the ones I've mentioned? Two simple words—what if—drive the process of maximizing and miniaturizing. For example, let's say you own an Italian restaurant and you and your employees are trying to come up with ways to get more attention. One of your waitstaff asks "What if we made a pizza the size of a shopping mall?" Of course, that's not very reasonable, but an idea like that could lead to having a pizza-making competition at your local mall that's sponsored by your restaurant. No notion is too absurd when trying to generate as many ideas as possible. Some of the crazier ideas will prompt laughter and a light, lively feeling—perfect for idea production!

Can you think of how you might apply this creative thinking technique to a situation in your line of work? You can begin to experiment with this method by starting with simple ideas to see how it works. Pick one aspect of your work—either within your particular job responsibilities or something that is more broad-based that affects your whole department. Start to notice products and services in the marketplace that could potentially be maximized or minimized. This will enhance your awareness and will help you when you want to use this tool in a real-life workplace situation.

CREATIVITY KEY

This concept doesn't have to be limited to the physical size of an object. For example, if you're a retailer who has a gift shop that has "something for everyone" with a large inventory yet sales are slow, you might ask "What if I got rid of my current inventory and only offered blue items?" On the surface, that idea may sound crazy and limiting. However, you begin to research the color blue and learn that it is known to have a soothing effect. You also learn that there are thousands of people with sleep disorders. Therefore, you decide to shift your entire retail focus by having a limited, specialized inventory and becoming a boutique shop called "True Blue." Everything in your shop is blue, including the painted walls, and you only offer items that are calming, relaxing, and sleep inducing. This illustrates how one idea, however impractical it seems at first, can actually lead to a viable concept.

Looking for More Than One Answer

Students are brought up through the educational system to look for the one and only right answer. So it's no wonder that as adults, that pattern continues. As I covered in Chapter 4, that's what happens when thinking convergently. The quickest way to end an idea-generating session, regardless of what technique is employed, is when you start by thinking there's only one correct solution.

This limited thinking can even hamper you with everyday work situations. For example, if you work in an open office environment and you're having to deal with an obnoxious co-worker who is loud, you might think the solution is to speak with her. But what if she doesn't get it and continues this behavior? Are there other solutions? Yes, if you allow yourself to look for more than one answer. You could put in ear plugs, wear your ear buds and listen to relaxing music, use noise-cancelling headphones, ask your boss to speak with her, request a different office, or discuss the possibility of working from home when you're under deadline and can't be distracted.

So whether you're dealing with a situation that involves only you or a group of your colleagues, make it a practice to look for more than one answer. Use one of the methods from this chapter or previous chapters to help you think more divergently. If you've spent hours trying to come up with answers, it's no wonder when one emerges that has any kind of value, you want to stop and accept it. Resist this temptation to stop the process just because you may be tired or frustrated. In fact, you'll read in the next section why this may be the very time to keep going.

Consciously Changing Your Routine

Shifting your perspective to one that's more creative doesn't always have to involve actively engaging in new thinking patterns. Sometimes it can be as simple as altering your normal routine, which opens your mind to new opportunities that can lead to creative ideas. This requires conscious attention; otherwise, you may find you're frequently in autopilot mode from the time you get up and go to work until you return home and retire to bed.

A slight tweak of your routines can also help you capture the right mood for the day. For example, if your morning routine includes reading the newspaper, which tends to be negative in nature, you may want to hold off on doing that if you're hoping to have a creative day at work. In a study, participants who were shown sad video clips were not as capable of solving problems creatively compared to those who watched uplifting videos. So if hearing about or reading negative news puts you in a downbeat mode, you would be better off watching a funny video or listening to comedy radio instead on your morning commute. When you're feeling positive, your mental processes are more flexible, whereas being in a bad mood decreases your cognitive ability.

Another reason to consciously change your routine is to expose yourself to new possibilities. In Chapter 9, one of the suggestions I made was to take the wrong way home. Think of other changes, however subtle, you can make that might open your mind to new horizons. For example, consider meditating for five minutes when you first wake. You may not consider yourself to be a good meditator, but if you give it a chance, you may find it helps to elevate your mood so you can start your day on a positive note. Plus, people are known to have creative insights hit them right in the middle of a meditation.

What can you add or take away from your daily routines that might help shift you to a more creative space? Examine your normal patterns both in the morning and throughout the day to see if releasing them would point you in a more creative direction.

If It's Not Broken, Break It

Why mess with success? Isn't that how the saying "If it's not broken, don't fix it" came about? However, now more than ever, with innovative technology changing the landscape of the work-place faster than any other time period, it's important to anticipate and act upon the need for change before it's obvious. If you don't, you better believe one or more of your competitors will. That's why that same adage has been adapted to "If it's not broken, break it." Keeping things as they are is playing it safe and is unlikely to lead to innovation.

The best time to implement change is when you're not under the gun to do so. Why wait for a crisis when you can use your creative thinking to proactively produce ideas that can lead to improvements in the workplace? This goes back to the importance of being willing to take risks.

Yes, it's much easier to maintain the status quo, but you and your co-workers should not become complacent and then be burdened with a lot of forced changes down the line.

A quick look at some of the industries that have completely changed reinforces the point of initiating changes before they're forced upon you. For example, the newspaper industry has vastly changed now that people can get their news online. Or think Blockbuster, Netflix, Borders, and Amazon. Why are Netflix and Amazon still around, while Borders and most Blockbusters have gone under? The music industry has also seen massive changes. You can still find a record store, but not like you used to. Now most people prefer to buy their music online and download MP3s. In all of these cases, the ones who thought ahead and were able to prepare for and adapt to changes in the market still survive, while the ones who were more reactive saw marked declines or even went out of business.

When it comes to your workplace, what's happening or not yet happening in your industry? What is the next stage of development for your line of work? How do you determine what may benefit from your attention when everything seems to be going smoothly? Following your gut instincts is one way. If you know your business or your job position well and you sense it's just a matter of time before some kind of changes will need to occur, don't wait to act, even if others don't see it coming. This is where you may have to challenge convention. Be ready for co-workers or even management to point out every reason why things should stay the same.

 INSPIRATIONAL INSIGHT

"If it ain't broke, break it (or someone else will break it for you)."

—Tom Peters

Getting in the Habit of Asking Questions

You've probably seen your share of ego clashes both at work and in personal situations. It's that feeling of "I'm right" and "You're wrong." Both people are hanging on tightly to their own beliefs and progress comes to a grinding halt. In reality, one of the best practices you can incorporate into your work is to learn how to ask questions and not stick to thinking you have all the answers. This can lead to self-discovery and insights that may lead to innovative ideas. In creativity coaching, the whole premise behind it is asking the client powerful questions to help her gain clarity. This same principle applies in business.

The following are some tips for how to put this into practice in your workplace:

- Slow down. Asking questions gives you a chance to really think about the issue at hand and not brush it off or move ahead before you or your co-workers understand it completely.

- Don't go into situations thinking you have all of the answers or be intimidated that others will look at you with less respect if you don't know everything there is to know about the given topic.

- When asking questions, be sure you are doing so in a way that is not undermining authority or being invasive. If you're asking questions as part of an ideation session, your intentions should be understood.

- Let go of your assumptions and be open minded as you pose your questions. You can start by asking broad questions and then narrow your focus as you gain more clarity.

- Answer questions with another question in order to make sure you cover all bases with the issue.

For example, as a freelance journalist, if I go into an interview thinking I have all of the answers, I'm not going to even hear what the interviewee has to say. I certainly do my homework before doing an interview, but I remain open as I ask questions. I listen intently because oftentimes the person's responses are what prompt me to ask questions that weren't even on my list and lead to a much more interesting discussion and story. You can do the same in your line of work.

Accepting Failure as Part of the Process

Being okay with taking risks when the situation is unpredictable ultimately means being okay with making mistakes. While there are known risks, there are also those that are unforeseen.

Throughout this book, I've given examples of how failure has been turned into success and how learning lessons emerge from mistakes. As I addressed in Chapter 13, a lack of success can occur when you take a risk that doesn't pay off. But even when there is no risk involved—you're simply acting on a new idea—you may experience a negative outcome. If you're going to be creative in the workplace, you must accept failure as part of the process. If you're a manager, it's imperative you also realize the importance of this; otherwise, your employees will be too afraid to try any of the creative techniques presented in this book. When the results don't pan out as you had desired or expected, you can look at them together as a team with an attitude of "We're all in this together." This is similar to the adage of finding a silver lining, which means finding the positive aspects in every situation despite disappointing results or downright failure.

As one who has been involved in the creation of numerous special events, the team of people with whom I worked made it a practice to thoroughly dissect each affair soon after it ended. There was always room for improvement for future events. Sometimes some of the biggest challenges prompted solutions that wouldn't have otherwise happened and made the events that followed even better. When you pursue ideas that don't work out, look for the blessing in disguise. If you can make that a practice, you'll start to look at failure in a different light.

Can you recall work-related times in your life when you were upset the outcome was different from what you wanted, only to realize later it was all for the best? Maybe you didn't get the promotion you wanted, but then you were offered an even better job by the competition. Or maybe you pitched your boss on a new idea that he turned down, which motivated you to rethink the situation and come up with an even better idea that was so great, the president of the company personally congratulated you. So it is when you accept failure as part of the process. Some ideas will fall flat on their face, while others can catapult the company to achieving financial success or superior customer satisfaction. Keep exercising your creative muscles. You can't lose!

The Least You Need to Know

- Using creative thinking techniques will help you generate innovative ideas by opening your eyes to seeing things in new ways. Looking beyond logic, brainwriting, role storming, changing your wording, and maximizing and miniaturizing are among the methods you can use.

- Don't wait for a crisis to implement change within your organization. Proactively pursue ideas that will put you ahead of the competition.

- Develop the habit of asking questions while discarding the need to be right. If you think you already have all of the answers, you're less likely to be creative.

- If you look at failure as a learning opportunity, you'll be more likely to take risks in finding and implementing innovative solutions.

Creative Teamwork

Sometimes competition can happen among employees, and as long as that happens in a healthy way, creativity can still flourish. However, if it happens amidst jealousy and threatened feelings, it doesn't matter how innovative the ideas; sooner or later that will catch up to the rest of the company, which will suffer as a result.

In this chapter, I touch upon how to lead your team; even if you are not in any kind of supervisory capacity, you should still be able to glean suggestions you can make to your boss. I also discuss the importance of you and your co-workers working together as a team and how you can become more motivated yourself by helping co-workers.

In This Chapter

- Tips for leading teams down vthe creative path
- How creating outside of the workplace helps organizations
- Mentoring or seeking a mentor
- How to be part of a healthy and productive team

Leading the Team

You might be the owner of the company, a director, a manager, or serve in some supervisory capacity. Regardless of the number of employees who report to you, are you prepared to lead them in your organization's quest for creativity? Assuming a creative climate has already been established, how will you motivate your staff to not just come up with new ideas, but also to know how to work with them and bring them to fruition? Are your employees being challenged enough in their work to have a desire to innovate on their own, or is so much getting piled up on their plate that they don't even know where to begin?

Many studies have shown that employees may be productive when given a tight deadline, but it's usually at the expense of their creativity. When given enough time and space to explore possibilities, creativity has a much better chance at flourishing. This section gives you some tips on how to best steer your staff down the road of creativity.

Setting the Example

A creative and innovative organization starts at the top. Therefore, make sure you are buying into the edict of a creative culture at every turn—from the way the office space is organized to how you conduct yourself. If you are looking at creativity as some kind of fluffy directive handed down by your boss or perhaps the owner of the company, your attitude will be apparent to those you supervise. In other words, you can't fake it! You really need to embrace the creative directive yourself to expect others to follow.

One of the keys to showing employees you embrace a creative culture is allowing them to do their jobs in their own way. Don't mistake this as employees being able to do whatever they want; they must still be aware of what objectives they need to achieve. It's about giving them some freedom in their approach. Unlike micromanaging—which can manage the creativity right out of employees and create a feeling of distrust—giving employees space to explore will spur ideas and increase motivation.

 INSPIRATIONAL INSIGHT

> "Capital isn't so important in business. Experience isn't so important. You can get both these things. What is important is ideas. If you have ideas, you have the main asset you need, and there isn't any limit to what you can do with your business and your life."
>
> —Harvey Firestone

Knowing how to promote risk-taking also is essential in leading the way. It's a fine balance between stepping beyond the comfort zone and not going so far as to seriously cause damage to not just your organization's bottom line, but also its reputation. In your role as leader, you can manage this by helping your employees weigh the pros and cons of carrying out their ideas. Again, it's about knowing when to step in and when to let your employees do their thing so ideas can be fully developed.

Employees who are entrusted to do their jobs in a supportive environment are more likely to be more creative, which means they're not afraid to take risks. For example, if they end up initiating and developing a major idea that takes hold and could change the course of the business or a specific product line, they are going to need support. As the leader, it's important you're there for them. Does your staff know they can turn to you in times of trouble without being admonished? They must be assured that if you've encouraged them to be innovative and ultimately their ideas crash, you'll still support them. Get in the habit of making a positive comment before you dive into any criticism, which must be delivered constructively.

Another key is to be sure your employees' work is challenging enough to keep them motivated but not so difficult they reach a point of feeling overwhelmed. It's a delicate balancing act. Employees often complain their boss doesn't have a clue about the details of their responsibilities and keeps piling more on. They may end up doing the work, but if they're snowed under, their creative efforts won't have a chance to begin. Because it takes time to develop ideas, consider what you can do to give them the breathing room they need to be creative, including providing a certain amount of flextime (as discussed in Chapter 13) they can use to think beyond what's right in front of them.

As a leader, setting the example also means realizing the creative process doesn't happen over-night. Exercising patience and doing what you can to keep the troops feeling energized will keep the process in flow. Can you think of actions you can take to accomplish this? This is where your own creativity comes in. You can start by asking your employees what will keep them going when they're involved in a lengthy creative process and then formulate a plan that takes their feedback into consideration. Certainly a paycheck is part of the equation, but remember, most people are motivated intrinsically by work they care about—that is, meaningful work.

 CREATIVITY COMPASS

Consider devising a program in which your staff may opt to take advantage of a half-day or a complete day off on a regular basis to engage in something creative. You could treat it like a holiday, which could mean once a year, once a quarter, or once a month. Challenge yourself to see if you can come up with a workable plan for your business. For example, perhaps you have them report back to you on how they spent their time. Encourage them to tell you about any innovative insights they had during this time off or if they've returned to the workplace feeling more refreshed. Imagine the goodwill this will create and, as a result, the increase in quality output for your business it will generate!

Creating Bonding Opportunities

Giving your employees opportunities to see you in a different light could open up creative pathways as they get to know you better in a more relaxed atmosphere. Consider devoting one day a week to a "Lunch with the Boss" type of open forum. The concept would be for each employee to bring a brown-bag lunch into a common area, such as a conference room, in which you would all sit and have lunch together. There would be no agendas and would be intended mostly for personal sharing. No RSVPs would be necessary, depending on the amount of space you could allot and the number of employees involved. As the boss, this is your opportunity to show interest beyond the workplace in the staff members who attend.

For example, one person I know set up an employee bonding opportunity that she called "Knitting with Nancy," in which staffers were invited once a week during their lunch hour to literally learn how to knit. Nancy, who supervised a team of directors who dealt with extremely stressful situations involving rape victims and battered women, taught them how to knit while they sat and chatted about nonwork subjects. This enabled the employees to get to know her better in an informal, creative setting and, at the same time, take a break and de-stress. She enjoyed getting to know her directors on a more personal level during knitting time, and she liked that they could see beyond her role of the boss who did the hiring, firing, and deadline enforcement.

Can you think of a creative skill you could share in a similar fashion? The idea wouldn't necessarily have to revolve around you teaching your employees. It could be a shared activity, such as challenging yourselves with writing poetry. The idea is to gather your team together to get to know each other better in ways that go beyond the typical manager-employee relationship.

Another activity that could take place would be monthly luncheons that are creatively themed with decorations and discussions centering around that theme. You could divide the employees into teams and divvy up the year, with each team taking on different responsibilities for their month. Each team could be charged with the task of coming up with a menu and providing the food. There would be plenty of creative opportunities between the food preparation and decorations. The structure all depends on your business and the number of employees, but this idea at least gives you a starting point to develop it further. In the end, it's about creating the perfect opportunity for teamwork in an informal way.

Encouraging Creativity Outside of the Workplace

It's important for employees to feel they are not completely defined by their work. Beyond flextime within the workplace, do you allow your employees to take time off occasionally outside of the office? Do you encourage your employees to be creative when they're not working or to take on a hobby or activity that has nothing to do with their job responsibilities? According to an informal online poll conducted by Mitch Ditkoff and Tim Moore of Idea Champions, the office is not where people said they get their best ideas. "In the workplace" ranked number 35 on the list, behind daydreaming, driving, walking, being in nature, being up late at night, surfing the internet, vacationing, showering, having fun, relaxing, dreaming, and taking a break. So not only does giving employees time away to explore their own hobbies not only make them appreciative, it also may lead to innovative insights. Plus, their participation in one of their passions outside of the office will help them to feel more relaxed and content.

You can take your support a step further by showing interest in your workers' outside activities. For example, if Stephen is involved with community theater, it would probably mean a lot to him if you went to one of his performances. Or perhaps there's a way to showcase your employees at your own events. For example, if you're hosting a reception and want to include background music, rather than look outside the company, check first to see if any of your staffers have the ability and would like the opportunity to perform.

If enough employees who have a creative craft, piece of art, or other talent to share that they practice outside of the workplace, you could even consider setting up a gallery in the office that features their work. You could designate an area in a common space or hang employees' creations throughout the building with a committee of employees who would set up some type of program that addresses the logistics and creative aspects. This type of commitment could go a long way to demonstrate you believe in creativity both inside and outside of the workplace.

CREATIVITY KEY

You also want an atmosphere in the office your employees will enjoy coming back to. You've already read about how humor plays a big role in personal creativity. The same applies in business. If you're always serious, that sets the tone for the rest of your staff. Does your organization's culture have a place for lightheartedness at appropriate times? Think back to your school days and professors and instructors who displayed an enthusiastic style of teaching. They may not have been telling jokes (though I can remember some who did), but they presented their information in a way that was memorable because they made learning fun. The really good ones piqued your curiosity, too, and inspired you to probe further. Creativity and innovation in the workplace follow a similar path, so make your workplace fun, inviting, and stimulating to your employees.

Leading Meaningful Discussions

Another aspect to be aware of is the dynamic of how your team members interact with one another. As a leader, it's up to you to notice their communication styles and patterns and whether they're conducive to advancing their creativity. You also need to recognize your own style. Do you truly listen to your staff when they speak during a meeting, or do you have an autocratic management style in which you do all of the talking? Notice if you have a habit of interrupting your employees and if you give them ample time to express their ideas.

It's also beneficial to create a climate in which employees are free to make a case for their ideas without being shut down. Egos will undoubtedly bump up against each other during the creative process. After all, it's very common for people to get attached to their ideas. You can even expect members who haven't yet adapted to the idea of creativity in the workplace to fight to keep things just the way they are. While this doesn't mean they can argue relentlessly and disrespectfully, give your employees leeway to propose and talk out different ideas while staying "on topic" and not attacking each other personally.

Beware of people who dominate discussions and also those who sit in silence. Team interaction could even be the topic of one of your meetings. Ask your staff for feedback on ways they can improve the overall process. Also, give them the opportunity afterward to submit ideas and observations anonymously in writing. This will give those who are reluctant to speak up—especially if they have negative feedback about you—to have their views heard and considered. Creativity can blossom even when there's conflict, as long as a strong level of trust has been established among and between employees. Working together as teams can help to build that trust.

Becoming a Team Player

If you're not in a supervisory position, what can you do to help build a creative culture within your organization? After all, it's not entirely up to your boss or management to instill a creative spirit within the organization. That happens with all of the team members contributing in their own way—including you. Just as with any team sport, such as football or baseball, if you all work together, you're more likely to have a winning team. Not everyone will be a quarterback or receiver or pitcher or catcher, but each member will have a designated position in the "creativity crew."

Tuning Into Resistance

When it comes to a workplace in which a new creative direction is being implemented, it's important to check in with your feelings. Does this idea excite, enthuse, and motivate you, or do you feel ambivalent, unwilling, or scared that you won't be able to contribute or be given the proper support to seek out new ideas and act upon them? Revisit the blocks outlined in Chapter 6 and see if any of them are coming up for you now. Also take a moment to close your eyes and breathe into your feelings. Don't deny what you feel; that will only delay the process. You want to be able to identify your feelings so you can work through them.

It's natural to resist change of any sort, especially if you're not sure what to expect or you have specific concerns. If that's the case, do your part and own your feelings. While it's easy to sit back and complain, it's more effective to offer innovative solutions that address the issues you've raised. Don't allow yourself to be a victim. Be willing to speak up. If you find it difficult to express yourself in a meeting with your co-workers, arrange a one-on-one meeting with your boss. If your boss is the problem, consider taking it to the next level. Remember, you're looking for optimal ways to be part of a successful team. A happy employee has a far greater chance to be creative and a team player. In fact, use your discontent to motivate yourself to come up with positive solutions.

Maybe you're on board with your company's new creativity edict but you notice certain co-workers are still reluctant. Rather than berate those co-workers or gossip behind their back, as a team player you can approach one of them to learn more about their resistance. You may not be in a managerial role, but you can still use your leadership skills to listen, discuss possible solutions, and offer inspiring words. Just as with personal relationships, people often cop an attitude because they feel like they're not being heard. Instead of speaking up, they keep their feelings to themselves. That behavior manifests in ways that appear to be unsupportive of the entire team when what they really want is to be part of a team that includes them more. You can wait for your boss to handle such situations, or you can take the initiative by seeing how you can involve others who seem to be out of the loop.

 INSPIRATIONAL INSIGHT

"It's easy to come up with new ideas; the hard part is letting go of what worked for you two years ago, but will soon be out of date."

—Roger von Oech

Finding and Being a Mentor

One of the best ways to foster your creativity is with the help of a mentor. You may find a mentor in your own office, a professional associate who works elsewhere, or someone who isn't even affiliated with your type of work. For example, I'm one of the lucky ones who had parents who supported and encouraged my siblings and me to engage in creative activities. In that way, my mom and dad served as mentors and I grew up believing I was creative. Neither of them were professional musicians, but they both served as good examples because they played different instruments just for the fun of it. The key is to develop a relationship with someone you trust and admire—one who inspires you. He should motivate you to be a better person, to explore and experiment, and to give more to others and to yourself. Good mentors will not be threatened as you become more knowledgeable and experienced.

You also can serve as a mentor to others. Whether you serve as a mentor to a co-worker or an associate, you're not only helping that person, you're also contributing to your own personal growth. Perhaps you know someone with whom you can swap roles, depending on the subject matter or skill. At times you'll serve as the mentor and in other situations, the other person will assume that role. The best way to mentor is through demonstration—not insisting that your mentee do something strictly your way. Allow mentees to observe and ask questions, and then allow them to carry out the task in their own creative way.

Creative Play: The Magic of Mentoring

It's easy to take for granted what you know. In this creative play, you'll be focusing on your knowledge and skills so you can become more aware of how you might mentor another person.

Tools Needed: Paper and a writing instrument

Take a moment to think about your education, training, and experience—not just as it pertains to the workplace, but in totality. Now write down 10 of your strengths. Write the first things that come to your mind.

Once you've done that, expand on each strength on your list. For example, if you listed "writing" as one of your skills, expound on what makes you a good writer. Is your expertise in grammar and spelling, or is it that you are able to convey messages in a powerful way through the written word? Be clear in your descriptions. After expanding on your strengths, review your list and think about how one or more of your skills would be helpful in mentoring or partnering with another individual.

Finally, look at your list once more so you can appreciate yourself. Be grateful for your gifts. You might want to take your list and turn it into a creative project. For example, you can take your key points and write them on a poster board or construction paper, making it colorful and decorated. Celebrate you!

You have now increased your awareness of what you have to offer others. Be willing to share what you know. They will thank you and you will feel better for giving back. If you mentor or partner with somebody in the workplace, your willingness to share your knowledge can only strengthen your organization.

 INSPIRATIONAL INSIGHT

"Tell me and I forget, teach me and I may remember, involve me and I learn."

—Benjamin Franklin

Creatively Collaborating with Co-Workers

You might feel you work better independently. I often feel this way, and I know there's a time and place for that. I also know that working with a team of people who are excited to join forces can be a rewarding experience for all involved. There are several guiding principles to follow to ensure you are part of a team that is both creative and productive.

For starters, trusting and respecting your co-workers is essential. Let go of your "rightness"— in other words, check your ego at the door and give equal consideration to ideas expressed by all members of the team. If you go into a group session thinking your ideas are more worthy than others, you're limiting what the team can achieve as a whole. It's perfectly acceptable to be confident and stand up for your ideas, but be willing to listen intently to your co-workers. On the other hand, you may feel you have little to offer or are afraid your ideas will be criticized. Remember, you're all on the same team. Any discussion that turns into a competition can become counterproductive.

No doubt personalities will enter the picture. The key is to not take comments and criticisms personally and also do your part to avoid personally attacking your co-workers. Stick with the issue. Keep it as impersonal as possible. You're all after the same goal—or at least you should be. When conflict arises—and it will—accept the differing views as part of the process. Disagreements can be healthy as long as they're constructively construed. You can still encourage one another and make your points in ways that are positive.

Collaborating effectively with your co-workers can be a tightrope act. You'll be considering off-beat ideas versus more traditional concepts, imaginative versus linear thinking, and ad-libbing versus organized thoughts. Remember the differences between convergent and divergent thinking? You may have the ability to think both ways but perhaps you favor one over the other. The same applies to your co-workers. If half of the team is more analytical and logistical in their thinking and the other half loves bouncing around off-the-wall ideas and experimenting with them, that combination is actually an asset. The beauty of working in partnership is that you can complement each other by combining your strengths.

As you test out the different innovative thinking techniques that were presented in Chapter 10 and Chapter 14, you will see which tools work best for your team. If you're part of more than one team, it's possible that certain methods may work for one team but not for another. The subject matter also may influence the technique. Through trial and error, you will learn what works best in various situations and with different types of teams. When it comes time to reach a conclusion, notice how your co-workers function with their thought processes. Some people like to take their time and analyze situations before deciding how to move forward. Others like to move quickly. If you're the latter, be careful not to judge the "analyzers" as procrastinators or being wishy-washy with their decisions. If you're the former, resist the temptation to label "quick responders" as impulsive. The important thing is to recognize differences among the different team members and decide as a whole how you will reach a consensus that works for everyone.

To encourage that understanding between you and your co-workers, it's important engage in *active listening,* a method of communicating in which you, as the nonspeaking person, carefully listen to the person talking and then feed back to the speaker what you heard. This serves as a confirmation that you understood what the person speaking was conveying. In this way, you can accurately build on what was just shared, which is the whole idea of working as a team. Like a snowball that gets bigger as it rolls down a snow-covered path, adding to each other's ideas eventually creates a synergy. How do you know when you've achieved this? You'll feel it!

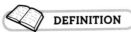 **DEFINITION**

> **Active listening** is when you listen carefully to what the other person is saying and then restate what you heard back to the speaker. This gives the speaker a chance to confirm or correct your feedback and creates a better understanding between the two of you.

Also, be sure each participant understands the purpose and the vision of the idea. If you can, clarify up front what you want to achieve without defining it with such minutiae that you inhibit creativity from the start. You and the other team members need to have a singular focus while keeping an open mind. That also makes it critical to schedule your group sessions at a time when everyone can really zero in on the mission at hand. If you and the others are worried you're not going to get your other work done, you'll likely rush through the process and not come to any real decisions, which would be a waste of time for everyone.

When it comes to generating ideas or making decisions, everyone should be participating in the process. If you notice someone who isn't engaged, call upon that person. If this is truly a group effort with no one serving as the leader, anyone should be able to encourage another to speak. Also, don't be afraid to speak up if you notice that one of your teammates is hogging the conversation. No one benefits from that. You'll find the more you work in teams and get to know one another better, the more the creativity and productivity of the group is likely to increase. You'll get to know each other's styles better and how to work with them.

In the end, while you may not achieve perfect symmetry as a group, at least everyone will have had the opportunity to weigh in and contribute toward achieving the goal you originally outlined. When everyone feels like he has been given a chance to contribute, and the team reaches a consensus that pleases all, that's when collaborating truly pays off.

 CREATIVITY KEY

> The same principles for creating solo apply to innovative teamwork. Keep an open mind, relax, be flexible, be okay with failure, and remember to laugh!

Creative Play: Now Hear This!

This in an exercise in making a case for a more creative organization. Two sets of instruction are outlined: the first is intended for people in managerial positions, and the second is for non-supervisory employees.

Tools Needed: Either paper and a writing instrument or a computer and the appropriate software

Instructions for Managers or Those in a Supervisory Position

The situation:

Your manager has given you a directive to create a culture of creativity within the organization. Assume you have already bought in to this concept. In fact, you can't wait to share the good news!

The task:

To get your team members to buy in to this concept, write a letter explaining the new direction and then determine a way to creatively distribute the information.

Instructions for Staff Members Who Do Not Supervise Any Employees

The situation:

You have been reading a lot about the benefits of creativity (this book and perhaps others, too!). You're totally on board with the idea of increasing creativity and innovation within your organization and want to convince your boss of the merits.

The task:

Write a letter that outlines all of the reasons why creativity within the workplace is essential and then figure out the best way, day, and time to present it. Will you do it as an email or make a verbal presentation and then present the letter to your manager for further consideration?

An alternative way to do this creative play would be to develop a PowerPoint or keynote presentation. Or perhaps you have the skills to create a video production. This creative play, or a variation of it, could turn into an actual task within your organization that you can carry out.

The Least You Need to Know

- Being an effective team leader starts by you setting the example. You can't just talk the game of creativity—you also must demonstrate it.

- Think empowerment over micromanagement. Clearly state the company's creativity goals and the staff's specific objectives, and at the same time give your employees the space and time to explore and exercise their creativity.

- Be patient with your employees' creative processes. Find out what's behind their motivation, so together you can co-create ways to make their job more meaningful.

- It doesn't matter if you're in management or not. You can do your part by developing a willing attitude to be part of a creative team at work. It's up to you to speak up and be heard and also to give your undivided attention when listening to co-workers.

- Mentoring others in and outside of the workplace can be very rewarding. Realize your strengths and how they may be helpful to others.

Developing a Creative Mind-Set at Work

Your boss may be putting pressure on you to be more creative or that directive may be self-imposed. Either way, rather than thinking of creativity as a separate entity, look at it as part of the everyday strategy that helps you thrive and drives your company's mission and business. It's the thread that keeps all of the parts stitched together. No, you're not going to hit a home run each day in terms of originality, and some actions you take will be more useful than others in moving you forward. But incorporating creativity into each day of your work life—as opposed to making it something you do in moments of crisis or when sprucing up the mundane—takes some of the pressure off.

In this final chapter on the workplace, you learn the importance of maintaining the right mind-set, the subtleties of creativity, what can happen when you deliberately set out to innovate when it seems there are no opportunities, and the causes and solutions to burnout.

In This Chapter

- Why creativity is no longer optional in the workplace
- How to create when it appears there's no opportunity
- Gathering ideas using the process of benchmarking
- What to do when you're feeling burned out at work

It's a Matter of Perspective

Read the following statements out loud:

- I *must* be creative.

- I *must* think of something no one else has thought of before.

- My creativity *must* help the company's bottom line.

- I *must* devise creative solutions to improve employee morale.

What feelings did these statements evoke inside of you? More than likely, they felt more like mandates. Whenever you demand something from yourself, you're more likely to intimidate the creative sparks right out of you rather than light them up. Being creative is a mind-set. You will be more creatively productive if you produce the conditions that are conducive to being creative: giving yourself time to play, to laugh, to engage in activities you truly enjoy, to take reasonable risks, and to follow your passion. When you do these things, you're supporting your inner being and putting yourself in a more relaxed state. That's when creative insights are most likely to occur. It's a mental shift to say "Every day I am creating" as opposed to saying "I must be creative every day."

Keeping the need to create and innovate as part of your everyday mind-set will prevent you from becoming apathetic. Companies that are comprised of individuals who become complacent and satisfied with doing the same old thing are likely to lose customers and supporters and may eventually go out of business. It's a thrill when you come up with a new idea that gets developed and implemented, especially one that makes a big difference to your internal or external publics. Remember how Chapter 3 talked about how motivation begets more motivation? If you can view creativity and innovation as opportunities that help your company thrive rather than something forced upon you, you can create some excitement of your own as you experiment with different ideas along the way.

Viewing Creativity as Essential

In college, some courses are required and some are electives. In the workplace and in general, creativity is often seen as something elective. However, if creativity were viewed more as a necessity well before higher education comes into play, creating would feel more natural, rather than an imperative being forced in the workplace. It's not too late to begin viewing creativity as an essential while still allowing your ideas to flow organically. If you can develop and maintain this viewpoint, your attitude is in alignment with many businesses today. No matter the industry, profit or not-for-profit, creativity and innovation are being seen more and more as crucial components.

In an article by Robert J. Sternberg in *Tulsa World,* he identified three primary reasons why creativity is not an option for businesses:

- You no longer have a hold on local customers. You're competing globally rather than only within your local community (think Amazon.com and other blockbuster consumer websites).

- Communicating with customers all over the world is far easier, thanks to the rapid rise of the internet.

- More competition has increased the speed of innovation.

 CREATIVITY KEY

Can you think of ways your company has used creativity? Do not limit your thoughts to innovative products. Creativity can extend to services, customer retention programs, promotions, and even creatively designed bathrooms. Make a list of five examples of creativity that have taken place within your own workplace and then list at least three areas in which you believe there are creative opportunities for improvement. Identifying them is the first step toward taking action.

There are many examples of companies that have gone under due to lack of creativity and innovation. For example, brokerage firm E. F. Hutton used to have the slogan, "When E. F. Hutton talks, people listen." Apparently not enough people, as it is now defunct. Compaq, Burger Chef, Montgomery Ward, Pan Am, and Woolworth's are other companies that weren't able to keep up with changing times.

But what about companies that have succeeded and innovated? How did they do it? For example, one company went from near bankruptcy to billions in 13 years. Do you know which one? Yep, you probably guessed it: Apple. While Apple has always had its critics and always will, you can still learn from lessons from one of history's greatest business comebacks. An online *Business Insider* article addressed how Steve Jobs returned as the CEO and put an end to products like the Newton and formed a partnership with Microsoft. He is quoted as saying "We have to let go of this notion that for Apple to win, Microsoft has to lose. … This is about getting Apple healthy, this is about Apple being able to make incredibly great contributions to the industry and to get healthy and prosper again." Despite the fact that both decisions were controversial, Jobs was willing to step out and take a risk, one that obviously paid off with products like iTunes, the iPad, and the iPhone. In terms of the latter product, customers are demanding and expecting more novel features and will even stand in long lines to be the first to buy the latest version, regardless of inclement weather.

So why don't more companies innovate and create like Apple? For the same reasons you may be hesitant: fear of failure, lack of patience, feeling threatened, declining motivation, being unwilling to take risks, not having the proper mind-set, and so on. However, if creativity is viewed as a day-to-day priority rather than something used only in times of crisis, you and your organization will be able to work through these roadblocks and be successful.

Creating Something Out of Nothing

While it's one thing to hear success stories about major million-dollar corporations and their innovations, what if you own and operate a small business with very limited resources and few employees, if any? Creativity goes well beyond the initial idea. In fact, what you may think of as a small idea can turn into a much larger and more successful initiative for your workplace.

For example, as a professional who has spent most of my career in the creative field of public relations, I was approached by a local chiropractor from a nearby small town who felt he needed more exposure in the community. This came at a time when the economy was faltering and many businesses and individuals were hurting financially. This chiropractor, whom I'll call Keith, wasn't doing anything in his practice that would be considered unusual or innovative that would warrant any media attention, so I told him we would have to consciously create something that was meaningful.

I suggested we create some kind of community outreach project. The challenge was that Keith didn't have many resources himself as a one-person office and dwindling revenues, but keeping an open mind, I knew it was still possible for the two of us to co-create a project that would serve both the community and his practice. I advised Keith to think of charities and causes he truly cared about; anything less would come across as a self-serving promotion, and the public would see through it. I suggested he take his time and reflect on this—again, removing any pressure that he had to be creative in that moment.

In the meantime, I began researching opportunities by reading the two major daily newspapers in our area, looking at televised news reports, listening to the radio, and seeking online stories for ideas. The recurring, dominant theme focused on the challenging economy. Specifically, there were many reports about how food pantries were struggling to keep their shelves stocked to help not only unemployed individuals, but also the "working poor." I brought this to Keith's attention, and he felt that helping the hungry was a cause in which he had a genuine desire to help. So we set out to create a community outreach program that would ultimately help adults and children in need. That became the intention (see Chapter 4 for a refresher on clarifying your intention).

We then brainstormed some ideas on how he could gather donations in his office and discussed them with employees at the local food pantry. We learned the program we were proposing had never been done before and they were very open to working with us to implement it to fill their void, particularly in the summer months. We called the program "Five for Free," which took place over a five-week period in the month of July. Anyone who made a Thursday morning appointment and brought at least five cans or boxes of food received a free office visit for chiropractic services. His office was normally closed on Thursdays, but he was willing to stay open during July and donated all of his time as part of the program. Because of the high response rate, he extended the offer to the entire day on Thursdays. In addition, each patient was offered an additional four visits for another five cans or boxes of food per appointment that could be made any weekday.

 INSPIRATIONAL INSIGHT

"Without the playing with fantasy, no creative work has ever yet come to birth. The debt we owe to the play of imagination is incalculable."

—Carl Jung

The program caught the media's attention in a big way, providing Keith with more positive exposure than he expected. All four local television networks—ABC, CBS, NBC, and FOX—ran stories on their newscasts. The benefiting charity shared these segments by posting to its website and on YouTube. The local major daily newspaper printed a front-page article, and the other major daily ran a full-color photo along with a profile on Keith and his efforts. Several monthly and weekly publications also picked up the story. In all, Keith's office collected a half-ton of food, or 1,000 pounds. To cap it off, a local massage therapist read about the donations and decided to create his own version of this program and also offered free services in exchange for food donations.

This community outreach program began with the objective of creating more positive exposure for the chiropractor. It became more about helping out a charitable cause and at the same time Keith's generosity garnered a plethora of media coverage, which brought attention to him and the need for more food donations. This story illustrates how creativity isn't always about million-dollar budgets and advancing technology. It starts with a desire and a willingness to create, even when it appears that limited resources will prevent you from innovating.

What perceived limitations is your business facing? Can you think of steps you can take to begin addressing them using one of the creative thinking techniques you've learned or an idea you may have gleaned from this example? Do you feel better equipped to tackle what may seem like an impossibility? Let the ideas start to fly! I challenge you to take one situation that's happening right now in your workplace that seems to have no fix and begin working on making something happen out of nothing.

Wipe out the notion that creativity requires millions of dollars, millions of ideas, or a million-dollar idea. Instead, check in periodically to notice if you're willing to be open minded, to see what's not there, to take risks, and to infuse yourself with the passion to make a difference.

Getting Inspired Through Observation

Another way you can get in the creative mind-set for work is through observing what others are doing. One process is known as *benchmarking*. This involves staying on top of your industry's best practices—in other words, the companies that stand out to you with their creative ventures. You can even identify companies or nonprofit organizations that aren't directly related to your type of business, too, to gather tips. Look at companies or brands you respect and appreciate and see what techniques they use, what risks they take, and what small changes they make that lead to big results. Again, most ideas are spin-offs of existing ideas, so study, learn, and improve upon what you see other companies doing.

 **DEFINITION**

Benchmarking is a technique used by people in business to track and evaluate other companies' most effective methods, systems, and procedures. This allows them to improve upon and incorporate these practices into their own organization.

Another good practice is trendspotting. By paying attention to trends—the general direction of what's happening in the marketplace—you'll gain a better understanding of whether you're on the right track and what's to come. What are people talking about? What online articles are generating the most comments from the public? The internet has literally become a free-for-all when it comes to people voicing their opinions, so check out articles, blogs, and other forms of social media to spot trends. Even comedy shows may be good sources of information for you, as the television hosts tend to capitalize on current events, which can be an indication of where things are headed.

Closer to home (or your business), begin to make more observations about the people whom you admire for their tenacity to create. You may find them within your own organization, leaders of different businesses, dedicated volunteers—anyone who inspires you to want to continue to improve your creative output. What is it about them that inspires you? How and why would you like to be more like them? It's a healthy practice to have a business hero or two. When you need an inspirational lift, you can look to them.

Causes of Creative Burnout

If you're not mindful, taking on new, creative initiatives in the workplace can eventually lead to a feeling of burnout. This is different from the blocks you identified in Chapter 6 that kept you from creating. I'm talking about that feeling of saying to yourself—usually in the middle or toward the end of a project—"I can't do this anymore." It reminds me of being in labor with my first son. Going into the twenty-fourth hour, I remember saying that very line. I was done, or at least I wanted to be—but then again, there was no turning back! With many creative projects, there's no turning back either. You've come too far, but you feel like giving up, or you simply need to be reenergized and reinspired before continuing.

When it comes to burnout, it's important to understand what caused it. How long have you been feeling this way? Has it been building over time, or did you all of a sudden throw your arms up in the air and proclaim "I'm done! I've had it!"? What's the primary feeling of your burnout? There's a difference between feeling bored and feeling beleaguered. Both can be the result of burnout, but it's helpful if you can put your finger on your innermost feelings to help you better address them. The following are some of the main contributors to burnout:

Your lifestyle. Simply put, have you been taking good care of yourself? The creative project itself might be a lot to handle but your other work and personal responsibilities may be pressing down on you as well. Are you so busy working or taking care of others that you have neglected your own needs? Have you been getting enough sleep—and do you even know what "enough" is for you? Are you eating the foods that nourish you or are you reaching often for junk food? Many people like to burn the candle at both ends, not thinking about the consequences until that burnout hits. Being surrounded by any kind of emotionally charged situations also feeds burnout. For example, working on a creative task while dealing with a divorce, the sickness of a loved one (or perhaps yourself), or any distressing circumstance involving drama can lead to an overall feeling of burnout.

 INSPIRATIONAL INSIGHT

"There's nothing that kills creativity faster than burnout. We are undermining ourselves and our own effectiveness by buying in to the myth, the collective delusion, that burnout is the way to succeed. It's not."

—Arianna Huffington

Taking on too much. The entire creative process—from ideas and the incubation of them to experimenting, analyzing, and implementing them—can place demands on your mental, emotional, physical, and spiritual energies. Pushing the limits of any of those areas can lead to burnout, especially during busy times in your workplace. An overloaded workflow can zap your zeal and throw your balance off.

Information overload. In these high-tech times, information overload can be a contributing cause to burnout. Just considering emails alone, the average corporate worker will send and receive 125 emails per day in 2015, according to the Radicati Group. Add in additional computer and phone usage, text messages, radio, and television, the amount of media that flows to individuals and households in a year is 6.9 zettabytes, or 6.9 *million* gigabytes, according to a study produced by the Institute for Communication Technology Management (CTM) at the USC

Marshall School of Business and visiting researcher James Short. The study didn't even include workplace consumption—only individuals in and out of the home. Too much of a good thing can be, well, too much!

Continuing to work on something you really don't care about anymore. It's also common for you to start off your creative activity with a bang. You're off and running, feeling energized as you reach different milestones, and like a marathon, you get to the midway point and you hit a wall. The enthusiasm you felt in the beginning has faded as you grow tired. *Hmmm … it seemed like such a great idea at the time,* you think to yourself. It's not so much about the initial inspiration now as it is about finishing the race, while wondering if you'll ever desire to do this again. This is especially common with people whose professions depend on creativity every day, such as graphic designers, photographers, and writers. If that's you, you may still be productive with your craft but you may feel like you're just going through the motions.

When it comes to understanding burnout and its causes, think of yourself as a smartphone. It takes on tons of creativity in a day—checking email and running apps of all kinds, serving as a voice recorder and MP3 player, taking requests and talking back to its owner, and more. Sooner or later, its battery drains and it has to be recharged. You are no different. So how do you plug in to recharge? What are the best ways get your game on again?

Helpful Remedies for Burnout

How you address your burnout depends on a variety of factors. In particular, just as with identifying your blocks, once you uncover the reasons for feeling less energized and motivated, you can start to figure out how to work through these feelings. Plus, if you can learn to spot the clues of creative burnout as it's just starting to build, you can address it while it's still manageable.

 CREATIVITY KEY

One mental technique that may be helpful in working through burnout is to remind yourself that the feelings you're experiencing are temporary. Nothing lasts forever. Situations evolve and change, and you will be a wiser person for having had a challenging experience. For more serious burnout you can't overcome on your own, you can always work with a therapist, spiritual counselor, or coach.

Now that you've looked into the potential causes of your burnout, consider some of the following solutions. Acting on one or more of them doesn't mean you have to ditch your creative project. You can still come back to your endeavor and focus like a laser beam. In the meantime, though, take time to feed your hungry soul.

Refocusing Your Attention

Sometimes all it takes to work through a burnout period is to adjust your focus. The following recommendations all deal with creating a change to refocus your attention. Change occurs when you make it happen, so try one or more of these to see if they begin to elevate your spirit:

- Shift your concentration to an activity that has nothing to do with your current project. This could be taking a few minutes to temporarily divert your attention or switching it up altogether by spending the next few hours on a different work initiative.

- Break up your routine—to, during, and from work—in some way, however big or small. Just make it different! A routine provides safety and security, but doing things the same way every day also can lead to boredom.

- Stagger your more intense work with mundane tasks in between. Ideally, break away from work entirely with mini-breaks throughout the day. Don't feel guilty about it either. What you're after is bringing back some of your creative spark.

- In your off time or during work breaks, read books that inspire you and have nothing to do with work. If reading tacky novels takes your mind away and relaxes you, go for it!

- Revisit the activities and interests that inspire you and make you feel good. Determine what it'll take to commit to one of them and then do it!

- Read through your "gratitude file" (see Chapter 9). You did set one up, didn't you?

Involving Other People

One of the biggest complaints people have in any kind of relationship—work or personal— is they feel like they're not being heard. Therefore, it might help to get back into the swing of things by turning to other people for help. Here are a few ideas:

- Tap into your co-worker's brain and see if she can offer a fresh perspective. This works especially well if you're feeling immobilized. Work collaboratively in discussing how to inject new life into the project or into yourself.

- Ask your boss for a mental health day and spend the time doing something fun and relaxing.

- Call or make lunch plans with a friend who has been in your shoes before. It helps to feel like you're being understood by someone who gets it.

- Don't assume that your boss knows what you're feeling or thinking. If necessary, have a heart-to-heart talk to take a load off your mind and get you back on the road to recovery.

CREATIVITY KEY

If you're struggling with a particular project, consider switching one or more of the involved tasks that are troubling you with a co-worker for a period of time before resuming work on it. The company may be better off to have someone with fresh eyes and energy working on it, and you also may be able to breathe new life into the other employee's project, too.

Getting Physical

Feeling good physically in your body and your workspace can positively affect your mood and decrease your stress level, helping you overcome burnout. Consider doing one or more of the following suggestions:

- Address your basic survival needs of getting the proper amount of sleep and healthy nutrition. A lack of sleep and poor eating habits are enough to throw you off balance. If necessary, see if vitamins and supplements make a difference.

- Commit to some form of exercise. It doesn't have to be long; in fact, quick bursts of intense workouts have been proven to provide health benefits.

- Take a quiet walk or one with stimulation, where you listen to music or an audio book using ear buds.

- Organize your workspace in a different way. Just as with changing your routine, making physical changes can give you a new perspective.

Centering Yourself Inwardly and with Love

Especially if you're still uncertain as to the cause of your burnout, it can help to take the time to understand what's really going on inside of you. Here are a few more steps revolving around self-reflection and treating yourself kindly:

- Are you doing your "morning pages" (see Chapter 9)? Even if you haven't committed to that practice, a great way to gain a better self-understanding is to write down your feelings. Sometimes just getting them out on paper can help to release them.

- Allow yourself to be still and meditate. There are a number of smartphone apps that offer free guided meditations, or you may opt to meditate on your own. Even taking five minutes at your desk in the middle of the day may be enough to fortify you.

- Build small treats into your workweek. For example, allow yourself to go out for lunch once a week to a restaurant that offers your favorite type of food.

- Step outside to get a breath of fresh air now and then.

- Hug a pet. Feel the unconditional love.

- Be gentle with yourself and remember to laugh!

 CREATIVITY KEY

Yet another way to look at your role in the workplace may be to see yourself as being there to motivate other employees. Perhaps some of them look to you as a role model. Knowing that you are helping to shape others' careers and perhaps influencing them in their personal life, too, may help your attitude by giving you more of a sense of appreciation. Perhaps you'll even feel more invigorated now! Positively assisting others may create more meaning in not just your work life, but your place in the world as a human being. When you can create more meaning, you naturally feel better and your attitude will slowly begin to improve. Think of other ways your job holds meaning that you may not have ever considered, however small. They may just make the difference you've been needing. Attitude is everything!

Creative Play: Interview Insights

This activity will help you get in better touch with yourself as you reconnect with what initially inspired you to pursue the field you're working in. Gaining additional insights may help you get a better understanding of what's at the root of your feelings on the job, whether you're feeling more stress than usual or experiencing full-blown burnout.

Tools Needed: Two chairs (optional: a video camera or a recording device)

You're going to play the roles of both a talk show host and the guest. To start, write down at least five questions that address what originally attracted you to your current profession. Structure your questions so the answer must go beyond a simple yes or no. For example, you might ask, "What inspired you to pursue your line of work?" or "Can you recall the creative impulse that got you started?" You might follow that with "What changes have you noticed through the years and how has that affected you?" Keep going until you've written down five or more questions.

Once you complete your questions, set up two chairs facing each other. Determine which chair is the host's and which is the guest's. Start by sitting in the host's chair and ask your first question out loud. Next, literally get up and sit in the guest's chair and answer the question, as if you're responding to a host other than yourself. Repeat this process until you go through all of your questions. As the host, depending on the answer you hear, you can add more questions on the go.

Give yourself permission to be playful and unstructured yet answer the questions authentically as if you are being interviewed for an actual television or radio program. Allow the space for a spontaneous answer to emerge that may even surprise you. This can be both a fun and revealing exercise. You may wish to record this process with a video camera or audio recorder so you can go back and review your answers for even more insight.

When you finish, write down any new realizations of what you learned through this process. A side benefit is that if you're ever interviewed, this activity will give you a little practice!

The Least You Need to Know

- Treat creativity as a given in the workplace—a priority that is part of your every-day strategy.
- Competition in the global marketplace means that creativity and innovation are no longer optional in the workplace.
- When you think there are limited possibilities to produce something innovative, dig a little deeper and put your creative thinking cap on. Involve others in the process and you may find that the impossible has become possible.
- If you don't take the proper steps to take care of yourself, burnout can occur. Pay attention to the signs and take the necessary steps to prevent it.
- If you're already feeling burned out, some of the solutions include refocusing your attention, seeking help from others, getting proper rest and exercise, and being loving with yourself.

Living Creatively Every Day

Once you've made a commitment to your own creative expression, you can't really separate that from your everyday life. It is now a part of you and manifests in different ways. You may have developed certain expectations about your abilities and find yourself feeling like you're going backward at times. Do not despair. This is normal, and in this part, you learn different recommendations to keep you going.

Children also may be a part of your everyday life. Whether you're rearing your own kids, teaching young students, or interacting with children in other ways, this part begins by taking a look at creativity in youngsters and teenagers. From there, I focus on how creativity continues to offer tremendous benefits to people as they get older, so if you're the caregiver of a parent or a loved one, you'll want to take note.

This part also addresses the advantages of showing your creative work, why you may be holding back, and how you can get comfortable with going public—or at the very least, sharing with your friends and family. You then revisit your blocks, tune in to your creative rhythm, and discover how handwriting can actually contribute to your creativity. You also get a chance to check in to see how far you've come and where you're at now. You are even given a few more creativity resources to consider and information on how meditation may enhance your creative efforts. To end this part, you get to read about what to expect on your ongoing creative journey, including whether you can and should force creativity, how to deal with personal burnout, and the importance of being authentic. At the end of this book, you will see you have now unlocked the door to creativity! Time to celebrate!

The Ageless Art of Creativity

Age 2 or 3 is usually the cutoff for free admission to attractions, you have to be 21 years old to legally drink in most states, and you usually have to be at least 55 years of age to take advantage of senior discounts. Fortunately for everyone, there is no age limit to creativity. Kids begin to express their own ingenuity before they're even walking, and adults may continue to follow their own creative path until their final days.

That's the beauty of creativity—it's inherent and available to all, regardless of age, ethnicity, or gender. You may be responsible for children in some way, as a parent, caregiver, or teacher. If kids are not a part of your world, you can still learn a lot from children about creativity. This chapter starts with considerations of the young and ends with a look at how creativity continues to provide benefits through midlife and beyond.

In This Chapter

- What we can learn from kids and their creativity
- How to prevent kids from losing their imaginative edge
- Reversing the negative effects of schools on creativity
- Keeping teenagers inspired and innovative
- How creativity can still stimulate older minds

Supporting Creativity in Your Kids

Children display amazing imaginations and have an insatiable curiosity. One example is getting caught up in the "Why?" game with a toddler whose questions of why and how the world works seem endless. Kids pose questions about matters that aren't even a passing thought to adults. They have entire conversations with imaginary friends, turn cardboard boxes into trucks, play "make-believe" with just about anything they can get their hands on, and oftentimes get more enjoyment out of the package a toy came in than the toy itself.

Unfortunately, little by little, most kids begin to disengage from their natural states of creativity and show less imagination as they grow older. Some of them become those adults I referenced earlier who say things like "I'm just not creative." Therefore, it's imperative to make creativity a priority for kids today so they can experience the inner joys and internal rewards that come with creative expression. If they experience those feelings on a regular basis, they will be more likely to carry creativity into adulthood.

Whether you have one child or more, the following tips are useful in fostering creativity. (I will be using the plural form, kids or children, in stating the tips.) As you and your children explore these, be careful not to let them—or you—become overwhelmed, which can negatively affect creative expression. Do what you can, and remember, it's not the end product that's most important—it's the enjoyment of the process itself.

 CREATIVITY KEY

When I talk about the process, I'm not necessarily speaking of the creative process that was described in Chapter 4. Kids' creative play is usually more fleeting and less structured, although you will probably see some elements of that process in action. For example, they get an idea, they experiment with it, act on it, and (hopefully) enjoy it. As you become more attuned to your own creative process, you'll notice theirs.

How Encouragement Goes a Long Way

If you ask most adults who think they're not very creative if they received a lot of encouragement to be creative as a child, their answer will probably be "No." To prevent that from happening to your kids, be very conscious of the need to offer some form of support every day.

One way is to encourage their curious nature. That's a quality all kids display when they're young but can lose quickly because they're being told "no" so much of the time. For example, while it's understandable you don't want your kids to touch breakables in the house, limit the amount that is within their reach and allow them to poke and feel appropriate items and ask questions. They can be curious without touching anything, too. You could show them common kitchen items that are unfamiliar to them and ask "What do you think this is used for?" Notice the different answers they give you and applaud them for their original answers before telling them how you use it.

Another area to encourage is spontaneity. This may be accomplished by not planning every minute of every day. Be sure they have unstructured time each day to choose their own activities. Notice how they may seem to jump from one interest to the next, which is okay, because it allows them to explore and experiment. It's because of their curious nature they easily switch gears. For example, if they're coloring a picture in a coloring book, and then decide in the middle of it to go outside and play on the swing set, show support rather than expecting them to finish coloring the picture first. As long as they're not jeopardizing their safety, be okay with their spontaneous choices.

Promoting your kids' independence also can aid their creativity. You could start by giving them simple choices, such as "Do you want to wear your red polo shirt or this blue T-shirt?" Having the opportunity to make decisions on their own will build their confidence and self-esteem—two important characteristics of creative expression.

 INSPIRATIONAL INSIGHT

"The hardest thing about reality is returning to it after an hour inside your child's mind."

–Robert Brault

Making Art Convenient

Artwork can be a way for children to express their feelings—good or bad—and provides a healthy, creative outlet. You can encourage this by making the tools for art available to your children at any time.

For example, always have crayons, markers, pens, paper, and other materials available for use. If you have the space, store the materials in a place that's visible and handy and designate an arts area where you can set up a child-size easel, table, or small desk. For most kids, the old "out of sight, out of mind" principle applies; if you choose a space where most of the family spends its time and keep things in places that are easy to get to, your children will be more likely to go there more often and engage in an artistic activity.

You can also guide them in the direction of artistic creation by deliberately setting a time to sit with them and organize the supplies in a way that's easy for them to create. If you're a neat freak, let go of that need and be tolerant of messes. The paints you use should be washable, and you can cover your floor with newspapers or buy an old sheet from a thrift store to use for protection.

Another way to support your children's exploration of art is to view all materials you may be tempted to discard as usable in a possible art project, such as buttons, pieces of cardboard, greeting cards, corks from wine bottles, old shirts with sequins, egg cartons, and so on. This will stimulate more curiosity in your kids and aid their creative thinking by telling them to look beyond how something is normally used. You can do the same in nature, too, by gathering pinecones, acorns, leaves, shells, and rocks as potential art pieces. Whatever the case, in collecting materials, ask them "How do you think you could use this in your artwork?" To give them more ideas on different resources for art, take them to an arts and crafts show and point out works that utilize common household items (such as spoon art). Museums and Pinterest are two other places to search with your children to get ideas.

As you encourage your kids' artistic expression, be careful with your feedback. For example, if you said to your son "I really like the house you drew," he might respond by saying "That's not a house. That's a box for my pet monkey." It's better to start off with a positive comment, such as "I really like how you used the color red," followed by "Tell me more about your picture." This gives children a chance to explain their own thought process and keeps you from attaching a name to the picture. By allowing your children to readily express themselves artistically in a way that avoids judgment, you give them a healing, positive outlet for creativity.

CREATIVITY KEY

Here's a fun and easy activity for your kids using natural resources: Put a leaf underneath a piece of paper and rub over it with a crayon. Your kids can then add watercolors or markers to decorate the leaf design as they'd like.

Putting a Creative Spin on Everyday Things

Creativity isn't just relegated to making artwork. There are things you do every day with your children that can be used to engage their creativity.

Chores are not typically something children—or even you!—look forward to. By adding a little creativity, you can show them even important tasks don't have to be completely serious. For example, in teaching your kids to clean up after themselves, take the opportunity to turn it into a game that will be fun for them. Tell them you'll time them to see how fast they can put their toys away. Ask them for their ideas, too, not only regarding chores, but any routine tasks they resist doing.

Story time can also be a place to inject more creativity. While reading stories to your children, stop and ask them about the characters. See if they would like to be friends with one of the people in the story and to tell you why or why not. After you've read the story a few times, ask them to make up a different ending. If they're stuck for ideas, prompt them with a question like "What if Cinderella didn't return by midnight? What do you think would happen?"

Introducing kids to music can also lead to a variety of creative activities. You can show them how to move around and dance with them. Or you can tell them they are the stars of the show and create a stage for them to be the entertainment, letting them pick out the pretend microphone they'd like to use to perform. I can remember my two older sisters and I pretending to be the Supremes because our mom was such a fan of this popular singing group at the time; we lip-synched the songs as we put on a show for our parents. By allowing your kids the fun and freedom of sharing music, you'll help them create unforgettable moments.

As for television, much has been written about limiting the amount of time children spend in front of the tube. You may use the TV to entertain and babysit your kids on occasion, such as when you are busy preparing dinner, but it's better if you can select programs that will stimulate their creativity and that you can watch together. Nowadays, you don't even need to buy videos. There are plenty of choices you can find for free on the internet, such as at watchknowlearn.org, which contains a number of educational videos for kids from kindergarten through grade 12 that have been suggested by educators.

The kitchen is another area to have your kids explore creativity. You can involve them in the preparation of meals, asking them to put the decorating touches on cupcakes or other baked goods. They may also enjoy making their own "play dough." There are easy recipes you can look up on the internet that call for cheap, common ingredients and don't involve baking.

 INSPIRATIONAL INSIGHT

"Children see magic because they look for it."

—Christopher Moore

Finding Creativity Outdoors

Taking nature walks provides many opportunities for children to get in touch with their creative side. It teaches them to appreciate beauty, which can someday be translated into such creative activities as paintings, photographs, and stories. For example, if you're into gardening, involve your kids in planting flowers and vegetables. Even if you don't have a full-blown garden, supervise them in planting seeds. They'll delight in watching the plant grow and take pride that they had a hand in it.

It doesn't matter what environment you live in; there are plenty of opportunities for creativity. The following are some ideas for a snowy climate:

- Fill a spray bottle with some type of food coloring or dye and water and create snow paintings. Brainstorm with your kids to think of other materials to use to add color to snow and then decide what to create.

- Make a snowman with your kids and ask them to come up with ways to dress him. What can they use for the eyes, nose, and mouth?

- Have a snowman- or snow sculpture–building contest with your neighbors. A friendly competition like this can stimulate creativity.

- Have your kids think of tools and common household goods that can make impressions in the snow and then try them out.

The following are some things to consider if you live near a beach:

- Bring cookie cutters with you and put sand mixed with water in them so your kids can make their own designs.

- Collect different types of shells and make a design in the sand. Or bring the shells home and help your kids create a wreath, centerpiece, or candles.

- Just as you can color snow, you can color sand, too. Use food coloring, dry tempera paint powder, or colored chalk. You and your kids can even do the old classic—build a colorful sand castle!

- Have your kids write messages in the sand with their feet. If it's a love message, take a picture and text it to the intended person.

Creative Discipline

Creativity isn't just about rewards and allowing any sort of behavior. In fact, how children develop depends largely on methods of discipline. The "do as I say," strict disciplinary model that often included corporal punishment, or spanking, was commonplace in the last century. However, today many parents are looking for more creative ways to discipline their children without being too stern or too lenient.

According to parenting coach and expert Ginny Luther, disciplining with shock and awe—such as shouting, shaming, and spanking—will always teach children, but that type of learning comes from a place of fear and doesn't allow them to access the problem-solving part of the brain. The creative part is letting go of trying to control kids and instead focusing on connecting with their gifts of creativity and then providing guidelines around those gifts.

Luther uses her own son, Bart, as an example. From the time he was 14 months old, he was turning toast into guns and making gun sounds, which was contrary to her belief system. The traditional approach would have been to stop his behavior by threatening, which would have exacerbated his defiance. However, Luther determined what he was really doing was displaying his leadership, a trait that serves children well later in life but can challenge parents to the max in the earlier years. She therefore realized she had to get very creative in how she parented him and began using a technique she calls *reflecting,* as opposed to using judgment and control.

 **DEFINITION**

> **Reflecting** is a technique used in creative discipline with children in which the parent reflects to children their expressed desires followed by providing guidelines that offer safe choices and redirection.

Reflecting means mirroring back to children what they are expressing and establishing guidelines around that, which includes ensuring safety and offering choices and redirection. Reflecting doesn't mean you're giving in; it means you're stimulating the higher parts of your children's brain, which enables decision making by them. For example, a controlling attempt might be for Luther to say "Bart, don't you dare point that at me! That's not nice. We don't use guns in this house. They are hurtful." On the other hand, if she used a reflective attempt, it would be something like "Bart, you like to play GI Joe. You want to help others feel safe. Let's build a safe place for them so they can be safe." This empowers him to make a choice that builds free will verses taking his power away.

At 14 months, reflection is more redirection, but if Bart was a 3-year-old pointing the toast gun at his mother because he was mad he couldn't have candy for breakfast, she would use reflecting by saying "You want me to know how mad you feel right now. You were hoping I would give you candy. It's hard when you can't choose candy for breakfast. You may have some eggs or cereal. What's your choice?" Choice and redirection become something children are willing to listen to. Luther looks at parents as the vehicles for their children's creative being.

In essence, creativity in parenting is the willingness to step aside and guide rather than control and make it about the parents' agenda, according to Luther. It still means structure, limits, disappointment, and crying. It's how parents respond that will make the difference between whether children exercise their own creativity or shut down. The connection between parent and child is that crucial. Luther's philosophy of discipline utilizes a more creative brain, one that is flexible and sees more than one option, as in whole-brain thinking. So by allowing your children to reflect upon their actions, you bring about awareness and teach them the ability to problem solve the hardest of situations by taking responsibility. This mindful awareness is what builds creativity, not the shoulds and shouldn'ts.

Some Final Dos and Don'ts

Most children are very sensitive and impressionable, and what you say to them can last a lifetime and potentially lead to creative blocks (see Chapter 6). Therefore, I'd like to close this section with some general dos and don'ts for supporting your kids creatively:

- **DON'T make comparisons.** Just as you should never compare yourself to anyone else, never compare your child's creative works and efforts with a sibling or anyone else!

- **DON'T pressure your children to perform on command.** If you sense they just need a little prodding, that's okay, but overall, let them initiate their sharing.

- **DON'T judge.** Judging can make your children feel like they're being evaluated and not living up to your expectations. This could then cause them to limit their creative efforts and focus more on pleasing you than being original.

- **DON'T try to relive your childhood through your children.** What appeals to you may not interest your children. Expose them to different opportunities but do not expect them to gravitate to your passions.

- **DON'T expect perfection.** It's okay for you to encourage your kids to do their best work, but do not ever expect or demand they strive for perfection. Be proud of your children—no matter the outcome of the project.

- **DO be a role model.** If your kids see you engaging in creative activity, they may wish to join you or be inspired by you.

- **DO emphasize the fun aspects of creativity.** For example, you can inject humor into creative play by telling knock-knock jokes and having your children make up some of their own.

- **DO praise your children.** I can't emphasize this enough. Praise, and then praise them again!

- **DO allow them to have imaginary friends.** If your children want to invite them to the dinner table, go along with it. It's their way of exploring and it may be comforting as well.

- **DO give them gentle guidance.** It's okay to give basic instructions, but once you do, allow your children to proceed on their own, even when you notice them doing it incorrectly. If you see them getting frustrated, you can offer to help. Honor their answer. It's always important to supervise to ensure safety but the more independently they can work, the more it will build their confidence.

CREATIVITY KEY

The ideas I've provided are just some of the considerations to promote creativity with your kids. Be creative yourself and think of some more ideas. Perhaps one of the tips prompted you to think of others already. If you had a creative upbringing yourself, revisit your own childhood to recall what helped your imagination soar.

Creative Play: Don't Lose Your Marbles

In this experimental activity, you and your child are going to create an abstract piece of artwork. If you'd like, you can even try this by yourself!

Tools Needed: A minimum of 15 marbles; tempura paints (red, yellow, and blue are good starters because as primary colors they make secondary colors when combined); three containers that will hold your paint, such as tinfoil pans or paper cups; a box that has four sides, such as a shoe-box for smaller kids or a pizza box for older children; computer paper or construction paper; and a plastic or regular spoon

1. Pour each color of paint into its own container.

2. Line your box with a piece of paper.

3. Start with a minimum of five marbles and drop them into the different colors of paint. Swish them around to cover the marbles completely.

4. Take the marbles out with a spoon (or your hands, if you don't mind getting messy) and drop them onto the paper that's covering the pizza box. Roll them around until all of the paint comes off the marbles. If you tilt too far, they can fly out, so be careful.

5. Keep going until you decide your masterpiece is complete! Wait for it to dry and post in a visible place. Perhaps it's even suitable for framing!

Reconnecting Teens with Their Creative Nature

Some of the same principles that have been addressed regarding younger kids apply to teenagers, too, but teenagers also have their own additional considerations. The main difference is that most teens are grappling with establishing their personal identity. They want to conform and at the same time they want to buck traditions and become their own person. They want to stand out without sticking out—out of place, that is. Hanging out with Mom and Dad isn't usually high on their priority list, yet they also need to know you support and love them. Figuring out who they are and what they stand for is a creative act. However, one study showed that while 98 percent of 3- to 4-year-olds use divergent thinking, only 10 percent of teens do so. One of the biggest reasons is because of the pressure they feel to fit in. As their parent, what can you do to support them in their quest to be unique yet accepted?

 INSPIRATIONAL INSIGHT

"There is a fountain of youth: it is your mind, your talents, the creativity you bring to your life and the lives of people you love. When you learn to tap this source, you will truly have defeated age."

–Sophia Loren

First, understand their fear of failure and looking stupid in front of their friends can override everything else and keep them from stepping out too far from the perceived "normal." To counteract that, let them know that healthy risk-taking is not just part of the creative process, but a big part of life overall. If they make a mistake, show them you love them unconditionally no matter what. You can even share your own vulnerability by telling them about some of the things you've attempted that didn't work out the way you had expected. Talk about your feelings and how you overcame the negative experience, including the lessons you learned and how some of your failures led you down a better path. This will not only make your teens more likely to take risks, it will also make them trust you through that personal sharing.

You should also ensure your home feels like a safe place where your teens can have both privacy and a comfortable space in which to explore their creative interests. As was discussed earlier in the chapter, supply the necessary materials so they can experiment. These can actually be the same as what you put together for younger children, as adolescents (and adults, too!) can also have fun with things such as scented markers and crayons. There may be a few items that are different from a toddler's creative basket due to safety concerns, such as a whittling knife if they're into carving, or more expensive paints and brushes if they're more serious about painting. The point is, making creativity convenient for them may inspire them to engage in it more often.

For most teenagers, their friends are of utmost importance, so if they have friends who have similar interests, let your teens know it's okay to invite their friends over to share in the activity (as long as you have the space to do so). When it comes to spending time on their own, encourage them to write their feelings in a journal that they don't have to share with you. I remember that I first started journaling when I was 14. It's a great way to deal with tender feelings that surface and cause confusion at this age that doesn't have to leave the privacy of their room.

Another way to encourage creativity is to discuss your teens' dreams and passions with them and show your support of these pursuits. For example, if they show an interest in learning to play an instrument, rent or buy what they desire to play and (if you can swing it financially) pay for private lessons. At least offer this as an option to show that you're behind them 100 percent.

Exposing your teens to a variety of options will open their minds to experiences they may not otherwise know about. For example, drama and dance workshops are an effective way teens can explore self-expression. Instructors who teach six-week classes in these and other disciplines say kids display more confidence at the end of the session. It's also a great way for them to learn teamwork. Technology is another option for expression. For many adolescents with camera phones and action cameras, it has opened up a whole new world where they can post creative videos on the internet. On the flip side, teens can explore nature explore creatively with projects that might include carving wooden utensils, decorative pieces, and furniture, or weaving baskets out of tree bark and pine needles. Another way for teens to engage their creative abilities is through community outreach opportunities. Many high schools require a certain amount of community service. Whether your teens' school does or not, getting your children to become involved with a need in the community helps build character. It's an opportunity to personally shine while helping out a good cause.

 CREATIVITY KEY

> While you may want to encourage your teens' involvement in different creative activities, also keep in mind the pressure of taking exams and their possible involvement with college prep or other plans after graduating. Just as you need to keep your life balanced, so do they.

To bring all of these creative outlets together for your teens, explain the concept of divergent thinking and how it will help them generate original ideas they can further explore. And when they approach you with a far-out idea, resist the temptation to immediately react negatively. After all, you encouraged them to think outside the box! Naturally, as their parent, you'll have to still weigh the pros and cons and check in with your own comfort level. If you decide against having them pursue a particular idea, be sure to explain the reason very clearly and simply— don't just slap it down with a flat "No." Maybe there's an aspect to their idea that may still be implemented.

Remember, teens often become rebellious because they're trying to form their own identity. Expect them to experiment with different things, such as hairstyles and outfits, and give them as much creative freedom as you can. Oftentimes the things they want to do are part of a fad that will pass. Plus, being rebellious is one of the common traits that creative people have; you don't want to completely squelch it. Ultimately, if you can come from a space of being a supportive co-creator having fun with them, rather than with an attitude of "I know more than you," this will help to foster a healthy and respectful relationship that is bound to advance their creativity even further.

Encouraging Creativity in Students

In Chapter 5, 12 common traits of creative people were discussed. If you saw the trait apart from this book—curious, adventurous, spontaneous, energetic, rebellious, and playful—you might think it was a list that describes children. It should come as no surprise that they exhibit many of the same characteristics of productive adult creators. However, a study by Kyung Hee Kim, PhD, a professor of education at the College of William and Mary, revealed that the United States' creativity levels among all age groups have been decreasing since 1990, with the most noteworthy decline being among young students.

What happens to derail these natural attributes that just about every kid exhibits to some degree, and how can it be corrected? The following takes you through the many reasons for stifled creativity in the educational setting and how you can counteract it as a teacher.

The Decline of Creativity in Education

While school systems and teachers cannot be blamed entirely, there are consistent findings that show kids lose their creative nature because of the ways they are taught in school. Traditional teaching methods are authoritative, which is focused on strict adherence to rules and regulations. This kind of organization is uninspiring to students and can lead to questioning of the established rules. When students challenge a teacher's authority, they're often viewed as rebellious, difficult, and disruptive. Before you know it, they're being sent to the principal's office. With each creative instinct that gets pinched—or, even worse, punished—children's creative expression begin to erode little by little.

 CREATIVITY COMPASS

While Deb was teaching an art class of ninth-grade students, she observed that many of them had doubts about their creative abilities and were extremely sensitive, with some reluctant to try the activities due to low confidence. To help turn them around, instead of focusing on their grades and drawing ability, she encouraged them to give their best effort, which would allow them to grow as a result. She continuously supported them by offering positive feedback and told them how much she believed in them. She also chose activities that helped the students make a connection between their emotions and expression in the creative process. She found this approach shifted many of the students' attitudes about their own creativity.

While the need for this is understandable so the classroom environment does not become chaotic or dangerous, some who have studied this subject say breaking the rules not only should be endured and encouraged, it also should be taught. Why? Because it promotes creativity, which is becoming one of the driving factors in business today and carries with it many life-giving benefits (see Chapter 2 for a refresher on those benefits).

Beyond the issue of rules and regulations, oftentimes children are taught to memorize material, which forces linear, noncreative thinking. In his book *A Whack on the Side of the Head,* Roger von Oech talks about how our schooling trains students to look for the "one right answer." This begins in preschool and continues through college and beyond. While math equations may have only one correct solution, when it comes to innovation, limiting students' search for answers and ideas can be a creativity killer. Even teachers complain about the expectations placed upon them, a "teach to the test" mentality, where scores on state-sanctioned standardized exams have become the priority because it's tied to funding and other rewards.

However, studies show this authoritative nature of direct instruction greatly affects how students approach learning and creative expression. Too much of that limits their ability to solve problems on their own or come up with innovative solutions. Instead, they merely imitate what they've been shown. When given some leeway to think on their own, they are able to offer creative solutions.

One study, The Rainbow Project by Dr. Robert Sternberg, set out to see if more learning would take place if students were taught with creative teaching techniques and instructed to think creatively about a problem rather than using the typical, passive lecture approach. The results showed that those who were taught in the nontraditional, creative manner received higher final grades than the control group who were taught with traditional methods.

So while kids need to learn certain facts that can be taught directly by their teachers, they also need to be given opportunities to arrive at their own answers through a discovery process. This encourages divergent thinking, which allows for *ambiguity* rather than one right answer. This is an important skill for students to develop over the long haul so they can continue to develop their creativity.

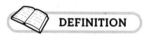 **DEFINITION**

> **Ambiguity** is to be unclear, to have multiple possible meanings, and to have a subject matter that's hard to grasp. Learning to be at ease with such uncertainty is a key ingredient of creativity.

Creative Teaching Methods

So is there a way to maintain a necessary structure and order in the classroom, teach certain facts and figures that really do have only one correct answer, and also encourage creativity in students? One way to start is to become more aware of what fosters and what destroys creativity. If you're a teacher, the following are a few simple guidelines you can follow to get back to the basics of creativity:

Give a few tips on a given subject or skill that's being taught and then allow time for students to explore on their own. Take something as simple as the definition of a line. You can teach students the Merriam-Webster definition—"a long, narrow mark on a surface"—and move quickly on to the next point or topic. Or you can stimulate their creativity by following that up by telling the kids that a line can be associated with an emotion. For example, if you're teaching an art class, tell your students to close their eyes and visualize a time when they were angry; you can then tell them to draw an angry line, which may be done with a heavy hand and appear dark and bold. Next, you can tell them to close their eyes and imagine a time when they felt happy, and have them draw a line representing that emotion, which might be drawn as a light, upward wave. By giving them time to experiment, they can play with their creativity.

Encourage students to ask questions and do not put them down if they ask a question that appears to have an obvious answer. One of the worst experiences I can recall from my high school years was being told by a teacher, in front of the whole class, that I asked a dumb question. He said "There are no dumb answers, only dumb questions." Funny how I can still remember that years later. That's how impactful it was for me. Therefore, keep in mind how your encouragement—or lack of it—can impact your students when they're exploring an idea through questions.

Challenge your students with situations that will motivate them to examine and experiment with finding their own solutions. They may protest and want you to hand them the answer. Don't give in to that. Let them know this is for their own growth, so they can tap into their own creative expression.

Let your students know it's okay to make mistakes. Help them to see that negative outcomes are learning opportunities that will help them grow. Give them ample time to explore how they can do it differently next time. During this contemplative process, they may even have an a-ha moment in which the "mistake" leads them to a far better solution.

Answer students' questions with a question. This technique works especially well for parents and their young kids, but also may be applied in the classroom. In other words, when students look to you for a solution, before answering, ask them what they think. Reward them with praise, even if the answer isn't correct, and then provide a proper explanation. If the answer is either right on or it's creatively crafted and could possibly work, reinforce that thinking even more with additional positive feedback.

By using these preceding techniques, you will allow students of all ages to develop their divergent thinking. Yes, they'll still need to expand their ability to think convergently as well, as that is part of the creative process, too, but there will be plenty of opportunities through the traditional learning methods that will allow for that. Just as modern medicine is beginning to take a more integrated approach to healing, advances in education to support students' creativity also will benefit from a multidimensional system, one that still allows for structure along with the free flow of exploration and independence.

 INSPIRATIONAL INSIGHT

"Creativity is an area in which younger people have a tremendous advantage, since they have an endearing habit of always questioning past wisdom and authority."

–Bill Hewlett

Creativity Knows No Age Limits

If your children are grown or you don't have kids, you may be in the position of caring for an aging parent or another loved one. While they may believe they're too old and missed their creative opportunities, studies tell a different story. After reading about the interesting research that follows, you can help them remove any reservations they have and remove any doubts you may have as well.

Research shows that creative expression actually stimulates and benefits older brains. Francine Toder, PhD, psychologist and author of the book *The Vintage Years: Finding Your Inner Artist (Writer, Musician, Visual Artist) After Sixty,* has been studying the field of neuroscience for years. She concluded that "novelty, complexity, and problem solving" were the three main keys to maintain the brain's vitality. She interviewed folks who took up art after the age of 55 and determined the expression of a fine art form is "inextricably connected" to brain health.

In other research, Dr. Gene Cohen, a psychiatrist and director of George Washington University's Center on Aging, Health and the Humanities, was the principal investigator of the Creative and Aging Study from 2001 to 2006. The results pointed to improved health and disease prevention when older people participated in community-based art programs run by professional artists. The study also showed this process reduces dependency and may have positive effects on maintaining independence, such as decreasing the risk factors that are tied into long-term care.

Any kind of arts participation for midlifers and beyond, including a more passive involvement, such as listening to music, helps to support overall well-being on all fronts—emotionally, mentally, and physically—and may alleviate symptoms. Other benefits that have been revealed in studies of those 65 and older who took part in arts programs were self-sufficiency, independence, increased intellectual activity, and emotional improvement. They also decreased doctor visits and had better health—mentally and physically—and didn't fall as often as those who didn't participate. Even people with dementia who participated in a painting program showed more engagement, enjoyment, and confidence compared to other, more typical activities.

Does any of this research surprise you? I found that it confirms my own experiences and beliefs. Some of the most creative people I know personally are over the age of 50 and are at the height of their creativity. It's never too late to get started or to continue to develop creative expression. So if you are caring for your mom, dad, or another loved one, what can you do to encourage them to pursue their creative expression? Here are a few tips:

- Don't let them get away with the excuse, "I'm too old." This was covered in Chapter 6. Share some of examples that were given and come up with some of your own.

- Inspire them by sharing Rhoda P. Curtis's book with them. She wrote a memoir titled *Rhoda: Her First Ninety Years* and makes a case that all people, regardless of age, are hard-wired for creativity, and this remains the same throughout the years.

- Talk with your loved ones about any creative opportunities they feel may have passed them by, and then do what you can to make at least one of them happen. For example, if they always wanted to paint, buy the necessary supplies. Perhaps you could make this an activity you can do together.

 INSPIRATIONAL INSIGHT

"The mind, once stretched by a new idea, never returns to its original dimensions."

–Ralph Waldo Emerson

Creating for the mere fun of it offers a feeling of freedom. By assisting your loved ones to engage with their creative sensibilities, you may see a light turn on inside of them that you haven't seen in a while.

The Least You Need to Know

- As a parent, caregiver, or teacher, make it a priority to do all you can to promote creativity in kids. Role model, offer praise, and supply the necessary tools are just some of the actions you can take to support this effort.

- Recognize that many teenagers are struggling to establish their personal identity. Proactively supporting their creative efforts will assist them with their self-esteem and the everyday peer pressure they experience.

- Creativity levels have been on the decline in education for the past couple of decades. This will continue unless changes are made within the system. You can help by consciously encouraging students to engage in creative activities and divergent thinking.

- The benefits of creativity are not age limited; in fact, studies have shown people 55 and older who are involved in arts programs can enhance their overall health.

To Share or Not to Share

One of the greatest feelings you've probably experienced is when you've been able to share a meaningful part of yourself with another person. Giving a gift to someone for no reason engenders warm feelings and pleasantly surprises the other person. Perhaps you've been on the receiving end of such an exchange, too.

But what happens when you share a part of yourself with others and the situation doesn't go as planned? This can happen when you decide to reach out and show your creative work and may be why you're not so sure you want to share. The flip side is that sometimes one act of sharing can move mountains. In this chapter, you learn the pros and cons of putting your work out there, which, in essence, is showcasing a piece of your heart. You also learn how to prepare yourself and your work for showing and how to accept both praise and criticism.

In This Chapter

- Preparing to show your work
- Overcoming your reluctance to share
- Dealing with feedback in healthy ways
- The gifts of sharing your creativity

Being at Peace with Sharing

The decision to share your creative efforts with others is a big one. Whether you paint, draw, sculpt, act, cook, quilt, sing, play an instrument, dance, write, take photographs, make films, or engage in some other kind of creative activity, eventually you must decide if you desire to share your talents with others. Those who make their living in a creative field must show their work or they won't be in that profession for long. But even professionals get disheartened when their creative work is questioned, or worse, criticized harshly or rejected altogether. A lot of people declare "I just do this for myself. I don't need an audience."

Do you fall into that category? If you do, do you secretly wish to change that viewpoint? I certainly did at one time, but I wasn't conscious of that for a long time. For literally two decades, I wrote songs and felt contented as I sang and played them aloud in an empty room. Yet when I reached into the inner depths of my soul, I knew someday I hoped to tap into the emotions of other people and touch their hearts in a way that would make a difference in their lives with both my singing and songwriting. That would only happen if I went beyond the bounds of my closed door and reached out to others. I finally did, and yes, it was scary and emotional, especially considering that my first public performance was at a friend's funeral. My fingers literally were shaking as I played my guitar and my voice was quivering. But I survived it and went on to do more public performances, which happens on a regular basis today.

If you are uncertain about sharing your work, can you also go well beyond the surface and reach deep within yourself to get to the bottom of what's behind your hesitation? What comes up for you? If it's fear, question that further. What is behind the fear? Are you afraid you're not good enough? If so, what constitutes "good enough"? Remember Chapter 6 and the blocks that were discussed? What's the worst that could happen if you reached out and shared your work? Keep in mind that "the worst" usually doesn't manifest. Can you recall a time when you feared "the worst" would happen and not only did it not go the way you had envisioned, but in fact there were no negative ramifications at all? Even the supposed "worst experiences" you imagine can have a happy ending.

The same can happen when you share your creative work. Whenever you go public with your work, you do risk criticism from others. You've read multiple times throughout this book how taking risks is a part of creativity. That includes stepping out of your comfort zone.

 CREATIVITY KEY

Sharing doesn't have to be a black-or-white situation; there are certainly shades of gray. In other words, most people don't go from creating on their own to sharing with a football stadium-size room of people. It can happen in stages.

"I'm Ready to Share—I Think"

Congratulations if you've decided to step beyond your private boundaries and go public or are at least willing to continue reading this chapter to consider the idea further. What does going public mean? That depends on your personal desires, dreams, and goals. Are you wanting to be a big fish in a small pond, a big fish in a big pond, or not a fish at all? Perhaps you just want to share your creative work with a few friends and family or are creating solely for your own personal pleasure.

Take a look again at your initial motivation and purpose, which will help you answer the question of what you truly desire to do. In Julia Cameron's book *The Artist's Way,* she talks about finding the "true north" of your goals on your "emotional compass." In other words, what's behind your creative goal? If you paint portraits and one of your goals is to have a solo exhibit in a gallery, perhaps respect as an artist is what's most important to you. Someone else may be after fame and fortune and is looking to make it big. Neither situation is better than the other. It's an individual aspiration and choice you make.

Also, if you are creating in more than one discipline, you may want to involve others with some projects and not others. For example, you may write poetry and make beaded jewelry. You may feel the poetry is too personal and you would feel too vulnerable sharing it, whereas you see the jewelry as more of an activity that would be fun to share as people try on colorful bracelets and necklaces you've made. With each of your creative endeavors, take a look at what drives you.

The following questions can help you decide what stimulates your desire to share your work:

- Are you drawn to share your work because you feel you have something important to reveal to others?

- Are you driven to make money from your creative venture?

- Do you want to transition your creative focus from an avocation to a vocation? In other words, do you want to make a hobby a job?

- Does the possibility of being in the spotlight motivate you?

- Does sharing mean you are you simply looking for approval?

- What would it mean to you to have your work validated by others?

- If the thought of sharing your work makes you feel nervous and uneasy, are you looking to work through this anxiety by confronting it head on?

- Will you be truly happy if you keep your creativity to yourself?

Assessing Your Work

If you still have some discomfort around the idea of sharing, you may feel a need to protect yourself. How can you do that? Assessing your own work can help you decide whether it's something you're truly ready to share or something you need to give more attention or put aside.

The trick is to do an honest evaluation without being too soft or hard on yourself. You're back to that "good enough" question again. Good enough in whose eyes? Yours or someone else's? That's an easy answer—it starts with you. You have to believe in yourself. At the same time, you need to establish your own measurement standards for judging your work. Do you have a sense of the criteria you'll use? What's a "must," and what's optional? Remember, one of the blocks that was discussed in Chapter 6 was procrastination. Are you judging your own work harshly as a way to avoid going public, or is your creation really not ready and in need of reworking?

 INSPIRATIONAL INSIGHT

"Part of the healing process is sharing with other people who care."

—Jerry Cantrell

To evaluate your own work, the following are some general criteria you can use:

- Reflect upon your motivation when you first began your creative project. This should tie in to your "true north." What were your feelings around the creative endeavor? Did you stay true to your original intention or did something change along the way?

- Are there steps you can still take to improve upon the work? Beware of the perfectionist popping up here! Remember, it's always best to strive for excellence, not perfection. As I presented in the chapter on your blocks, perfection can become an excuse to procrastinate.

- Are you happy with the way your project turned out? How do you truly *feel* about the final outcome? If you intend to sell your work, the marketability of your work becomes part of your criteria. If you were after a certain type of feeling, make that an important part of your evaluation.

In short, to properly assess your work, look at your original goals and see if you accomplished them. If you've accomplished them, you can feel ready to share; if you haven't, you can go back and see what you can do to make your work ready to share.

Deciding Whether It's Truly "Share-Worthy"

Even after you've gone through an evaluation process, it's understandable if you're not completely sure your work is "share-worthy." If you're at the point in which you think you're ready to share but still have reservations, stop right now and make a list of what's holding you back. I mentioned fear earlier in the chapter. Tune into that feeling more now and write down your reservations, starting with the words "I fear …." Examples might be the following:

- I fear there's nothing special about my work.
- I fear others will secretly laugh and make fun of my work.
- I fear my work isn't very original.
- I fear anyone could do what I've done.
- I fear this just doesn't stand out.

Just writing down your fears will help you get in better touch with where you're at psychologically. Once you've examined the statements in black and white, it's easier to be objective. Take the first statement in the example. What really makes a work of art (or whatever your creative activity is) "special"? If this is one of your fears, it's probably because you're comparing yourself to someone who has been out there sharing her work for a long time. Remember, you have to start somewhere, just like other people did! Go through each of your statements and evaluate them for their truthfulness. If there is any truth to them, ask yourself "Does it really matter?" Again, that ties into your motivation and purpose.

Take your time in digesting your fears and in determining an evaluation system for your work. You may be overly critical of your work, but it is possible to share prematurely. I remember doing that with two songs that I had written. In both cases, I knew that they weren't my best songs, yet I put them out there anyway. With the first song, it was just in the draft stage and I shared it with one of my biggest supporters. I could tell by his reaction that he wasn't that crazy about it. I wasn't upset with him, but I was kind of mad at myself because I knew I should have waited. I was excited about the direction it was going because it was a different type of song for me. In other words, I let my excitement to share overtake my gut instincts to wait. In the second case, I knew the song could be improved but I let go of the need for it to be perfect and told myself it was "good enough for now." I don't regret that decision, but I now know the difference in how I feel when I share a song that isn't quite there compared to when I sing one that I feel is ready.

Creative Play: It Starts with You

One way to step into the idea of sharing is to practice with yourself. This activity takes you beyond just imagining what it would be like and takes you into a more realistic realm before actually stepping out into the "real world."

Tools Needed: A hanging mirror, paper, a writing instrument, and your creative work (if you have several from which to choose, select one)

Stand before a mirror with one of your creative works, such as a piece of art, photograph, poem, or speech. If your craft doesn't involve an item—perhaps your talent is dancing—stand by yourself in front of a mirror. If it's cooking a specialty dish or something that doesn't fit perfectly into these instructions, do the best you can to adapt this exercise. Be creative! This activity is like doing a dress rehearsal with no audience other than you.

Now look in the mirror and talk with yourself as if you're speaking with either one person, a few other people, or a big audience. Start with an introduction of what you would say if you were really sharing it with others. For example, if you've never done this before and you're presenting to a small group of friends, you might say something like the following:

> "Thank you for gathering here with me. Tonight, I am taking a giant step forward in my quest to advance my creativity. I have been [doing this creative project] for years but have never before shared my work with anyone. I am excited that you are my first audience and I hope you will find my work to be inspiring."

A more creative introduction related to this example would be to write a fun, rhyming poem. It's really all about what feels right to you and what kind of a tone you want to set.

After your introduction, either show your work, perform your dance, sing, or play guitar—whatever is involved. Do it in a way you would imagine doing it "for real." While rehearsing, fully feel and express your enthusiasm for what you've created. Notice if reluctance or judgment comes up and work through it until you can remove those feelings.

Once you finish, while it's still fresh in your mind, write down how you felt during this exercise (aside from the fact that you may have felt awkward or silly talking to yourself). Address each one of your observations. For example, if you noticed you didn't really know what to say in the introduction, that gives you a starting point. This is your opportunity to work out the "bugs." Doing so will help increase your confidence level and you'll be closer to sharing! Repeat this creative play until you feel more confident about sharing your work with others. It's great practice!

Sometimes, you may need an outsider's input to help you decide if your work is truly ready to share, as well as whether you're emotionally prepared. If your reluctance in sharing is because you've determined your creative venture is lacking something but you're not quite sure what, this would be a good time to consider consulting a friend, a mentor, a creative person whom you admire, or someone whose opinion you value. Research shows that interacting with others and discussing your challenges can lead to a breakthrough you might not achieve on your own, especially if you pair up with someone who thinks differently than you do or takes approaches that vary from yours. If you recall, I presented the idea of teaming with another individual to create in Chapter 10; however, it's also a useful technique at any stage of the creative process—in the beginning, when you first get an idea, in the middle when you're experimenting and exploring, or during the evaluation stage.

If you feel you're not ready to share because you still have fear or are unsure of yourself and you've done the creative play in which you've practiced with yourself, you could reach out to a trustworthy friend for support. When seeking out that support, use discernment in selecting the right person. Sometimes even the best of friends can come from a place of insecurity and even jealousy, especially if your life is taking off in a positive direction and their life is going downhill. That doesn't necessarily mean a problem-plagued friend will let you down. My point is to choose carefully, especially if you're sensitive to feedback that could feel like rejection. Even the most confident person can be shaken by that feeling. You also could consider sharing your work with your mentor first, if you've established that type of relationship, in order to gain confidence to share with a wider audience.

Once you have determined the right person or people with whom to initially share, give yourself enough time and space to "show and tell," followed by a meaningful discussion. In all likelihood, you'll feel most comfortable doing that in your own home. From there, you can make whatever adjustments come out of that session and then branch out and invite a few more people over. Little by little, you're building your confidence by sharing with people who you already know are on your side but who also will be honest with you.

You can improve your chances of receiving truly helpful advice on whether your work is "share-worthy" by structuring the gathering in a way that's specific. For example, consider asking them to provide written notes so you'll really be able to take their comments in and appreciate the information more. Your supporters will be more likely to give meaningful feedback rather than speak "off the cuff." And instead of telling the participants something as vague as "I'd appreciate your opinion," it's better to be more explicit. Ascertain what would be most beneficial to know in order to determine whether your work is ready to share. For example, if you're sharing a short story, you may want to know if your characters are believable or descriptive enough. Or perhaps you want their viewpoint on whether the ending was a surprise or predictable. Form your questions based on your creative goals and see whether your audience thinks you've accomplished them. In the next section, I talk about the different types of criticism you might hear once you have reached out and shared and how to prepare yourself to deal with each comment most effectively.

You may choose to limit sharing your creative talents to one person or a small group of supportive friends and family, or you may strive to go for the gusto and shine in a much bigger, public way. In the end, your choice is about what is going to bring you the greatest joy. However, don't lose sight of how you also may touch others' lives by sharing your gifts.

Handling Feedback Once You've Shared

So now you've prepared yourself mentally and emotionally and you're feeling good enough about your work to step out and share. You may never feel 100 percent ready and may still feel a little bit nervous; that's okay. If you take the following tips into consideration, you can save yourself from potential heartache if you receive feedback that doesn't sit well with you.

You can't please everyone. I know you already know this, but it bears repeating. For example, I'm always amazed when I view a video on YouTube that seems positive or remarkably creative in every way but see that some people gave it the "thumbs down." I think to myself, *How could they possibly not like that video?* Yet I know better. Everyone thinks differently and comes from their own perspective. If you're putting yourself out there, not everyone is going to like what you do. That doesn't make you a bad person or a lackluster creator. Not everyone is going to like you or your work, whether it's due to envy or something else. Accept that as a fact and spare yourself the agony of overanalyzing where people are coming from. You'll probably never know.

Teach others how to treat you. What I mean by this is if someone mistreats you, perhaps by putting you down or being sarcastic, and you allow it to happen frequently over time, in essence you are sending a message to that person that it's okay to treat you that way. I'm not talking about the occasional slip people make; I'm referring to a pattern of behavior toward you that an individual has established. Decide what you're willing to tolerate and either confront the person, who may not even be aware of her conduct, or ignore the situation altogether.

It also may not have anything to do with you personally; some folks have a negative disposition regardless of the person or situation. Realizing there are people with a negative outlook on life overall is an awareness to keep in mind as you put yourself in the public eye.

Establish boundaries around what you are willing to tolerate. If you find people go beyond what you wish to hear—perhaps their critique feels hurtful and unproductive—speak with them politely to let them know you only wish to hear information that is useful. You have to establish your own boundaries on what you deem as valuable.

Don't immediately discount someone's feedback. Whether you receive feedback in a safe environment that you've set up or you're in the public eye at large, as long as the people in your audience are being kind and supportive, hear them out. For example, if someone offers a suggestion you don't agree with, do not automatically reject her idea. First of all, you may be reacting negatively because you're "attached" to the way you've been expressing your creativity and it's natural to resist change. To combat this, allow some space and time before determining if it's valid. In the moment, you can simply say "Thank you. I'll think about that."

The more comfortable you get with your own creative expression, the more you'll have a sense of what you are willing to change based on others' comments. While you may know right then and there that there's no way you're going to proceed with their idea, there's no reason to let them know that. It can't hurt to listen as long as the conversation is respectful.

Don't take it personally. In Don Miguel Ruiz's book *The Four Agreements: A Practical Guide to Personal Freedom,* one of the agreements is to not take anything personally. This is great advice for everything in life, and your creative work is no different. Remember that any critiques you receive that seem cruel are not about you. It's about your work, which goes back to point number one. Not everyone is going to like what you do. Oftentimes people who critique in an unkind way are projecting their own feelings of unworthiness onto you. It's their baggage. Don't carry it for them!

Of course, if you receive disappointing feedback from people with whom you have a close relationship, you may feel like it's personal. To get past this, have a heart-to-heart talk to find out why they didn't respond more positively. People who care about you are more likely to give you honest answers that you can take as constructive criticism. They care enough about you to provide feedback that could help you improve.

CREATIVITY KEY

Sometimes as soon as you hear a negative comment, you automatically shut out any praise that is given, even if you received 10 other compliments. In receiving feedback, make it a habit to listen for the positive. Take it into your heart and then say "thank you."

Consider the source. How do you decide whether to respond to someone's unsolicited advice, particularly if it's negative? Start by determining whether it's worth your time. Remember the discussion of time in Chapter 6—that immovable commodity of seconds you have every day? If it's someone you don't know well, you may decide to not go forward with learning more about the feedback. But if sharing your creative project happens in the workplace and your boss criticizes your work, for example, obviously you just can't ignore her. If you encounter such a situation and you disagree with the assessment, request time to discuss the comments so you can gain a better understanding of the person's rationale and to ask for suggestions for improvement. Such a meeting also gives you an opportunity to provide more clarity around your intentions and can even shift the person's perception of your work.

You don't always need to defend your work. When getting feedback, be aware if you are being needlessly defensive, especially if all that may be required are a few minimal adjustments. Yes, sometimes major changes are necessary and you'd rather remain firm, but those changes could make all the difference. Work through your resistance by keeping an open mind. You may ultimately find that the alterations you make result in a change for the better.

Give yourself time to process your emotions. All of the preceding suggestions are simpler to say than to actually implement. It's easy to say you're not going to take criticism personally; it's much harder to actually dismiss negative comments. Therefore, if you're truly upset or disappointed after feeling criticized, give yourself time to process your emotions. Otherwise, you're just brushing them aside.

Use a creativity booster to get out of a "feedback funk." Rather than replaying negative feedback in your head, instead take action to get your creative spark back. You can revisit some of the earlier chapters that talked about techniques to inspire your creativity. By engaging in one or more of them, you can reconnect with your original reason for creating, which will help move you into a more positive emotional state. And if you have a gratitude file, this is a great time to pour through it. A situation like hearing disappointing feedback provides another reason why it's good to have something to go back to that boosts your confidence and makes you feel better.

Creative Play: Feeling Your Feedback

In this exercise, you are going to prepare yourself to respond to both positive and negative feedback.

Tools Needed: Paper and a writing instrument

First, describe the feedback that would make your heart sing after someone experiences your work. Make a list of at least five words or phrases that would be most meaningful to you. Next, make a list of at least five remarks that would feel most damaging to you.

Now decide how you will *respond* ahead of time to each of these statements so you don't have to *react* when the time comes. This will prepare you for when you actually receive any kind of opinions—complimentary or critical. Sometimes the tendency is to deflect praise and to immediately defend yourself against disapproval. You can revisit these lists prior to any sharing you do, whether it's formal or informal, to better prepare yourself.

CREATIVITY KEY

Take note that the biggest critic often resides within you. Remember the inner critic that you read about in Chapter 6? This voice of doubt can start to speak loudly at the end stage of the creative process—not just in the beginning. This is especially true if you're new to creating and sharing. Your censor may speak up if you've reached out in the past and experienced rejection. That voice says, "Remember the last time you tried this? You don't want to feel disappointment again." If you've read this far, you have the tools to silence this faultfinder. Select one of the many techniques you've learned and start using it. Happiness awaits you!

How Sharing Your Creativity Touches Others

I don't want to underestimate the courage it takes to put yourself out there and I hope you feel better prepared now to respond to criticism should that happen. At the same time, I don't want you to leave this chapter thinking that sharing your creativity will frequently result in a negative experience. In fact, the opposite is usually true. Perhaps the best way to overcome your fears is to experience the joys that come when you share and receive uplifting feedback. Imagine how wonderful you will feel when you are approached by people who tell you that your creativity touched them in a significant way.

It's a heartwarming feeling to know you can make a positive difference in others' lives by sharing a part of you. That's what Melody, a visual artist, learned while doing her first art show. A woman visited her booth several times throughout the day. She kept coming back to look at an original painting titled "Seek," which was part of a series called "The Journey." About an hour before the show closed, she came back and bought the painting. As she was paying Melody, she began crying. She told her that she had lost her daughter earlier that year and had been seeking to find a way to move on without her. She was drawn to the painting because it reminded her of her daughter. She and Melody both cried and hugged.

Melody told me she remembers how vulnerable she felt that day. She feared her first show would be a bust and imagined how awful she would feel if she didn't sell anything. In Melody's own words, she said, "I have always strived to live a meaningful life but have struggled with knowing how to serve and make a difference for others in a way that serves me also. Never did I imagine that I would realize my own journey of finding a way to follow my pleasure while making a difference in the life of another." Since that initial show, the woman bought every original painting and several prints from "The Journey" series.

I've also experienced this impact firsthand. During a church service, I once sang a song titled "My Angel on Earth," which I wrote in the wake of my best friend's sudden death. Afterward, a woman came to me with tears in her eyes and told me how much the song comforted her because she had just lost her father. Cherish moments like that. Do not undervalue what you have to offer. You may never have aspirations of becoming a creative professional, but the good news is that you don't have to be a pro to connect soul to soul with another human being. You just have to be willing to share your creative essence!

As you can see from these stories, you never know how your contribution can make a difference in another's life. In his book "Show Your Work!" author Austin Kleon said that if you want people to know what you're all about and the things you love, you have to share. This will help you find your own "voice." To build up to that confidence in sharing, he recommends sharing something small once a day. If you do that right from the start of your creative project, you'll develop a healthy habit and feel better equipped to share a bigger creative endeavor once it's complete. You can also take the time to explore the different ways you might step outside of your safe sanctum. For example, sharing doesn't always have to happen in person; depending on the nature of your work, you can become an artistic contributor to online galleries. You might even consider doing a "show and tell" with elementary students. You'll probably hear all kinds of praise from the children—and you may serve as an inspiration at the same time. Whatever way you decide to do it, share with others and experience the joy of the give-and-take that is creativity.

The Least You Need to Know

- There's a certain amount of risk involved in showing your creative work to others. Remember, though, taking risks is an important part of creativity.
- Re-examine what you wish to receive from your creative expression. This will help direct you in how and with whom you wish to share your creative output.
- Develop a system of your own to evaluate your creative work to determine when and if it's "share-worthy." Feedback from others is helpful but you must feel good about it first.
- Constructive criticism from others can lead to improvements that may not have happened on your own. Keep an open mind, and after thoughtful consideration, do what feels best to you.
- You can literally change a person's life through your creative efforts. Be aware of this whenever you resist sharing due to fear of being rejected. Your creativity is a light in the world. Let it shine!

CHAPTER 1

Applying Creativity in Everyday Life

Many people who go on diets complain they don't work. They go from one type of weight loss plan to another; one of them may work for a while, but then they get off track. Your creative life can be the same way—unless you start to look at creativity as a lifestyle, not just activities, hobbies, or passions you choose to engage in when you feel like it. Creativity is a way of life, a way of being, all the time. It's an attitude, a habit, a perspective, and a choice.

While sometimes you may feel more creative on some days compared to others, if you incorporate even a fraction of the tips you've read in this book, you are already on your way to developing a creative lifestyle, one that you truly can maintain for life! In this chapter, you begin to consciously apply different strategies and techniques you've already learned and are given a few more tips to consider to make creativity a natural part of your daily life.

In This Chapter

- How your creative essence is who you really are
- Being on the lookout for synchronicity
- How handwriting helps your creativity
- Finding balance between creativity and other daily tasks

Keeping Creativity Alive and Well

If you look at creativity as an entity that falls outside of yourself, you are putting separation between "you" and "you." In other words, you can't detach a wave from the ocean any more than you can separate your creative essence from who you really are. While you may not choose to consciously exercise your creativity every day, that doesn't mean it's not there. It's an innate part of you that's available whenever you decide to make it a priority. This doesn't mean that deeming creativity as important will necessarily lead to a multi-million-dollar innovation, but it does mean your life will be more attractive and rewarding as you are nourishing your inner being's calling.

 INSPIRATIONAL INSIGHT

"There are no rules here—we're trying to accomplish something."

—Thomas Edison

If you embrace your creativity daily, you may find it not only impacts you, it also touches others. A great example of this is Matthew Hoffman's campaign to add a little sunshine to someone's day. It began with an idea in 2002, when, at age 23, he decided to print 100 stickers with the simple but powerful message "You Are Beautiful." He began handing them out to friends and soon afterward, the stickers began showing up everywhere—including China—bringing joy and smiles to the faces of those who encountered the message. He expanded the campaign with the creation of a website inviting people to request his ready-made stickers (You-Are-Beautiful.com), and people got them and started taking snapshots of where they placed their stickers and sending them to him. The campaign has since gone global, with more than one-and-a-half-million stickers posted in public places throughout all seven continents. It's an affirming message Hoffman believes everyone needs to hear every now and then. In a YouTube video, Hoffman said "It all comes down to intention. I'm interested in creating moments."

Just as Hoffman had no clue that his idea would be so embraced, you also should not underestimate the effect of your own creativity. However, your idea does not have to spread worldwide to have significance. Positively impacting just one person's life makes creating worthwhile, even if the only life that is affected is your own. Therein lies the real beauty of living a creative life. It's putting you in touch with a power greater than yourself. Some people call that power God, the divine, the universe, nature, or your inner being. Regardless of what name you give it, when you are engaged in your own form of creative expression, you are conveying the essence of who you are meant to be.

Fun with Synchronicity

Psychiatrist Carl Jung first coined the word *synchronicity* after a session he had with a patient who was not responding well to therapy. She told him she had dreamt that someone offered her a golden scarab, a rare and expensive piece of jewelry. Just when she was describing the dream, Jung noticed a large insect that was flying and hitting the window. He opened it, and in flew a scarabaeid beetle. The story goes that he caught the bug in his hand and said "Here is your scarab." It was enough to cause a breakthrough in her therapy.

According to Jung, synchronicity like what happened to his patient is "a meaningful coincidence of outer and inner events that are not themselves causally connected." The more significant the events, the more amazing they seem. The key is they are meaningful in some way. While a lot of people pass off these moments of synchronicity as "out of the blue," "happenstance," "dumb luck," or "serendipity," some describe these synchronicities as "mind-blowing" or "gifts from the universe," depending on the meaning they hold.

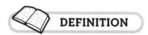 **DEFINITION**

Synchronicity is when two related events occur unexpectedly in a meaningful way.

The following are a few examples of situations that demonstrate synchronicity. Think about how you'd describe these if they happened to you:

- You're thinking about calling your mom. However, before you can pick up the phone, it starts ringing. When you answer it, it's your mom.

- You make a purchase at a fast-food restaurant and the cashier hands you 31 cents in change. As you're waiting for your order to be filled, the person behind you in line places an order and his total comes to $6.31. You then notice the 31 cents in your hand, which causes you to look at the person in line. It turns out he's a long-lost friend you had been trying to track down.

- You're driving home and the song "Who Let the Dogs Out" comes on the radio. When you arrive home, you notice your backyard gate is open and your dog is not in the backyard. Fortunately, he's not far off.

One of the most synchronistic events that has happened in my lifetime is the how book you're now reading came into my experience. I was traveling from Florida to Vermont when I stopped in Maryland to visit with my cousin. Over dinner, I told her I wanted to write a book on creativity. We started having fun brainstorming possible titles. A few days later when I arrived in Vermont, I met some friends and started telling them about my intention to write a book. Five days later, the publisher of this book contacted me to see if I would be interested in writing a book about creativity. I would say that chain of events falls into the "mind-blowing" category!

What about you? Can you think of any synchronistic events you've experienced? It's possible that a synchronicity will just pass you by if your head is stuck in the sand, oblivious of what's happening around you. However, if you engage in daily creativity, you will be operating with an open, aware, and receptive mind and therefore will be more likely to experience synchronicity.

You can have a lot of fun with the whole concept if you start paying attention and inviting such synchronistic experiences into your life. Whether or not you're someone who believes there's no such thing as a coincidence because everything that happens is meant to be, I recommend writing down or recording your "coincidences," even if they seem like small occurrences at the time. Sometimes events build on each other and what may seem insignificant at first glance becomes meaningful later as the pieces get fitted together. By recording these events and exercising your creativity daily, it's very likely you will notice an increase in these meaningful coincidences.

Boosting Your Creativity with Handwriting

Another opportunity to live creatively every day comes in the form of writing longhand. Do you remember learning how to print the alphabet letters by hand? Years ago, students typically were taught how to print in the first grade and began learning cursive writing in the second grade. Today, far less emphasis is being put on teaching kids how to write in cursive; instead, with technology at the forefront, more and more students are simply learning to type on a keyboard. Handwriting is becoming a lost art.

However, writing by hand offers benefits that typing on a keyboard does not. Studies have shown that typing on a keyboard, printing, and cursive writing are associated with different and separate brain patterns. When you write, you automatically stimulate a neural circuit in your brain that is prompted solely by writing, according to Stanislas Dehaene, a psychologist at the College de France in Paris. While you may be able to type faster than you can write by hand, you may be losing ground when processing new information. When you write by hand, you give yourself more of a chance to process what you've written, which can lead to additional insight and memory function.

 INSPIRATIONAL INSIGHT

"Poets don't draw. They unravel their handwriting and then tie it up again, but differently."

—Jean Cocteau

Other research points to additional benefits. An online article by Meredith Knight of the Genetic Literacy Project said "Writing by hand may open a conduit to human creativity." She noted that studies have shown a link between handwriting and three key areas: creativity, reading comprehension, and information retention.

You can find countless examples of creatives who have benefitted from handwriting. For example, self-help guru Wayne Dyer, PhD, has written more than 30 books by hand—no small feat. Novelist Ernest Hemingway, who won the Nobel Prize in Literature in 1954, usually wrote his first drafts with pencils and is quoted as saying "Wearing down seven number-two pencils is a good day's work." Director Quentin Tarantino doesn't use keys of any kind, instead opting to write his own screenplays using pens. Amy Tan, a Chinese American novelist, also writes her initial drafts longhand. She stated in an interview with *The Atlantic,* "Writing by hand helps me remain open to all those particular circumstances, all those little details that add up to the truth." The book you're reading also illustrates this point. I am writing it using a combination of longhand and typing on my Mac. Personally, I have found it helpful to initiate and flesh out ideas by writing them down first and then finalizing my thoughts when I type them.

As you can see, many people have established for themselves that the pen (or pencil) is mightier than the keyboard. This doesn't mean you should ditch your keyboard altogether, but as part of your daily creativity, you might try experimenting to see if writing by hand rather than typing makes any kind of difference for you, especially if writing is your forte. You may not notice anything right away, but be open to the possibility that you will be more creative as a result. After all, science backs up the notion that writing by hand can make you smarter and more creative!

Creative Play: The Lost Art of Handwriting

The purpose of this task is to mentally stimulate those areas of the brain that are accessed through handwriting. This creative play also should make someone else's day!

Tools Needed: Notebook paper, decorative paper or stationery, and your favorite writing instrument

For this exercise, you are going to write a good, old-fashioned letter. Rather than picking up any old pen or pencil, select one of your favorites. Do you prefer a ballpoint, fountain, or rolling ball gel pen? What about the color of ink—do you like black, blue, or maybe purple? For those who prefer pencil, do you favor the changeable lead type or a regular number-two pencil? Pick one that will feel good in your hand as you write.

Now decide who will be the lucky recipient of your letter—your spouse, partner, mother, father, son, daughter, best friend, or long-lost friend. This will be a positive, uplifting letter, so select someone with whom you have a loving relationship. (This is not about forgiveness work. That's reserved for a different book!)

Next, begin writing; the content is up to you. Cover at least both sides of the paper to give yourself a chance to experience this lost art of handwriting. You might even tell the person you are reading a book on creativity, which said writing by hand can enhance your creativity. It's also an opportunity to convey how much your recipient means to you. Once you finish your letter, either mail it or deliver it in person, if that's possible. Go ahead, make their day—and yours, too!

Now spend a minute or two thinking about how it felt to write a letter by longhand. Do you think you would have felt differently if you had typed this letter on a keyboard, be it your computer, smartphone, or tablet? Did writing by hand prompt you to be more deliberate and more thoughtful with your words? If you made a mistake, were you okay with scribbling through or crossing out the wrong words? Just notice how this exercise made you feel. The beauty with this tool is that it's readily available for you to use anytime, anyplace—no batteries or electricity required!

Creating a Balance

There's a whole world of possibilities that awaits your creative expression. However, you might be thinking "But wait! I have more ideas than I could possibly execute!" Combined with the other responsibilities in your life, that can feel like a heavy weight. Whether you're working for a living, taking care of children, caring for your aging parents, or volunteering for a charity, sometimes the tasks can feel so overwhelming, you may not always feel you can take the time to engage in one of your creative passions. Paradoxically, those responsibilities are the reason you should create. Creativity can help relieve some of the daily pressure you feel to complete tasks. It's all about achieving a balance and remembering that being creative doesn't always involve a monumental task.

To help find that balance, challenge yourself by taking one small step each day that represents your unique voice. Consider one way you can explore your creativity each day in some way without it feeling like yet "one more thing to do." For example, when I got my new iPhone, I started capturing at least one nature photo a day while taking my morning walk. At first, I was just testing it out to compare the quality to my old phone's camera. However, I soon decided to start sharing the images on Facebook with the hope of inspiring others to pursue a creative aspect of themselves.

INSPIRATIONAL INSIGHT

"Happiness is not a matter of intensity but of balance, order, rhythm and harmony."

—Thomas Merton

It doesn't take that much time for me to take a few pictures; I'm already carrying my mobile phone with me. I also don't always get around to posting them on Facebook, but I've decided in advance that's okay! Decide for yourself what's okay and what isn't, what's realistic and what's better left undone until another time. You can always switch things up, which will keep your experience fresh. Just make it something you look forward to doing.

If you're stuck on ideas, here's one that's fairly simple and at the same time will cause you to think and use your imagination: Do one nice, unexpected thing a day for at least one person either at home or in the workplace. For example, compliment a co-worker on her dress, make breakfast for your spouse (if that's not something you normally do), or put a love note in your child's lunch box. Don't tell anyone you are making this part of your everyday routine. It's kind of like being a "Secret Santa" without the ho-ho-ho and the fact that your gift isn't materialistic. The real present is your presence with another human being and taking the time to be supportive.

The key is that you must be sincere in whatever action you choose. See how creative you can be with this commitment and what kind of difference you feel within yourself as you try to capture a balance of work and play in your life.

Times When You Have to Force Creativity

Even when you maintain a creative awareness and try to keep a nice creative balance, there will be times when you're not feeling very inspired and you either feel you need to be, perhaps due to a work initiative, or you simply want to be because you now have everything you need to start your project. During these times, no matter how many times you repeat that old cliché "Think outside the box," all you can do is picture yourself inside the symbolic four walls and a cover. You're feeling boxed in, with not a creative thought coming to you. Can you force yourself to be creative? While the outcome may not be as desirable compared to creativity that arises more spontaneously or genuinely, it is possible to force creativity.

If you're in a situation where it's absolutely essential that you must force your creativity, such as a work project with a critical deadline, it may be helpful to shift your perspective to view the project in front of you as more of a discovery process. Even if it's something you've done many times before, what can you do to make it fresh and new? "But I can't think of anything; that's the problem," you tell yourself. That's when you must rely on one or more of the many techniques you read about in this book, such as developing a playful mind-set, lightening up with laughter, writing in your journal, thinking in metaphors and similes, involving the five senses, combining unlike ideas, mind mapping, and so on.

Another technique is to recall experiences in which you felt on top of your game, energetic, driven to produce, and stimulated—that "in the flow" feeling. Can you remember with any clarity what brought on those feelings? Is it possible to recapture them at a time when you're being pushed to create? Perhaps you wrote about your creative moments in your idea journal; you can either reflect upon ones that motivated you in the past or look for ideas you wrote about but never developed to spur you. And for those times you're really having trouble on a mission-critical project, you can even look into hiring a creativity coach (see Chapter 12).

But what if you're simply getting antsy all on your own, feeling restless and wanting to get beyond that boxed-in feeling? When the pressure isn't so demanding as to threaten your job or diminish how others view you, sometimes you can force creativity in a light and fun way. For example, I used this approach for the first song I ever wrote. My college roommate and I were both taking a guitar class as one of our electives. Toward the end of the semester, once we learned the basic chords and some picking patterns, we challenged ourselves to write a song, even though neither of us had ever attempted this before. We went into our individual rooms with our guitar, some paper, and a pen, and made a rule that we couldn't come out of the room until we wrote a complete song. I can't remember how long it took us, but the mission was accomplished, and we emerged from our rooms at about the same time with a complete song. This self-imposed directive started me down the path of songwriting.

 CREATIVITY KEY

Sometimes what can keep you from creating is overthinking. You imagine all of the possibilities, oftentimes focused on what might go wrong, which keeps you from beginning. However, when you finally take action and complete your creative project, you realize you spent more time thinking about it (otherwise known as procrastinating) than it took to go through the steps and finish. Stop thinking and start doing!

Sometimes you can use an activity you've never tried before as a springboard to tackle the creative project you really wish to take on. For example, if you're a watercolorist and you're feeling uninspired as you sit before the blank canvas, step away from it and try another creative interest in which there is nothing at stake. You might attempt cooking a dish using an untried recipe or sitting down to write a poem. Another option to force creativity is to pursue something you already know you're good at. It doesn't even have to be what you would consider a creative undertaking—just something that gives you a feeling of accomplishment, pumps up your self-esteem, and takes your mind away from the other task. Perhaps you enjoy gardening or working out. Choose your activity and when you return to your original creative project, see if your inspiration has returned.

Remember, the more you practice being creative, the less likely you will need to force it. With creativity as a part of your daily life, these moments will hopefully be few and far between.

Fighting Burnout

Feeling energized and alive usually only happens when you're balanced in all of the main areas of your life. However, when you repeatedly force yourself to be creative or participate in activities that previously inspired you but have since lost their glow, you can feel burned out.

A key to avoiding burnout is setting reasonable expectations for yourself. It's so important to give yourself the space you need—mentally, emotionally, physically, and spiritually—and to not place demands that bring any of these areas out of alignment. If just one of these gets out of whack, that's when signs of burnout surface.

Once you're feeling burned out, it's already too late to stop it—you've arrived. Fortunately, burn-out doesn't mean going to a place of no return. Using any or a combination of the following tips, you can work your way back to a healthy and creative state of being:

- Take whatever time you need to feel at peace again. Realize that in the beginning, you may only be able to capture fleeting moments of calm. Be patient with your progress.

- Reflect upon your original motivation. What prompted you to get involved with your creative venture in the first place? Do you still have the same interest or passion and just need a break or have you lost interest?

- Don't worry about taking on even more or using creative thinking techniques. However, do engage with some of your "loves," perhaps activities that you put on the backburner because you were so intensely involved with a creative activity. Examples are getting together with friends, reading a book, taking a walk, or anything that comes naturally to you and doesn't add to your stress.

Also, if you haven't already, take a look at Chapter 16, which presented information and tips regarding creativity burnout on the job. While it is geared to burnout in the workforce, the effects of work burnout are similar to exhaustion you may feel from a personal situation.

 CREATIVITY KEY

In coming up with ideas or solutions, you can consciously select a creative thinking technique or choose to walk away from a project to distance yourself and give it space. Both are valid. The paradox is that these opposing tools both work in creative situations. It's about achieving a balance between the two.

Creative Play: Achieving Alignment

In Chapter 11, you were asked to categorize how you spend your time. In this creative play, you are going to break those categories down into priorities and tasks to see if you're using your time effectively. You will take an honest look at how you utilize your time and how you can achieve a better balance. You also will bring to mind a creative activity you've thought about doing to see if you can make room for it.

Tools Needed: Sticky notes (2-inch or 3-inch square notes work well), one poster board, paper, and a writing instrument

Without giving too much thought, use your sticky notes to quickly write down all of the activities you do in a week on a regular basis. Write one task per sticky note and the approximate amount of time you spend doing it on an average day. Include everything that comes to mind, including the basics, such as preparing and eating meals, household chores (such as laundry), napping and sleeping, watching TV, computing, and so on. Put the completed sticky notes on a piece of paper for now.

Next, take your poster board and draw a line down the middle of the page. On the left-hand side, write the words "Must Do." On the right-hand side, write the word "Optional." Take your filled-out sticky notes and place them on the appropriate side of the board.

On your paper, write down your top five priorities in life. The following are some examples of what you might write:

- To be in a loving relationship

- To nurture and help my children grow

- To live a creative life

- To be financially secure

- To be spiritually connected

Now look at your poster board and see if the tasks you wrote on your sticky notes align with your priorities. Notice where there are gaps between your priorities and where you are actually putting your time. Also, evaluate whether anything on your "Must Do" side could be moved to the "Optional" side. Would making a shift or two bring you into greater alignment with your priorities?

Once you've made your decisions, stop for a few minutes, close your eyes, and take a few deep breaths. Visualize a creative activity you would like to do that's not on your list. Picture yourself doing it. Allow yourself to breathe in to the feelings you anticipate this interest could bring. Once you have a clear vision, open your eyes and return to your board. Is there a place for this interest on either list? Does it align with any of your priorities? If so, write in on a sticky note and add it to your board.

Make a commitment to either adjust your priorities or how you spend your time until they are in alignment. See if there are any optional tasks you can drop to make room for the new activity you pictured.

Developing a Daily Creative Practice

In establishing your daily creative practice, remember that it's not so much about the projects that you engage in—although they are an important part of the overall creative process—it's more about the attitude I spoke about at the start of this chapter. Tell yourself every day that you are a creator and that you open yourself to the opportunities that are presented to you and the ideas that you initiate and act upon. If you can maintain this awareness most of the time, you will find that ideas, as well as synchronicities, begin to flow more naturally to you.

The following are some tips to help you create your own practice:

The old adage, "Practice makes perfect," may not actually be true, but it doesn't matter when it comes to your creativity. I've already established that perfection is not what you're after with your creative expression. However, practice *is* important. Make a commitment to work on some aspect of your creativity every day, and eventually it will develop into a healthy creative habit.

Become keenly aware of your creative "high times" and "low times." Yes, time of day is part of what I mean. I'm also referring to other factors that I covered in previous chapters, including your ideal surroundings and where you find your inspiration. This may require some experimenting, but once you know what works best for you, build them into your creative routine.

Focus on what matters to you. How often do you get stuck in negative thoughts that go around and around? Instead of paying attention to what you want, your mind churns worrying about situations happening that you don't want. Catch yourself doing that and immediately shift your thoughts to what you really wish to create. You can use the affirmation technique you learned about in Chapter 7 or simply bring images to mind of your most meaningful desires. Take a multidisciplined approach to what you want to create and write it, speak it, think it, and sleep (on) it!

Be consistent with your creative efforts. Consistency leads to continuity, or flow. This may seem counter to a suggestion I made earlier in the book, which was to mix things up occasionally. That still holds true for times when you're feeling uninspired or your habits have become too routine. But being consistent means finding exercises or techniques that will help your creativity grow more each day. It could be writing in your journal or walking your dog to clear your head. Or perhaps you enjoy reading a poem to start your morning or listening to a favorite song that motivates you. It's better to do something small every day than to have a "creative explosion" once or twice a year.

These are just a few suggestions I hope you find helpful. Revisit previous chapters for additional ideas and talk with other creative people whom you admire to find out what works for them. You may be able to "steal" some of their methods or adapt them to better fit you.

The Least You Need to Know

- Living creatively every day means focusing on the true essence of who you really are and then engaging in your own form of creative expression.
- You cannot separate yourself from your creative expression. It's always there, just waiting for you to tap into it.
- You'll begin to notice that the more you are in tune with your own creativity, the more you'll experience synchronicity—those seemingly unrelated incidents that coincide at just the right moment to create meaning in your life.
- Make it a point to write by hand every day. You'll open up different neural pathways to your brain that can actually aid in creativity. Many famous creatives pen their works by hand before getting to the final draft.
- Use creativity as a fun way to balance out the more stressful parts of your daily life.

Reviewing and Re-Energizing Your Creative Practices

Now that you've tried some of the creative techniques in this book, it's time to think about what works for you and what more you'd like to do. Maintaining a creative practice is a continual process of reviewing and appreciating your progress, making adjustments along the way, and finding ways to keep you going when you feel you could use a creative lift.

In this chapter, I cover all three of those steps as you review the progress you've made since you picked up this book, which includes recognizing your achievements and revisiting your creative blocks. I then guide you to reflect upon how to close the gap between where you are and where you'd like to be. I end the chapter by giving you a few more opportunities you can draw upon when you need to be re-energized. This includes taking a look at meditating to help get and keep you in a creative space—even if you've never tried meditation before. Most of all, I want to continue to cheer you on. I believe in you, and hopefully now you also believe in yourself!

In This Chapter

- Appreciating your creative accomplishments
- Revisiting your creative blocks
- More ticklers to infuse your creative practice
- The effects of meditation on creativity

Reviewing Your Creative Progress

To effectively evaluate your creative progress, I suggest you take out your idea journal or any kind of notepad and jot down your thoughts to the following questions and considerations.

To start, recall where you were mentally and emotionally when you first started reading this book. What were your feelings at the time? Were you feeling uncertain, dubious, excited, or energized? Come up with the adjectives that best capture your feelings, and then reflect on your intentions. What was your primary interest in reading about how to unlock your creativity? Did you have a mild or burning curiosity about the subject? Were you feeling stuck, or was the idea of having a more creative life an interest that came about recently? What did you hope to accomplish?

 INSPIRATIONAL INSIGHT

"Don't wait until everything is just right. It will never be perfect. There will always be challenges, obstacles and less than perfect conditions. So what. Get started now. With each step you take, you will grow stronger and stronger, more and more skilled, more and more self-confident and more and more successful."

—Mark Victor Hansen

Next, think about what you have achieved along the way. It's important to recognize how far you've come. Look at all the positive aspects first. Do you now believe that everyone is creative, including you? Do you feel more inspired and vibrant and connected to your creative spirit? Have you been turned on by new ideas and pursued them? Have you had any epiphanies? Have you set up your ideal creative space, incorporated any new activities into your daily routine to spur your creativity, found a mentor, organized a new creativity group, started writing the book you always wanted to write, or undertaken any new creative projects? Record your thoughts pertaining to these questions along with anything positive you can identify since deciding to make creativity a commitment.

For the next part of your review, write down any blocks you may have encountered on your path to creativity. I hesitate to have you do this when you're in a positive space based on the previous considerations, but it is a natural part of the creative process. Obstacles will come into your space; it's a matter of how you deal with them. What were the biggest, most persistent blocks that materialized for you? Were you able to work through them—and if so, how did you overcome them—or are you continuing to address them?

Did you notice any patterns—the same barriers popping up with regularity? Perhaps you dealt with them and now they're back; or maybe they're all gone except for one. Wherever you are now, realize that just because you may deal with your blocks and successfully overcome them doesn't mean they won't rear their ugly heads again at some point. Take comfort in knowing that's a normal part of the process. Write down your thoughts along with any other negative pieces.

Closing the Creativity Gap

Looking at your creative achievements and blocks, notice where there are gaps between them and notate your observations. For example, maybe you accomplished your goal of buying a guitar because you always wanted to learn to how play one, but a procrastination block surfaced and kept you from finding a teacher and taking lessons. Or maybe you took steps to act on your idea for organizing a unique community event but haven't followed through due to a lack of confidence. Perhaps you have followed a lot of the suggestions in this book but your inner critic continues to tell you that you're still not that creative.

Once you've noted the gaps, look at your gap list and write down what you think it will take to get you to close that space. Be honest in your assessment. For instance, using the guitar example, are you not taking action because you're telling yourself you are short on money, aren't good enough, don't have the time, or something else? Once you're able to get to the core of your block, ask yourself "What can I do about it?" If you are really interested and committed to your creative idea, you will find a way. If you've lost interest in pursuing the idea, now is the time to realize that. Don't berate yourself in the process! This is where a total reality check with yourself comes into the picture.

Now bring yourself into the present moment. Where are you today with your overall creativity? How do you feel mentally, emotionally, spiritually, and physically? If you're not feeling well in any one of these areas, you'll find it's more challenging to be creative. Write about your attitude toward creativity, your habits, your frustrations, ideas you're considering, and your hopes and dreams. Are you connected enough with your creative spirit to hear what it is telling you? You'll know you're in alignment with it when you feel you have a zest for life, or as it was said in the previous chapter, you'll feel like you're "in the flow." The following creative play will give you an opportunity to reconnect with and solidify the relationship with your true creative essence.

CREATIVITY COMPASS

On the brainpickings.org website, Maria Popova describes John Steinbeck's *East of Eden* book as "a gorgeous meditation on the meaning of life and the essence of the creative spirit." In the novel's thirteenth chapter, it reads, in part: "Sometimes a kind of glory lights up the mind of a man. It happens to nearly everyone. You can feel it growing or preparing like a fuse burning toward dynamite. It is a feeling in the stomach, a delight of the nerves, of the forearms. The skin tastes the air, and every deep-drawn breath is sweet." This is the feeling you're after when it comes to creating.

Creative Play: Reconnecting with Your Creative Spirit

Read through all of the steps before starting this activity. This exercise is especially timely to do if you're feeling like your creative energies are scrambled. Even if you are feeling balanced and in alignment, it's still a worthwhile activity because it will help solidify your connection to your creative spirit, that inner part of you that supplies you with your creative life force. It's guidance that's always there if you take the time to access it.

Tools Needed: Paper, a writing instrument, and objects for your "oasis"

Begin with an open mind. Let go of any preconceived notions about your creativity and any attachment you have to previously held ideas. This is an exercise in listening carefully.

Next, create a type of temporary oasis, whether indoors or outdoors, that addresses the five senses. For instance, if you do it inside your home, you may put on a favorite piece of relaxing music for sound and plug in a fountain with gently running water. You can also consider burning a flavored candle or incense for smell before sitting down in a comfortable chair. To address the sense of sight, close your eyes and visualize whatever relaxing images come to mind or place an inspiring piece of artwork in front of you and gaze upon it. Engage your sense of touch by gently running your fingers down your cheeks and up your arms.

If you're outdoors in nature, either sit on the ground, set up a lawn chair, or bring a cushion. You can tap into the sense of hearing by listening to birds chirping or bring your MP3 player and wear your ear buds to listen to a peaceful song. Become aware of the subtle smells around you, such as freshly cut grass or the scent of fragrant flowers. Take your shoes off, wiggle your toes, and feel your feet upon the earth for a sense of touch, or simply feel the breeze caressing your face. To engage your sight, you might choose to do this as the sun is rising or setting to take in the view of the moon. Whether outdoors or inside, for the sense of taste, allow yourself to have a bite of chocolate or another treat. These are just ideas; use whatever will put you in a calming space.

Once you have all of your accoutrements set up, sit in your designated spot, close your eyes, and take at least five centering breaths, inhaling and exhaling slowly. Connect with your external surroundings, taking as much time as you need to enter into a pensive space. When you feel you have done that, silently ask yourself questions along these lines:

- What is mine to do?

- What shall I create, share, and offer to myself and to the world?

- What will expand my inner being so that I may feel creative, joyful, and alive, both inside and out?

Do this active mind meditation for as long as necessary. Then quickly, without judgment, write down everything that came to mind. You may be tempted to discard an answer you received by thinking, "I could never do that" or "That's stupid." Now is *not* the time to evaluate. You asked for guidance. See if anything new popped up or if you feel you were directed to revisit a creative commitment from your past. Listen to your inner being—your creative spirit. This is a great exercise to repeat whenever you're feeling scattered, confused, or frustrated with your creative direction.

More Resources to Re-Energize Your Creativity

Connecting with your creative spirit also can be accomplished by engaging in activities that will fill you up. Just as with your car, if you continue to drive it without refueling every now and then, sooner or later it will come to a halt. You don't want that to happen with your creativity any more than you do with your vehicle. Throughout the chapters, you've been given many tips, tools, and techniques to try out. You may have discovered additional methods and props on your own to support your creative efforts. Good for you!

I now offer you a few more to consider, particularly if after completing your recognition and review process, you feel like your creativity could use a boost. Take in these concepts and integrate those that are most valuable to you.

Eyeing Your Creativity

Did you know that the simple action of moving your eyes horizontally can potentially enhance your creativity, depending on which hand or hands are dominant? In a study conducted by Elizabeth Shobe, 62 men and women were asked to do a creativity test where they thought of alternative uses for some common items. She and her fellow researchers noted the participants' handedness—whether they were "strong-handers" (used one hand dominantly) or "mixed-handers" (meaning they used both hands equally)—since previous studies had indicated that strong-handers had less communication between the two sides of the brain than mixed-handers.

During the study, participants did one round of the creativity test and then were either asked to shift their eyes back and forth horizontally for 30 seconds or stare straight ahead. The purpose was to see if the eye exercise would increase the crosstalk between the two brain hemispheres and increase creativity as a result.

Upon repeating the test, the strong-handers who moved their eyes bilaterally showed a considerable increase in their originality both in more ideas and usage categories compared to the ones who stared straight ahead. While the mixed-handers achieved greater creative results than the strong-handers during the two rounds, the study also showed that doing the horizontal eye movement didn't make a difference for them. However, the strong-handers showed as much creativity as the ambidextrous group once they did the eye exercise.

While the researchers noted their findings didn't necessarily apply to those who are deemed "highly creative" and couldn't conclude that 30 seconds of this eye movement will turn you into an artist or a scientist, you never know what effect this simple exercise may have on you if you use one hand dominantly. It doesn't hurt to try experimenting with this back-and-forth eye movement to see if you notice any creative improvement or stimulation. You can even try it out using the same test. For example, take a common household item, such as a cotton ball, and write down as many uses as you can. You can then move your eyes back and forth for 30 seconds, repeat the same test, and see if you come up with even more ideas the second time around.

Zentangle—An Artsy Meditation

Another tool you can use to boost your creative energy is to add the Zentangle Method, created by Rick Roberts and Maria Thomas, into your creative practice. It involves drawing structured patterns that blossom into your unique expression. The black-and-white drawings are done on $3^1/_2$-inch-square pieces of paper, called *tiles,* and you make your symbols, shapes, and patterns using pens. The artwork is not intended to have an up or down side. In other words, you can view them from any direction because they're abstract. Each drawing also is meant to be completed in one sitting, which usually takes about 15 minutes. Just about anyone can take part in this practice. In fact, no prior drawing experience is necessary.

CREATIVITY KEY

The creators sell a kit that includes everything you need or you can use your own materials to make your own "Zentangle-inspired" images. You can learn more about this kit and more at zentangle.com.

While this activity may remind you of doodling, one of the key differences is that each stroke is done with a deliberate focus. Most people doodle when they're preoccupied with something else, such as listening to a lecture or sitting in a meeting, whereas with the Zentangle approach, it's intended to be an activity to which you give your full attention. It provides a way to shift your focus and perspective while letting go of any expectations of the outcome. It's akin to a type of meditation because the idea is that you become totally absorbed in what you're doing in the moment. Just as with intrinsically motivated creativity, you concentrate on the process, not the outcome.

An example of a Zentangle Method drawing.
(Inspired by the Zentangle Method of pattern drawing)

Upcycling

You've probably heard of recycling, where you take the primary elements of recyclable materials (such as newspapers, plastic, and glass) and produce a new product that isn't necessarily better quality or more aesthetically pleasing than the original. But what is upcycling? No, it's not bicycling uphill (smile). With upcycling, you're taking materials you would normally trash or recycle and making them into either something useful or eye-catching, which puts your creativity to the test in a fun way. Unlike recycling, upcycling is more about taking a shabby material and making it into something better.

For example, while you could take an old orange crate, flip it over, and use it as a stool, you could be even more creative and paint the crate and turn it into a planter or add other crates to it to make a coffee table. The idea is to give the items that many people see as trash a better purpose—not just a new purpose.

The process of upcycling isn't really anything new, except that it has a trendy name now. If you look through the annals of history, you'll see how financially challenged folks from previous generations made the best of the few resources they had. Some people upcycle today because they love the DIY (do-it-yourself) creative nature of this activity and want to help Mother Earth.

So before you throw that old briefcase away or recycle your beer bottles, stop for a minute and think of ways you may upcycle them. A quick scan of upcycling pictures on the internet shows an amazing display of ingenuity. Take a look yourself for a healthy dose of inspiration. Upcycled items can take on an art form of their own; it's only limited by your imagination. Let yourself go crazy with ideas!

> **INSPIRATIONAL INSIGHT**
>
> "When I say be creative, I don't mean that you should all go and become great painters and great poets. I simply mean let your life be a painting, let your life be a poem."
>
> —Osho

Watching Your Language

This is something you can do every day to help keep your creative efforts in check. Whether you're participating in a creative group process or creating alone, there are a lot of common phrases you use or hear others say when you or they think something isn't possible. The following are some common examples:

- "That'll never work."

- "We've tried that before."

- "Don't be ridiculous."

The preceding statements and any like them can put an instant halt to the creative process. So how do you avoid these verbal creativity obstacles?

To start, take a few minutes to think of the ones you hear most often or those you tell yourself. Once you've done that, get out your idea journal or a piece of paper and write down everything that came to your mind. Next, write down positive phrases to counteract the negative expressions. An example would be "You never know. Let's give it a chance." This is a quick exercise that may not seem like a big deal now, but by paying attention to your language, you will be more aware the next time you're participating in an idea session and someone blurts out something negative, or you're creating on your own and your inner critic decides to speak up. You can catch yourself or others in the moment, which may keep your creativity from croaking.

Particularly in a group setting, your words can make a difference when they are encouraging instead of negative, potentially leading to a home run of an idea instead of strikeout. Therefore, be willing to be the "cheerleader" of the group on occasion, especially when you notice your fellow members are slowing down or getting frustrated. Even saying something as simple as "C'mon guys, we can do this" can keep others motivated to continue generating ideas.

Creative Play: Fun with Poetry

Because you've been reading about a few additional ways to rekindle your creativity, here's yet one more way to awaken and call upon your creative expression. Whether you write poetry regularly or haven't written a poem since your high school English class, this activity is for you. You may be a poet and not know it. Have some fun!

Tools Needed: Paper and a writing instrument

There are no "musts or shoulds" and no rules for writing your poem, other than to challenge yourself in a fun way, which means not judging yourself.

You can pick any style of poetry—rhyming or freestyle. If you want to have a particular structure to your poem, you can search the internet to read about the different forms of poems (haiku, sonnet, list, and prayer poems, to name a few). I also highly recommend the book, *Unleash the Poem Within,* by Wendy Nyemaster. Your poem may be thoughtful or funny, short, or long. Remember—no rules.

Your topic is, what else, "creativity"! Open up your mind and heart, take a deep breath, reflect, and write! As you're doing this, notice if any negative "voices" try to get into your head. If so, you might incorporate them into your poem.

Meditating to Connect with Your Creativity

I hope you've had some fun in this chapter engaging with new and familiar activities. It's important to create just for the fun of it from time to time, even if you're a full-time creative professional. It's also essential to realize that if you're not feeling very creative or simply not in the mood that this temporary feeling is just that—it won't last forever, especially because if you've reached this point in the book, your knowledge and awareness of creativity has substantially expanded since you began reading it.

Not every deceleration you experience is due to a block, deep seated or otherwise. Sometimes your body is just telling you that it's time to take a rest. The ability to calm yourself and be still can be just as vital as taking action to stimulate your creativity. Once again, it's that fine balance. If you're always on the go, your energy can eventually get scattered, which can impede your creativity. This is one reason some people swear by a daily meditation practice.

Your first thought upon reading this might be "I'm not into meditating," "I don't know how to meditate," or "I have way too many thoughts on my mind to sit still." You may never release every thought or any thoughts during a meditation session, and that's okay and to be expected. It's quite common for thoughts to come in and out. So what's the point of meditating? Deepak Chopra, a meditation guru, says meditation is "tuning in … to find peace within … a way to get in the space between your thoughts … a space of infinite creativity, infinite imagination." So if a thought comes up, simply notice it. No judgment. No resistance.

There are both anecdotal stories and research that have revealed some positive links between the act of meditating and creativity. If you meditate regularly, you may find that your memory, concentration, and clarity improve. You'll likely approach your day in a calmer state if you start your day meditating. You may even stumble upon an unexpected insight during your meditation or later in the day. A study by cognitive psychologists revealed that divergent thinking was shown to increase when participants used an open monitoring technique, which involves being open to receiving whatever thoughts and feelings enter the mind and not focusing on anything particular. For individuals who used a focused attention meditation (concentrating on a specific item or thought), the study showed no measurable effect on convergent thinking and problem-solving.

CREATIVITY KEY

Approach the idea of meditating without expectation. In other words, do not enter meditation presuming it will make you more creative. Just be open minded as you enter into the quiet space and let the experience be as it is. You may notice benefits immediately, or they may occur to you over time.

There are numerous ways you can meditate. In the back of the book in Appendix C, which contains additional creative plays, you'll find the Meditation Minute exercise, which details a simple way to meditate. Additionally, I'll share a couple of ideas with you here, and if this practice intrigues you, I encourage you to further explore it.

One of the more common styles is a sitting practice in which you focus on your breath. The goal is to become present to each moment as it's happening while concentrating on your inhalations and exhalations. You observe if you're feeling tension in your body, gently dismiss thoughts as they arise, and notice your feelings and surroundings. Mindful walking meditations are another approach. Some are informal where you can stroll right in your neighborhood. Or you may prefer to meditate walking in nature or along a path. Don't get hung up on what you assume meditation is supposed to look like in terms of how you sit, stand, think, or breathe. You can't do it wrong.

Experiment with different styles to see what feels the most comfortable to you. You may want music playing in the background or select one of many guided meditations that are available for free on YouTube and other online resources. Or you may prefer silence. If you've never meditated before, start slowly, in a way that feels manageable to you. You might only start with two minutes a day a couple times a week and then build the time and frequency from there. If you can create a consistent schedule, you will begin to develop a routine and the process will become easier. As with all of the other suggestions, find out for yourself if you enjoy this practice and derive benefits from it, which may go well beyond creative results.

The Least You Need to Know

- Check in with yourself at regular intervals to determine if you're happy with the creative life you're living. Notice any blocks that still come up and also remember to note all of the positive strides you're making.
- Allow yourself to be guided by your creative spirit—that inner voice within that may speak gently or loudly, depending on how in tune you are with it.
- If you're in the 90 percent majority who are dominant-handed, you may benefit from an eye movement exercise in which you shift your eyes back and forth horizontally for 30 seconds. Research has shown that practice can enhance your creativity.
- Be conscious of your language. Both your self-talk and what you say to others can be elevating and encourage creativity or it can slow or stop the flow. Catch yourself being negative and immediately flip the thought to a positive statement.
- You don't have to be an artist to sketch a Zentangle-inspired drawing. Give yourself permission to partake in creativity-stimulating activities for the fun of it.
- Studies have shown that meditation can improve not only your overall physical and emotional health, but also your cognitive ability and creative thinking.

Creativity Is Not a Destination

As long as you are alive, you are creating. Perhaps not in the artistic sense of paints and brushes, but on a much grander scale. Every day you are presented with opportunities to create the canvas of your life with whatever colors you choose to feature. Whose life will you touch today? When you come from your heart space and truly understand that your creative expression is yours and yours alone, you realize the vast potential of what you bring into the world. That's creativity at its finest.

In this last chapter, you are given some inspiring thoughts to ponder, as well as some final tips on navigating your creative journey. It's time to celebrate your success!

In This Chapter

- The continuous nature of creativity
- Finding creativity in everyday life
- Staying true to yourself
- Taking the time to celebrate

The Journey of Creating

One of the common questions that children ask when going on a long road trip is "When are we going to get there?" You may ask yourself that same question when looking at certain goals or dreams you've been working toward. Sometimes it seems you'll never get there. With regard to creativity, I like to use one of my favorite personal sayings: "There is no there." There's only the journey that keeps going as long as you're alive. You may stop many times along the way to rest, and other times you may be so enthused and inspired that you're joyfully skipping down the creative path. Your jubilation may be fleeting or last indefinitely.

Creativity is about possibilities in every realm of your life. You can choose to lay the groundwork to advance your creativity, or you can let your ideas stagnate. Either way, your journey will continue. You can persist in dwelling on the painful experiences of your past, let them go completely, or capitalize on them by taking your creative energies to transform the past into a more vibrant future. There are thousands of examples of people who have overcome adversity by using their creativity, and in some cases, they have literally saved their lives with creative thinking. Hopefully, you'll never be in that position, but regardless, realize the power to create is always there for you in any situation.

Maintaining Creative Awareness

Maintaining creative awareness will strengthen your creative muscle during your journey of creativity. One way you can do that is by noticing the small things that represent creativity. For example, recently I received an email from Teavana Tea that read "Brew some creativity. Infuse your recipes with tea." In those two lines, the tea company was suggesting another use for their tea. When I clicked on the banner, it took me to a page of tea-filled recipes for pies, ice cream, cupcakes, and chutney. I took note of the creatively crafted email and what it represented.

Even checking product names can show you creativity in action. For example, what do Atomic Tangerine, Banana Mania, and Salmon have in common? At first glance, you might think they're all foods. In fact, these are the names of crayons produced by Crayola. How about Phish Food, Chunky Monkey, Chocolate Therapy, and Cherry Garcia? If you're a Ben & Jerry's fan, you already know they're the names of ice cream flavors. And then there's tricycle red, oriental iris, and rolling hill green, which are among the many paint selections offered by Benjamin Moore Paints.

Can you think of other examples in which you see creativity in action in small ways? Observing examples that come your way every day will help you continue to exercise your creativity. That will come more naturally when you're coming from a consciousness of creativity. It's easy to take creativity for granted if you're not paying attention, which may result in opportunities passing you by. But if you pay attention, you will learn about many opportunities to use your ingenuity to dress up what could otherwise be ordinary.

 INSPIRATIONAL INSIGHT

"You have brains in your head. You have feet in your shoes. You can steer yourself any direction you choose. You're on your own. And you know what you know. And YOU are the one who'll decide where to go …"

—Dr. Seuss

Realizing the Ebb and Flow of Creativity

When your overall life seems to be flowing effortlessly, it's likely your creativity will move along steadily as well. How do you know when you're "in flow"? That's when you experience those moments of being lost in time and space. You can literally forget where you are supposed to be next because you're so caught up in the moment of what you're doing. You lose track of time, you want to be exactly where you are doing precisely what you're doing, and you feel energized.

Noted psychologist Mihaly Csikszentmihalyi, whom I referenced in Chapter 5, described flow as "a particular state of heightened consciousness." He, too, found that time flies during flow; you're no longer self-conscious, and you feel you have a sense of control and proficiency. (In other words, you're not afraid of failure.) These same feelings also apply to group flow. That's when successful collaborations occur. It's no surprise that research shows that when groups are in the zone, there's a greater chance they'll find innovative solutions to problems.

Csikszentmihalyi also discovered the following elements contribute to achieving flow:

- **Skills that line up with the challenge at hand:** If the project is too difficult, you get frustrated; if it's too easy, you get bored.

- **Well-defined goals:** Being clear about your desires and focusing your attention on them will keep you moving—or flowing—in the right direction.

- **Getting immediate, regular, and clear feedback:** This keeps you from wondering if you're on the right track and allows you to make positive adjustments along the way.

- **The freedom to focus solely on the activity:** With such focus, you don't allow your thoughts to interfere with what you're doing, nor do you let other things distract you. You get lost in the activity itself.

Csikszentmihalyi also makes the point that you don't have to engage in a long-term, detailed commitment to experience flow. Simple activities, such as cooking, playing an instrument, or another favorite activity can also propel you into this feeling of flow. It's all about creating a stronger self. He also believes that if you're in a state of flow the majority of the time, you're able to see a difficult or threatening situation as a challenge—even an enjoyable one—as opposed to a stumbling block or major blow. Chances are, when you've experienced flow, you had a more positive outlook compared to when you felt out of sync. The saying "Go with the flow" came about for a reason. Think of a time when you felt in flow and were totally engrossed in a creative activity, and get out your idea journal to recapture what you remember from that experience.

 CREATIVITY KEY

Be happy! You will experience more creativity and flow when you're in a positive frame of mind.

Now contrast that with an occasion when you desired to be creative but felt stuck, uninspired, a lack of motivation, or bored—otherwise known as an ebb in your creativity. Were you disappointed when you thought it was 5:00, only to see the digital digits on your mobile phone reveal the time was only 2:59 P.M.? What about your energy level? Did you feel like quitting in the middle of it and taking a nap? Did you realize the source of what felt like a dead end? Was it a long-lasting or temporary feeling and what did you do to get past these feelings? Recall one of the times that you were struggling creatively and write down everything you can remember. Mainly, you want to capture the feeling and what you believe led to it. More than likely, you felt the opposite of how you were when your creativity was flowing.

In writing about both your inspired and challenging periods, you are developing more of an awareness of what each of these circumstances feels like. As you become more conscious, your creative muscles will become stronger and you will be able to produce more moments of creative flow and make sure the ebbs have less power over you.

However, realize your creative projects and feelings are not an "either-or" proposition. You could be rolling right along on a long-term creative project and little by little begin to lose steam. This doesn't mean you ditch the whole project; it just means you have to get re-energized by using one of the many techniques that have been discussed. And regardless of the nature of your undertaking, it's always a good idea to take mini breaks every hour. This can be as easy as stepping outside for some fresh air, taking a walk, or doing some stretching exercises right at your desk. Experiencing an ebb and flow is a natural part of creativity; embrace it.

Creative Play: Celebrating Your Mileposts

Taking time to recognize your achievements along the way, however small, will help keep you in flow. The act of creating and pursuing your passions is a reward in itself because of the joy, contentment, and peace it brings to your inner being. At the same time, you deserve an external reward as well, which is what this exercise will do for you.

Tools Needed: Paper and a writing instrument

First, decide what creative success means to you. If you're engaged in a long process, you might break the creative project into stages and see the completion of the different steps as an achievement. In other words, you don't have to wait until the end to feel a sense of accomplishment. If you're more likely to be involved in a short-term process, doing one creative task per day for a month may give you a triumphant feeling.

Next, consider different ways you can reward yourself. Think of some of the smaller things in life you enjoy. Perhaps a trip to the ice cream shop, a thrift store hunt, a massage, a bubble bath, an online song purchase, or lunch with a friend would make a nice gift to yourself. Now think of bigger treats, such as a weekend getaway, front-row seats to a concert, or purchasing an item from your wish list. Once you've done that, make a list of at least 20 small and big gifts you can give to yourself. Include activities that you wish you got to do more often. Your rewards don't have to cost money. If you're someone who seldom slows down, allowing yourself to lie on your sofa reading a favorite book for a few hours could be a reward.

Keep the list handy and when you've reached one of your mileposts, look at your list and pick whichever reward serves your fancy. Or if something occurs to you spontaneously that's not on your list, such as "I feel like checking out a yoga studio," go for it.

The list is a handy reminder to take good care of yourself. Refer to it whenever you feel you've earned it. You will already have done the creative thinking in terms of how to reward yourself.

Being True to Who You Are

An ongoing cause for celebration is knowing that you're being authentic with yourself and others. There will always be rules and regulations to follow, and many people—from your significant other and kids to your boss and family members—will likely place expectations upon you. Because of that, it's easy to lose sight of your genuine self as you aim to please them and stay within their boundaries. Be aware of how easily this can happen. There are authors and screen writers who have hesitated to write what they really wanted to because, even as adults, they're afraid their parents might disapprove. Yet to hold back what's really in your heart and on your mind is to curb your unique creative expression, meaning you can miss out on opportunities.

To be truly creative, you have to let go of what other people think. That's easier said than done, but anything less means you're relinquishing a principal part of yourself. A block can begin to form at that very moment and continue to build if your acquiescence persists. How can you embrace and share the person you're meant to be? By taking on some of the challenges that have been discussed in this book, which include the following:

- Continue to work through the blocks you've identified.

- Experiment with undeveloped ideas, even if they appear to be half-baked at first glance.

- Be willing to try new activities.

- Go outside of your comfort zone.

- Take reasonable risks.

- Allow yourself to be vulnerable.

As you continue to do this inner work, your confidence and self-esteem will increase and you can more readily dismiss what others think of you. Listen to yourself above all others!

Whether you feel you have a creative beast within you that's dying to break free or a creative mouse slowly edging through the mouse hole, you have to find your way out and be willing to take the necessary action to burst forth into your real creative essence. As you navigate your creative path and the "true you" begins to shine, you may surprise others who had maintained a certain view of you or had no idea of your capabilities. What a wonderful feeling it is to share a creative part of yourself and to hear someone exclaim "I had no idea you could do that! You're amazing!"

You honor yourself by being authentic. Yes, it takes courage and strength, but it drains you even more when you hide the real you. I liken it to a person who tells perpetual lies. He has to remember the last lie for the next one to make sense. After so many lies, it gets really difficult to recall the story. It requires so much less energy to just tell the truth. There's no tale to remember. Deep within yourself, you already know who you are; you just have to be willing to go beyond your fears and express yourself. You can still maintain your privacy, as you don't need to reveal every detail of your life. But when it comes to your creativity, go for the gusto. Unleash the real you!

CREATIVITY COMPASS

Jean was literally a "closet artist" during her teen years. She secretly had been doing all kinds of artwork that she then stored in her bedroom closet. She hid her art because she didn't want to compete with her oldest sister, who was always perceived as the artist in the family. It wasn't until the elder sister went off to college that Jean began sharing her artwork. So while she remained true to her creative self, that part of her didn't publicly surface for years. Being an artist was a very real part of Jean, and she continues today creating beautiful works of art. Unlike Jean, do not wait another minute to show the world who you are and what you have to offer!

You Now Own the Keys!

By reading this book and participating in the creative plays, you have obtained not one key, but many keys to unlocking your creativity. You may find it helpful to revisit certain chapters for the details on specific techniques you may wish to apply when the right opportunities present themselves. Just remember that while on your creative path, you have to crawl before you walk and walk before you run. Be willing to allow yourself to go slowly. Stay on all fours creatively until you feel you're ready to stand upright and take a few baby steps. Be okay with "falling down" on an endeavor a few times. You certainly wouldn't reprimand a baby who's learning to walk and then falls down; you would be gentle and encourage him to get back up and try again. Do the same with yourself. Don't be afraid to lower your standards if that makes you feel better and moves you forward.

I have thoroughly enjoyed taking this creative excursion with you. This chapter ends with a creative play that involves a fun proclamation in which you will put your artistic skills to use—and yes, you have them! But before doing that exercise, get out your journal or a piece of paper and a pen or pencil and complete the following sentences:

- "Creativity is important to me because …"

- "Before I picked up this book, I would not have even considered doing the following things …"

- "Now that I have done them, I feel …"

- "When it comes to my creative expression, I am willing to …"

- "My greatest takeaways from this book were …"

- "I am going to take what I learned and …"

- "Expressing myself creatively makes me feel …"

- "Therefore, I am going to …"

Once you complete these sentences, be sure you take time to celebrate! You now own the keys to unlocking your creativity!

Creative Play: Creativity Proclamation

In this activity, you are going to make a document that will serve as your very own creativity proclamation, which you can proudly hang in your ideal creative space.

Tools Needed: Writing instruments (the more colorful, the better!), paper of some kind (construction, colored, or so on), and decorations (such as stickers)

On your paper, handwrite the following words:

CITY OF (your city), (your state)

CREATIVITY PROCLAMATION

WHEREAS, (your name) has successfully completed reading *Idiot's Guides: Unlocking Your Creativity*; and

WHEREAS, (your name) is a creative being committed to practicing some aspect of his/her creativity every day; and

WHEREAS, (your name) will be sure to nurture him/herself along the way; and

WHEREAS, if creative adventures involve other people, (your name) will play well with others; and

WHEREAS, (your name) pledges to always get the necessary support, especially when he/she feels a block emerging, so that he/she may forever stay out of the creativity closet or, at the very least, remove the lock so he/she will never again be a prisoner to his/her own creativity; and

WHEREAS, (your name) will remain true to his/her creative calling.

NOW, THEREFORE, the City of (your city) does hereby proclaim the day of (select date) as

CREATIVITY CELEBRATION DAY

In (your city, your state), whereby (your name) will be recognized for his/her progress and achievements from the past year and will encourage all human beings to exercise their creative expression in the fullest way possible.

IN WITNESS WHEREOF, I have hereunto set my hand and caused the official seal of (your city, your state) to be affixed at the (your last name) residence.

Dated this day of (today's date)

By Captain Creativity

Now decorate your proclamation and hang it where you'll see it every day. (You may even consider framing it!) Finally, congratulate yourself!

The Least You Need to Know

- Creativity is a journey that continues as long as you're alive. It will wax and wane, but it's always there waiting for you to turn it on.
- Noticing the small, everyday examples of creativity and how it infiltrates different corners of your life will strengthen your imagination.
- Be sure you're authentic with your creative expression. This will bring you the greatest joy and will open you to more opportunities. Creativity is about expansion. Be the creator you were meant to be!
- Take the time to celebrate and reward yourself when you achieve noteworthy mileposts. Doing so will help you to stay in flow.

Glossary

active listening   A technique of listening carefully to what another person is saying and then restating what was heard back to the speaker. This gives the speaker a chance to confirm or correct the listener's feedback and creates a better understanding between the two people.

adrenaline   A hormone secreted by the body's adrenal glands, especially during stressful or stimulating circumstances, which can cause increases in bodily functions, such as heart rate and blood flow. You may experience this in the excitement of creating.

affirmation   A positive declaration that uplifts, encourages, and strengthens a particular feeling or viewpoint and can be helpful in bolstering your creativity.

ambiguity   This refers to the subject matter being unclear, having multiple meanings, and being hard to grasp. Learning to be at ease with such uncertainty is a key ingredient of creativity.

aptitude   Having a natural ability or inclination to do or learn something. It's not required to partake in a creative activity, but having an aptitude for it might make it seem to come more naturally and easily.

benchmarking   A technique used by people in business to track and evaluate other companies' most effective methods, systems, and procedures. This allows them to improve upon and incorporate these practices into their own organization.

convergent thinking   A type of thinking that is analytical, deductive, logical, and usually focused on one right answer.

creativity   Initiating, activating, and implementing ideas that are original, unusual, useful, or innovative. The ideas may advance an existing concept or seemingly spring forth from nowhere.

divergent thinking   A type of thinking that is novel, creative, and looks in different directions and at many possible solutions.

extrinsic motivation   A drive that comes from outside forces such as rewards, awards, promotions, money, and grades.

hot desking   A way of organizing the overall workspace so employees do not have a designated desk of their own. They are free to choose a different desk, table, sofa, or station each day.

intrinsic motivation   An internal drive to create due to your commitment or passion for the activity itself.

muse   A term that originated with Greek mythology in which goddesses represented the arts, music, poetry, and science. A muse is cited in creativity as an unseen guiding force or spring of inspiration.

paradigm   A set of beliefs that drive your thoughts and actions. Sometimes paradigm shifts are necessary if your belief structure is getting in the way of your creativity.

paradoxical   A way to describe highly productive creatives who display characteristics that are contradictory.

reflecting   A technique used in creative discipline with children in which the parent reflects to the child his expressed desires followed by providing guidelines that offer safe choices and redirection.

simile   A figure of speech that links one thing to another using the words *like* or *as* to make the comparison more memorable.

synchronicity   The concept of two related events occurring unexpectedly in a meaningful way.

talking stick   An effective visual tool used by Native American tribes and groups to control who is speaking. Only the person holding the stick may talk, while others listen and wait their turn to hold the stick and speak.

Resources

To support you on your creative journey, I encourage you to explore some of the books, materials, and website references that follow.

Books and Audio

Benzel, Rick, ed. *Inspiring Creativity: An Anthology of Powerful Insights and Practical Ideas to Guide You to Successful Creating.* Playa del Ray, CA: Creativity Coaching Association Press, 2005.

Cameron, Julia. *The Artist's Way: A Spiritual Path to Higher Creativity.* New York: Jeremy P. Tarcher/Putnam, 2002.

———. *The Vein of Gold: A Journey to Your Creative Heart.* New York: Jeremy P. Tarcher/Putnam, 1996.

Digh, Patti. *Creative Is a Verb.* Guilford, CT: skirt!/Globe Pequot Press, 2011.

Gelb, Michael J. *How to Think Like Leonardo da Vinci: Seven Steps to Genius Every Day.* New York: Bantam Dell/Random House, Inc., 2004.

Kleon, Austin. *Show Your Work: 10 Ways to Share Your Creativity and Get Discovered.* New York: Workman Publishing Company, 2014.

———. *Steal Like an Artist: 10 Things Nobody Told You About Being Creative.* New York: Workman Publishing Company, 2012.

Maisel, Eric, PhD. *Coaching the Artist Within: Advice for Writers, Actors, Visual Artists & Musicians from America's Foremost Creativity Coach.* Novato, CA: New World Library, 2010.

———. *Fearless Creating.* New York: Jeremy P. Tarcher/Putnam, 1995.

Maziarz, Mary Beth. *Kick-Ass Creativity.* Charlottesville, VA: Hampton Roads Publishing Company, Inc., 2010.

Michalko, Michael. *Thinkertoys*. New York: Ten Speed Press/Random House, 2006.

Myss, Caroline, and Sandra Joseph. *Your Creative Soul: Expressing Your Authentic Voice*. Sounds True, 2014. Audiobook.

Nyemaster, Wendy. *Unleash the Poem Within: How Reading and Writing Poetry Can Liberate Your Creative Spirit*. Naperville, IL: Sourcebooks, Inc., 2008.

Tharp, Twyla. *The Creative Habit: Learn It and Use It for Life*. New York: Simon & Schuster, 2009.

Toder, Francine, PhD. *The Vintage Years: Finding Your Inner Artist (Writer, Musician, Visual Artist) After Sixty*. Palo Alto, CA: Aziri Books, 2014.

von Oech, Roger. *A Whack on the Side of the Head: How You Can Be More Creative*. New York: Warner Books, Inc., 1990.

Zander, Rosamund Stone, and Benjamin Zander. *The Art of Possibility*. New York: Penguin Books, 2000.

Online

AFTA, Arts for the Aging, accessed November 29, 2014, aftaarts.org.

Amabile, Teresa, Constance N. Hadley, and Steven J. Kramer. "Creativity Under the Gun," *Harvard Business Review*, August 2002, hbr.org/2002/08/creativity-under-the-gun/ar/1.

"Association Problem Solving: An Open Thinking Process to Aid Your Creativity," Business Survival Toolkit, accessed August 6, 2014, business-survival-toolkit.co.uk/stage-three/creative-problem-solving/association-problem-solving.

Beecher, Henry Ward. "Doodling as a Creative Process," Enchanted Mind, accessed August 12, 2014, enchantedmind.com/html/creativity/techniques/art_of_doodling.html.

Begley, Sharon. "When Is a Brick Not a Brick?" accessed December 6, 2014, www. sharonlbegley.com/how-to-make-yourself-more-creative.

"Being Bored at Work Could Boost Creativity, Study Suggests," *Huffington Post,* accessed November 18, 2013, huffingtonpost.com/2013/01/14/bored-at-work-creativity-daydreaming_n_2450104.html.

Bellis, Mary. "Liquid Paper—Bette Nesmith Graham (1922-1980)," About.com Inventors, accessed July 10, 2014, inventors.about.com/od/lstartinventions/a/liquid_paper.htm.

Blank, Steve. "Using SCAMPER to Play with Your Business," Five Whys, May 30, 2012, fivewhys.wordpress.com/2012/05/30/using-scamper-to-play-with-your-business/#more-849.

Bratskeir, Kate. "Color Me Creative: Study Says Green Sparks Inventiveness," *Huffington Post,* accessed April 3, 2012, huffingtonpost.com/2012/04/03/green-colors-creative_n_1386190.html.

Breen, Bill. "The 6 Myths of Creativity," Fast Company, accessed December 1, 2004, www.fastcompany.com/51559/6-myths-creativity.

Brown, Sunni. "Doodlers, Unite!" TED, accessed September 2011, ted.com/speakers/sunni_brown.

———. "What We Learn from Doodles," CNN Opinion, accessed September 2, 2011, cnn.com/2011/09/01/opinion/brown-creativity-doodles/.

Buss, Dale. "Messy-Deskers Unite: New Study Hints That We're More Creative," *Forbes,* accessed September 19, 2013, forbes.com/sites/dalebuss/2013/09/19/messy-deskers-unite-new-study-hints-that-were-more-creative/.

Buzan, Tony. "How to Mind Map," ThinkBuzan, accessed August 11, 2014, thinkbuzan.com/how-to-mind-map/.

Chopra Center Meditation, "What Is Meditation?" accessed October 8, 2014, chopra.com/ccl-meditation/21dmc/meditation-tips.html.

Clear, James. "How Long Does It Actually Take to Form a New Habit? (Backed by Science)," James Clear, accessed September 19, 2014, jamesclear.com/new-habit.

Cohen, Gene D., MD, PhD, primary investigator. "The Creative and Aging Study," National Endowment for the Arts, accessed April 30, 2006, arts.gov/sites/default/files/CnA-Rep4-30-06.pdf.

Couch, Robbie. "Stylist Who Spends Every Sunday Cutting Hair for Homeless: 'Every Human Life Is Worth the Same,'" *Huffington Post,* accessed August 17, 2014, huffingtonpost.com/2014/08/17/mark-bustos-homeless-haircuts_n_5678454.html.

"Creativity—the Key to Proactive Aging," Creativity Toolbox for Seniors, accessed November 29, 2014, creativitytoolbox.org.

Csikszentmihalyi, Mihaly. "The Creative Personality," *Psychology Today,* accessed June 13, 2011, psychologytoday.com/articles/199607/the-creative-personality.

Currey, Mason. "Daily Rituals," The Daily Routines of Famous Creative People, accessed July 25, 2014, podio.com/site/creative-routines.

Curtis, Rhoda P. "Why the Elderly Are *More* Creative," *Huffington Post,* accessed January 21, 2012, huffingtonpost.com/rhoda-p-curtis/creativity-and-aging_b_1002737.html.

Desta, Johana. "10 Famous Writers Who Don't Use Modern Tech to Create," Mashable, accessed February 15, 2014, mashable.com/2014/02/15/modern-writers-technology/.

Ditkoff, Mitch, and Tim Moore of Idea Champions. White paper on "*Where* and *When* Do People Get Their Best Ideas?" Idea Champions Informal Online Poll, accessed June 18, 2008, ideachampions.com/downloads/Best-Ideas-Poll.pdf.

Donnelly, Tim. "9 Brilliant Inventions Made by Mistake," Inc.com, accessed August 15, 2012, inc.com/tim-donnelly/brilliant-failures/9-inventions-made-by-mistake.html.

Eby, Douglas. "The Urge to Create: Jane Piirto on Motivation," PsychCentral/The Creative Mind, accessed July 14, 2014, blogs.psychcentral.com/creative-mind/2011/05/the-urge-to-create-jane-piirto-on-motivation/.

Fenn, David. "A Management Lesson from Walt Disney," Quality Digest/Inside Quality Insider, accessed June 4, 2014, qualitydigest.com/inside/quality-insider-column/management-lesson-walt-disney.html.

Fields, Jonathan. "Clutter Can Kill Creativity and Innovation," Unclutterer, accessed September 26, 2011, unclutterer.com/2011/09/26/clutter-can-kill-creativity-and-innovation/.

Franks, Hunter. "Artist Uses Creativity to Build Community Connections," Knight Blog, accessed February 25, 2014, knightfoundation.org/blogs/knightblog/2014/2/25/artist-uses-creativity-build-community-connections/.

"Frito Lay's Creative Approach to Cost Improvement," Basadur Applied Creativity, accessed September 3, 2014, web.basadur.com/publications/case-studies/frito-lays-creative-approach-to-cost-improvement.

Gargiulo, Susanne. "Daydream Believer: Is a Wandering Mind a Creative Mind?" CNN Thinking Business, accessed October 30, 2013, edition.cnn.com/2013/10/30/business/daydream-believer-is-a-wandering/.

Generations United, accessed November 29, 2014, gu.org.

Giles, Jeff. "Paul McCartney Still Gets Songwriting Advice from John Lennon," Ultimate Classic Rock, accessed October 25, 2013, ultimateclassicrock.com/paul-mccartney-john-lennon-songwriting/.

Gilliard, Martin. "Colors That Inspire Creativity," Innovation-creativity.com, accessed August 4, 2014, innovation-creativity.com/colors-that-inspire-creativity.html.

Glassman, Edward, PhD. "Creativity as a Learnable Skill," Creativity Portal, accessed June 9, 2010, creativity-portal.com/articles/edward-glassman/creativity-learnable-skill.html.

———. "Ways to Shift Paradigms & Think Outside the Box," Creativity Portal, accessed December 14, 2011, creativity-portal.com/articles/edward-glassman/shift-paradigms-outside-box.html.

Grant, Katie, ed. "Having a Messy Desk Makes You 'More Creative,'" The Telegraph, accessed August 6, 2013, telegraph.co.uk/news/newstopics/howaboutthat/10225664/having-a-messy-desk-makes-you-more-creative.html.

"The Greatest Comeback Story of All Time: How Apple Went from Near Bankruptcy to Billions in 13 Years," Business Insider, accessed September 13, 2014, businessinsider.com/apple-comeback-story-2010-10#1997-partnering-with-the-enemy-microsoft-1.

"Hallmark History & Timeline," Hallmark Corporate Information, accessed November 15, 2014, corporate.hallmark.com/Company/Early-Innovation-1910s-30s.

Heid, Markham. "Boost Your Creativity in 2 Seconds," Prevention, accessed March 2012, prevention.com/mind-body/emotional-health/looking-color-green-enhances-creativity.

Hofman, Scott Barry. "The Creativity Crisis: The Decrease in Creative Thinking Scores on the Torrance Tests of Creative Thinking," Taylor & Francis Online, accessed November 9, 2011, tandfonline.com/doi/full/10.1080/10400419.2011.627805#tabModule.

"How Oprah Winfrey Changed America," Discovery Newsletter, accessed May 25, 2011, news.discovery.com/human/oprah-winfrey-changed-america-110525.html.

"IBM 2010 Global CEO Study: Creativity Selected as Most Crucial Factor for Future Success," IBM, accessed May 18, 2010, www-03.ibm.com/press/us/en/pressrelease/31670.wss.

Interview between Joseph Campbell and Bill Moyers, accessed August 17, 2014, Joseph Campbell Foundation, jcf.org/new/index.php?categoryid=31.

Jarrett, Christian. "Performing Horizontal Eye Movement Exercises Can Boost Your Creativity," Research Digest, accessed November 8, 2009, digest.bps.org.uk/2009/11/performing-horizontal-eye-movement.html.

Kaufman, Scott Barry. "The Real Neuroscience of Creativity," Scientific American/Beautiful Minds, accessed August 19, 2013, blogs.scientificamerican.com/beautiful-minds/2013/08/19/the-real-neuroscience-of-creativity/.

Kim, Kyung Hee, PhD. "Yes, There IS a Creativity Crisis!" The Creativity Post, accessed July 10, 2012, creativitypost.com/education/yes_there_is_a_creativity_crisis.

Kleon, Austin. "10 Ways to Share Your Creativity and Get Discovered," Austin Kleon, accessed February 19, 2014, austinkleon.com/2014/02/19/10-ways-to-share-your-creativity/.

Knight Foundation. "New Creative Placemaking Project Led by Hunter Franks to Inspire Civic Participation with More Than $55,000 From Knight Foundation," Knight Foundation, accessed February 25, 2014, knightfoundation.org/press-room/press-release/new-creative-placemaking-project-led-hunter-franks/.

Knight, Meredith. "Writing by Hand May Open a Conduit to Human Creativity. Have We Evolved to Write?" Genetic Literacy Project, accessed June 12, 2014, geneticliteracyproject.org/2014/06/12/writing-by-hand-may-open-a-conduit-to-human-creativity-have-we-evolved-to-write/.

Konnivkova, Maria. "What's Lost as Handwriting Fades," *New York Times,* accessed June 2, 2014, nytimes.com/2014/06/03/science/whats-lost-as-handwriting-fades.html?_r=0.

Kuszewski, Andrea. "The Educational Value of Creative Disobedience," *Scientific American,* accessed July 7, 2011, blogs.scientificamerican.com/guest-blog/2011/07/07/the-educational-value-of-creative-disobedience/.

Levy, Paul. "Catching the Bug of Synchronicity," *Awaken in the Dream,* accessed October 4, 2014, awakeninthedream.com/wordpress/catching-the-bug-of-synchronicity/.

Lilyquist, Mindy. "How to Be Creative? Change Your Morning Routine: 5 Tips on How You Can Boost Your Creativity," *About Money,* accessed September 9, 2014, homebusiness.about.com/od/worklifebalanceathome/a/How-To-Be-Creative-Change-Your-Morning-Routine.htm.

Ma, Moses. "The Power of Humor in Ideation and Creativity," *Psychology Today,* accessed June 16, 2014, psychologytoday.com/blog/the-tao-innovation/201406/the-power-humor-in-ideation-and-creativity.

May, Matthew E. "The Neuroscience of Creativity: Why Daydreaming Matters," American Express, accessed March 22, 2012, americanexpress.com/us/small-business/openforum/articles/the-neuroscience-of-creativity-why-daydreaming-matters/.

McNerney, Sam. "What Motivates Creativity?" Big Think, accessed May 31, 2012, bigthink.com/insights-of-genius/what-motivates-creativity.

Menge, Fred. "Business Viewpoint: Avoid These Five Email Mistakes," *Tulsa World,* accessed June 26, 2014, tulsaworld.com/viewpoint-fred-menge-avoid-these-five-email-mistakes/article_f4fe4ae6-d2c4-5a13-9cc3-44ef0a25ea04.html.

"Mihaly Csikszentmihalyi," Pursuit of Happiness, accessed December 6, 2014, pursuit-of-happiness.org/history-of-happiness/mihaly-csikszentmihalyi/.

The National Guild for Community Arts Education, accessed November 29, 2014, nationalguild.org.

Poh, Michael. "6 Ways to Unleash Creativity in the Workplace," Hongkiat.com, accessed September 2, 2014, hongkiat.com/blog/unleash-creativity-workplace/.

Popova, Marina. "John Steinbeck on the Creative Spirit and the Meaning of Life," Brain Pickings, accessed February 27, 2014, brainpickings.org/2014/02/27/steinbeck-east-of-eden-meaning-of-life/.

Radicati, Sara, PhD, ed. "Email Statistics Report, 2011-2015," The Radicati Group, Inc., accessed October 15, 2014, radicati.com/wp/wp-content/uploads/2011/05/Email-Statistics-Report-2011-2015-Executive-Summary.pdf.

Riggott, Julie. "Americans Consume Media in a Major Way, Study Finds," USC News, accessed October 30, 2013, news.usc.edu/56894/americans-consume-media-in-a-major-way-study-finds/.

"Rolestorming: Improving Group Brainstorming," Mind Tools, accessed September 6, 2014, mindtools.com/pages/article/rolestorming.htm.

Root-Bernstein, Robert, and Michele Root-Bernstein. "Einstein on Creative Thinking: Music and the Intuitive Art of Scientific Imagination," *Psychology Today*/Imagine That!, accessed March 31, 2010, psychologytoday.com/blog/imagine/201003/einstein-creative-thinking-music-and-the-intuitive-art-scientific-imagination.

Sawyer, R. Keith. "Group Flow: How Teamwork Can Foster Creativity," Daily Good, accessed February 1, 2012, dailygood.org/story/171/group-flow-how-teamwork-can-foster-creativity-r-keith-sawyer/.

Silverman, Rachel Emma, and Robin Sidel. "Warming Up to the Officeless Office," *The Wall Street Journal*, accessed April 17, 2012, online.wsj.com/news/articles/SB10001424052702304818404577349783161465976.

Smolensky, Michael, and Lynn Lamberg. "Are You a Lark, an Owl, or a Hummingbird?" excerpts from Chapter 5 of *The Body Clock Guide to Better Health*, accessed November 30, 2014, nasw.org/users/llamberg/larkowl.htm.

Spiegel, Alix. "Bored? Try Doodling to Keep the Brain on Task," NPR, accessed March 12, 2009, npr.org/templates/story/story.php?storyId=101727048.

Sternberg, Robert J. "Business Viewpoint: Creativity No Longer Optional in Business," *Tulsa World*, accessed May 19, 2011, tulsaworld.com/business/business-viewpoint-creativity-no-longer-optional-in-business/article_5457b042-ebf6-5525-b677-864a78fcdb87.html?mode=story.

Stillman, Jessica. "Go Ahead, Daydream," *Inc.*, accessed June 12, 2012, inc.com/jessica-stillman/go-ahead-daydream-for-creativity.html.

"Study Reveals Global Creativity Gap," Adobe, accessed April 23, 2012, adobe.com/aboutadobe/pressroom/pressreleases/201204/042312AdobeGlobalCreativityStudy.html.

"Susan Boyle Biography," *Biography*, accessed November 17, 2014, biography.com/people/susan-boyle-454696.

Trautmann, Maria, with references from Joseph V. Anderson, "Weirder Than Fiction: The Reality and Myths of Creativity," Celestra, accessed November 16, 2010, celestra.ca/top-10-creativity-definitions/.

Universiteit Leiden. "Meditation Makes You More Creative," ScienceDaily, accessed April 19, 2012, sciencedaily.com/releases/2012/04/120419102317.htm.

University of British Columbia. "Effect of Colors: Blue Boosts Creativity, While Red Enhances Attention to Detail," ScienceDaily, accessed February 6, 2009, sciencedaily.com/releases/2009/02/090205142143.htm.

Wetlaufer, Suzy. "Common Sense and Conflict," *Harvard Business Review,* accessed January 2000, hbr.org/2000/01/common-sense-and-conflict/ib.

"What Is Creativity?" Creativity at Work, accessed February 17, 2014, creativityatwork.com/2014/02/17/what-is-creativity/.

"What Is Upcycling, Anyway?" Hipcycle, accessed October 3, 2014, hipcycle.com/what-is-upcycling.

Widrich, Leo. "The Science of How Temperature and Lighting Impact Our Productivity," buffersocial, accessed February 14, 2013, blog.bufferapp.com/the-science-of-how-room-temperature-and-lighting-affects-our-productivity.

Winfrey, Oprah. "What Oprah Knows for Sure About Creativity," *The Oprah Magazine,* accessed February 2011 oprah.com/spirit/What-Oprah-Knows-for-Sure-About-Creativity.

Wong, May. "Stanford Study Finds Walking Improves Creativity," *Stanford News,* accessed April 24, 2014, news.stanford.edu/news/2014/april/walking-vs-sitting-042414.html.

Woollaston, Victoria, and Fiona Macrae. "Messy People Rejoice! Working in a Cluttered Environment Makes You More Creative (But a Clean Desk Means You Are More Generous)," accessed August 6, 2013, dailymail.co.uk/sciencetech/article-2385384/University-Minnesota-study-finds-working-cluttered-environment-makes-creative.html.

You Are Beautiful, accessed October 3, 2014, you-are-beautiful.com.

Zentangle, accessed October 6, 2014, zentangle.com.

Zimmerman, Eileen. "Career Couch: Hobbies Are Rich in Psychic Rewards," *New York Times,* accessed December 2, 2007, nytimes.com/2007/12/02/jobs/02career.html.

More Creative Play

Here are some "bonus" creative plays to help keep your creativity flowing. They address some of the points that were discussed in the book and are designed to increase your awareness of what motivates you and brings you joy, to rid yourself of persistent blocks, to enhance your sense of appreciation and confidence, to tune into your kid-self, to de-stress, and much more. Some of the tasks are more basic, while others are more sophisticated. Choose whichever tasks appeal to your creative spirit!

Meditation Minute

The purpose of this exercise is to allow yourself to feel free of having to do anything. While following these steps, you are going to meditate for one minute every day for 30 days.

Tools Needed: A chair and a timer

1. Sit in a comfortable chair. Or you can sit outside in nature, weather permitting. Set a timer for one minute, and then close your eyes and place your hands, palms up, in your lap.

2. Take a deep breath in, and then slowly exhale.

3. Empty your mind as much as possible. When a thought enters your mind, replace it with the silent mantra "I am breathing in" as you inhale and "I am breathing out" as you exhale—nothing more.

4. After the timer goes off, observe how you feel. Do you feel differently than you did before you began the meditation? Less stressed? More creative? Like you want more of this feeling?

You may decide to do this meditation for longer than a minute or for more than 30 days. If it feels good, do it!

Awakening and Observing

This activity will enable you to tune into thoughts you might otherwise ignore that may be helpful in providing you with additional creative insight.

Tools Needed: Paper and a writing instrument or an audio recorder

As soon as you wake up each morning, write down or audio record the first thoughts that come to mind before you can be interrupted. Do not judge your thoughts, analyze them, or ponder their meaning; that will come later. Just write them down or dictate them—as silly, logical, or nonsensical as they may seem—as quickly as you think of them. Do this for seven days in a row.

After one week, see if you notice any patterns. Are they positive or negative? Are there any common themes? Can you create meaning from them and apply them to your life in a creative way? See if this practice provides insight into the direction of your day. If so, consider doing it on a regular basis.

Your Wish Is My Command

In this exercise, you are going to create a magic wand and become your own wizard to grant your wishes. You can really have fun with this one! Allow yourself to become childlike and let go of any worrisome thoughts you may have been having.

Tools Needed: Some kind of a stick (see suggestions in the text) and decorating materials

First, decide on the material to make your magic wand. You could start with a stick from the woods, a wooden spoon from your kitchen drawer, a straw, a chopstick, or the inside cardboard from a paper towel roll. Be creative! Come up with your own idea. Try to use materials you already have in or around the house. This activity does not have to cost money.

Decorate your magic wand with stickers, feathers, glitter, or whatever else comes to mind. Continue dressing it up until you feel the wand is complete. Enjoy yourself in the process!

Then, every time you think of a creative idea or activity, reinforce the thought by picking up your magic wand, becoming the wizard, and saying out loud "Your wish is my command!" Sound corny? Good. Don't ever let silliness get in the way of your creativity. In fact, sometimes childlike activity can help you overcome whatever barriers are hampering you. Be open and watch your creative expression flow!

Curiosity Doesn't Have to Kill Anyone

… not even the cat! What are you most curious about and what have you done about it? This experience is intended to inspire you by having you tune into your curiosity.

Tools Needed: There are no particular tools needed for this activity. You will determine that based on the decision you make. (Read on for details.)

Pick a free day in your schedule and declare it "Curiosity Day." Put it on your calendar now. Next, complete this sentence:

"I have always been curious about _____."

When "Curiosity Day" arrives, go out and explore the topic you came up with in the preceding sentence. For example, if you're curious why birds chirp, go visit your local Audubon society and talk with some of the volunteers or experts on hand. You could also go out into nature and listen to their different sounds. Learn what you can the "old-fashioned" way first before looking for more information on the internet.

Be open to where your exploration takes you. Make this experience as "hands-on" as possible and see if it sparks any creative ideas. Maybe you'll be motivated to write a short story or a magazine article about it or paint a picture. And who knows? Maybe it could lead to a career change!

Daring to Dress Differently

This activity will help you develop more courage and risk-taking abilities.

Tools Needed: Clothes you don't normally wear

What type of clothes are you most comfortable wearing? Are you known for dressing conservatively, wildly, or something in between? Do you wear bright, pastel, or muted colors? Low cuts or turtlenecks? Ladies, do you mostly wear high heels or flats? Men, what kind of shoes do you typically wear? However you normally dress, pick one day and clothe yourself totally opposite of that. You may borrow the clothes from a friend or really commit yourself and buy a new, different outfit. It doesn't have to cost a lot of money; you can check out your local thrift stores and consignment shops.

Now, put on your brave face and go out into public, even if it's just to the grocery store. If you're really feeling courageous and it won't get you fired, go to work dressed differently. Notice how it makes you feel. Comfortable or uneasy? Self-conscious or more empowered? If you feel comfortable and empowered, who knows? Maybe you'll enjoy the feeling and begin to change your wardrobe and style of dress! Change can be scary … and fun, too, if you'll allow it!

A Peek at Your Peaks

In this exercise, you will look more closely at your creative peak periods to increase your awareness and inspire you toward greater creativity.

Tools Needed: A pad or piece of paper, a writing instrument, markers or paints, newspapers and/or magazines, a large piece of cardboard or foam core, glue, and decorating materials

First, recall a time in your life when you felt like you were experiencing a creative "peak" or "high." Make a list of words and phrases that describe your feelings when you were in that space—for example, in the moment, no sense of time, happy, in the flow. Take this list and see if you can find similar phrases in newspapers and magazines. When you do, cut them out.

Now, take your cardboard or foam core and at the top of it, write the following statement:

"When I am in the flow of creativity, I feel …"

Take the words and phrases you cut out and glue them onto the cardboard. You can use your markers or paints to add any of the descriptive words you wrote on your pieces of paper that you could not find in newspapers or magazines. You can also decorate your collage with stickers or any other materials you wish to add.

Finally, hang your piece of artwork where you'll see it every day. This may serve to inspire you to act upon your creative interests.

A Speedy Space Shifter

This is a great exercise to undertake when you catch yourself feeling negative and want to shift into a more positive space. You can do this in the middle of your work day or anytime you need to give yourself a break with a "time-out."

Tools Needed: Paper and a writing instrument

Start by thinking of activities you can do quickly. This may involve physical exercise, such as doing jumping jacks; a mental activity, such as completing the Meditation Minute creative play at the beginning of this appendix; or indulging in your favorite snack. For example, one thing that works for me is a mini-music break. I have multiple guitars and other instruments in the room next to my office. Sometimes I will grab one of them and play a song. When I return to my work, I feel lighter with a renewed sense of energy. This works if I'm feeling down, if I simply need a momentary diversion, or if I could use quick break. Your ideas should focus on actions you can take that don't require materials—unless they're handy—or you can do without much preparation. Now write down all of your ideas and keep this list nearby.

As discussed throughout this book, awareness is key. How will you know if you need to shift your space? Here are some clues. You may notice that your neck and shoulders are feeling tight or your lower back is aching from sitting too long. Perhaps you've had some fleeting negative thoughts, repeating thoughts that are not serving you, or some unsettling news that keeps going around in your head. Maybe you just need time to refresh yourself.

Whenever you wish to shift into a better space or just need a time-out, take out your list and pick one of your activities. Keep your list accessible so when you think of other activities, you can add them. If you do this exercise on a regular basis, the ideas on your list will start to come automatically to your mind and you'll no longer need your list as a reference.

Rock 'n' Release

Because creating is a journey, there will be twists and turns that may lead you temporarily back into the creativity closet. Turn to this activity when that happens.

Tools Needed: Paper, a writing instrument, rocks, and a marker

To begin, tune into the block that has reared its ugly head. It may be a barrier you've overcome in the past or a new snarl you're experiencing. Take note if you feel there's more than one. Write down your block or blocks as a single word or a phrase.

Next, find one rock for every barrier you wrote down, being sure to gather larger rocks for any phrases. Depending on where you live, finding rocks may be easy or prove to be challenging. By now, I trust you are creative enough to figure out where you might find a rock!

Once you have gathered the rock or rocks you need, take your marker and write the word or phrase on each rock. Now find a place where you can rock 'n' release. Ponds, lakes, or rivers are ideal places to throw your "rock blocks" if you live close to one of them and they're not on private property. Or you may want to cast away your rocks into the woods or an empty field. Again, use your imagination to determine what works best for you, as this is a symbolic exercise of letting your blocks go.

Catching Yourself Comparing

If you recall, I discussed "the comparison game" in Chapter 6. You may have more awareness of this now, but at some point you may find yourself playing this game again, either in the workplace or at home. This exercise will help you work through that.

Tools Needed: Your idea journal and a writing instrument

As suggested before, be sure to carry your idea journal with you at all times—not just for this exercise, but so you can capture ideas on the fly.

Every time you catch yourself doing any kind of comparison *whatsoever*, write it down in your notebook. For example, it could be a passing thought at work in the middle of a meeting when your co-worker suggests a wonderful idea and you think to yourself "She's always coming up with good ideas. Why can't I do that?" Continue making notes each time you become aware you are comparing yourself to another person.

After one month, analyze your notes. Look for patterns. Is there a common thread? Also, take an honest look at your comparisons and see if there's any truth to them. Chances are, you were just having a weak moment. If you do find any of them to be true, or they are simply thoughts you are having a hard time turning off, then develop an affirmation for each one. Using the preceding example, your affirmation might read "I am a great source for generating good ideas" or "Thinking of good ideas comes easily to me." Write down your affirmations and repeat them out loud every day until you've conquered those unconstructive viewpoints.

Even once you have gotten past the negative beliefs, it's still a good practice to continue saying your affirmations daily. This practice will reinforce them.

From Compassion to Creation

In this exercise, you will be looking at acts of creation or creative items in your everyday life you take for granted.

Tools Needed: Paper and a writing instrument, along with whatever comes of your imagination

Look back to Chapter 1, which said that everything in life is a creation. Think of all of the items or actions you encounter most days that you take for granted. Examples would be the pen you write with or daisies that line the road on which you travel to work.

Now use your imagination to think of how you can use one of those items to bring joy to another person's day. For example, you could use your pen to write a note of encouragement to your child and place it in her lunchbox, or stop and pick the daisies, put them in a vase, and give it to a co-worker who has been struggling. These "calls to creation" will not only help support someone's day, they also will keep you in the flow of creation and make you feel good, too!

To Me, with Love

This activity is a confidence builder, one in which your "inner child" will speak to your adult self.

Tools Needed: Paper, a writing instrument, construction paper, crayons, and stickers

Make a list of five people you admire. Beside each name, write down the reasons you selected them. What are their traits? Look over your list carefully and see if you spot any of those traits within yourself.

Now pretend you are 8 years old. Take a piece of construction paper and fold it in half. Using crayons and the folded construction paper, which helps you get into that childlike space, you are going to make a card. The layout can be horizontal or vertical. Fill the card with all of the wonderful expressions your inner child would like to say to your older self, including all of the qualities your 8-year-old self admires about you today. Decorate the card with stickers.

When you're finished, examine your feelings. How did you feel as you were making this card? Did you have trouble coming up with encouraging words, or did the compliments flow freely?

The wonderful traits you possess never go away. Sometimes, it just takes a little bit of prompting to get them out of hiding. Put this card where you'll see it daily as a reminder of the beautiful being you are—both as an 8-year-old child and a grown adult!

Snatching a Sunrise or Sunset

There are at least two occurrences that can be counted on every day: the sun will rise and the sun will set. Usually, most people take these wondrous acts of creation for granted. And sometimes clouds get in the way when taking in a sunrise or sunset. Regardless, no one doubts that this act of nature will create itself every day. In this exercise, you will use this natural occurrence to fuel your creativity.

Tools Needed: Paper and a writing instrument

Make a commitment this week to watch a sunrise or sunset. Look at a weather forecast to select an ideal day and actually schedule this viewing into your calendar as if it's an important meeting.

On your scheduled day, take your paper and writing instrument with you. As you are watching the sunrise or sunset, begin writing observations of the beauty you see. Go into detail about the colors, the streaks in the sky, the backdrop, and any other finer points you notice.

Once you've done that, create a poem, rhyming or otherwise, that includes your observations. Do not judge what you write! Instead, focus on appreciating the magic of the start and finish of each day. Remember, this experience is available to you every day and evening!

Treasure Hunt with a Theme

This activity will heighten your ability to focus and then creatively craft a collage based on a theme.

Tools Needed: A large piece of cardboard, foam core, or the equivalent; glue; markers, colored pencils, paints and/or crayons; and odds and ends found during your treasure hunt

Think about a subject matter you will have fun creatively illustrating. You could focus on a single color and all of the shades that go with it, the beauty found in nature, or comforting music.

Or you can make your theme action-based. Perhaps you enjoy helping seniors or caring for rescue animals.

Once you have selected a theme, spend a day noticing how this theme comes into your life. Remember, what you put your attention and intention on manifests in your life.

Now it's time to go on a treasure hunt! With your theme in mind, look in your junk drawer, garage, attic, closets, or anywhere you may find "stuff" that fits your theme that you can put on a 3D collage (which is unlike a typical collage of flat magazine images). Gather the items until you feel you have enough to create your collage.

Use your imagination to assemble your collage as a type of mixed-media art. It doesn't matter if this is a first-time activity of this nature or you've done a similar project in the past. This is a brand-new creation!

Once you're done, rejoice in your creation! You can keep your artwork or give it as a gift.

Songs That Make Your Heart Sing

One of my favorite television programs in the 1990s was *Ally McBeal*. In one of the segments, Ally's therapist told her to select a theme song. This exercise plays off of that idea for the purpose of giving you "musical support."

Tools Needed: Paper and a writing instrument, a recording of your selected songs, and a unit capable of playing your tunes (such as a CD player, an MP3 player, or your computer)

What songs can help support you in your creative journey? Will listening to an upbeat song get you into the groove of creating, or would a relaxing, soothing instrumental put you more in the mood? Perhaps a mix of songs works best for you. For example, being a singer-songwriter, I am inspired by other singer-songwriters whom I admire. Four of my inspirational favorites are "Living in the Moment" by Jason Mraz, "For a Dancer" by Jackson Browne, "Tapestry" by Carole King, and "Part of the Plan" by Dan Fogelberg. What songs or artists move you and make you want to create? Make a list of your top 10 inspirational songs.

If you own a copy of these songs (and if you don't, you may want to invest in yourself by purchasing them), make a playlist on your computer or burn them onto a CD. If you don't wish to add the songs to your personal collection, you can probably find them on YouTube. The idea behind this exercise is to identify the songs that will help to rouse your muse and then listen to them whenever you need that.

A Game from Yesteryear

In Chapter 17, I discussed how research points to the importance of encouraging kids to be creative. Yet you'll hear parents and even those without children observe how kids are spending more time with video games and other electronic devices. What has happened to good ol' board games or activities that don't depend on technology? For example, remember the game Red Light, Green Light, an outdoor game that required no technology or props whatsoever (or am I showing my age)?

In this exercise, you're going to use your imagination to create a game that does not use technology in any way. You can create a kids' game or one for adults—your choice. If you have children, you can actually test your game with them. Who knows? You could be the next Milton-Bradley!

Tools Needed: Your imagination—and whatever props go along with your idea!

First, determine the age group you're targeting. Next, consider your game's category and theme. Will it be educational, humorous, historical, romantic, or something else?

Now think of the logistics. Will you need any props, or will it be a game like Charades? Will the number of people who can play be limited? Can it be played indoors, outdoors, or both? Are any particular skills or knowledge necessary to play? Is there a particular objective you have in mind, or will you allow this to evolve as you develop the game? Consider existing games. Are there any current or old games you can play off of to further develop into another game? (Remember, some believe there are no original ideas—only the advancement of existing creations!)

Create your game and then try it out on your target audience. Listen to their feedback and if you think you're really onto something beyond doing this simply as an exercise, work to improve your game and continue to develop it until you're satisfied. You can then test it out again.

One way to complete this exercise is to plan a game night and invite 10 of your friends. The game you're going to play is to create a game! Divide your friends into two groups of five and follow the rules I've given. You can then present your game ideas to each other and see what happens. It's possible you'll come up with two great games or combine the ideas of both groups into one fun game. If you don't feel like you came up with anything "game-worthy," at least you had fun in the process!

A Picture of Love

Chances are, you've taken pictures before, even if you're not a professional photographer. For this exercise, don't worry if you feel you don't have the proper training or skills (one of the blocks that was discussed). You will need a camera, but mostly you will need to focus—literally and figuratively—on love.

Tools Needed: Any kind of camera, as long as it's working; paper (construction, card stock, or whatever you have that's handy); and markers

Your job is to take pictures of love, whatever that looks like to you. That could be images of couples holding hands, babies, a dozen roses, or your favorite easy chair (yes, you may love sitting in it!). You can spread this activity throughout the week or take a day and focus on picture taking.

Once you've taken them, print your favorite photos, either with your own printer or by taking them to be developed at a nearby photo lab.

Now fold your paper in half and make at least one card using one or more of your photos. Think of the person you wish to give your card to and add your sentiments. You can make more than one if you are so inclined. You can even make a bunch and bring them to a local nursing home to distribute to folks you've never met. Go ahead—make their day!

What Happened Next?

In this activity, you will exercise your mind by writing a short story after reading the prompt.

Tools Needed: Paper and a writing instrument

Start by reading the following prompt:

> I am walking down the sidewalk of a city street in a northern city. Signs of spring are blossoming, yet it's still fairly cold outside. In fact, on this day, a cool breeze permeates my skin. Brrr … I can't wait to get to my office so I can warm up. As I turn the corner, I see a trash can—one I pass every day on my way to work. Usually, I don't even notice it, but today I see a spotless winter coat strewn over its side with one shoe positioned on the ground in front of it. *That's odd,* I think to myself.

Now finish the story. What happened? How will you solve this mystery? Will you introduce other characters, or will you limit the story to your own actions and observations? Give yourself time to develop the story. You might play with different scenarios, or you may already be set on a plot line. Be open to ideas that come to you. While there is no need to rush this activity, I suggest you give yourself a deadline so you actually finish the story. Do not be tempted by procrastination!

Once you've finished, check in with yourself to see how doing this activity made you feel, especially if you do not consider yourself to be a writer or have any interest in writing. Did it spark a further interest in writing? Did you doubt yourself as you wrote? Note all of your feelings. Finally, share your story with someone you trust. Take the risk!

A variation on this exercise is to make this a group activity. Gather some friends for a potluck dinner followed by this exercise. Give yourselves a time limit and then end the evening by sharing your stories.

Inside the Box or a Box Full of Inspiration

You've heard the saying "think outside the box." This creative play directs you to take action "inside the box!" I'm literally referring to a box in which its contents will serve to inspire you.

Tools Needed: Magazines, newspapers, and other objects you find while exploring, index cards, a writing instrument, and a box of your choosing (one made of cardboard, wood, metal, or any other material—even a shoebox)

To begin, think about what inspires you and makes you feel happy. Using your index cards, write your own inspirational "directives," starting with the words "Today is my day to ..." and completing it with words such as "... spread joy to the world," "... smile at everybody," or "... fill my soul with hope." Write at least 10 of them to get you started. Put them in your box. You can write more cards as you feel inspired and keep adding them to your box.

Next, flip through magazines, newspapers, or publications of any sort and find phrases or pictures that inspire you. Cut them out and put them in your box.

Now go for a walk in the woods, along the beach, or any place you enjoy exploring and look for any items that may be suitable for your box. Select things that speak to you in some way—for example, an unusual-looking rock, a multicolored shell, or birch bark from a tree. If you find a penny, you could include that if it has any meaning to you. For example, whenever I find a penny, I say to myself "pennies from heaven," because each one says "In God We Trust" and they serve as a reminder of that for me.

Whenever you feel you need an inspirational lift, reach into your box without looking and randomly select a card or an item, and then carry that thought or token with you throughout the day as a reminder of your intention. Notice how events, people, or opportunities may present themselves to you that relate to your inspirational message. You may even wish to reach into your box daily for consistent inspiration.

Creative Explorations

This activity will open you to new possibilities as you go on an intentional exploration outdoors.

Tools Needed: A comfortable pair of walking shoes

Take a walk by yourself outdoors and explore. Go to a park, the woods, a new neighborhood, or wherever your intuition leads you. If possible, turn your cell phone off so you are not distracted during this exercise. Be curious and have fun as you observe your surroundings. If you're in a place you've been to before, notice how you may see things that you were never aware of before. While exploring, select items you're drawn to, such as a leaf, stick, flower, weed, feather, or bottle cap.

When you return home, do something creative with your find. Examples are to create a story about it, write a poem, paint it, draw it, make a collage, or frame it.

Appreciate the experience you had with this exploratory process and your creation! If you had any insights, you may wish to write them in a journal or speak them into a recorder.

Embracing Your Childhood Spirit

In this exercise, you are going to revisit your childhood to help you reconnect with the sense of play you experienced in your youth.

Tools Needed: Paper and a writing instrument (and other items, depending on what you include based on the information I give you)

Select a day you can devote at least a few hours (if not an entire day or weekend) to engaging in this activity. On the day you've set aside, at the top of your paper, write down the words "As a child, I used to love …." Recall as many things as you can that you enjoyed as a child. To jog your memory, use your five senses—things you liked to taste, touch, look at, listen to, and smell. Include whatever comes to mind, such as making cookies with your mother, eating candy (be specific as to what kind), riding your bicycle, collecting baseball cards, sleeping with your stuffed teddy bear, the smell of an apple pie baking, listening to Beatles records, or playing Monopoly. Write them down as they come to you.

Now select several of the activities you can revisit today. You may have to adapt them slightly. Do whichever items you listed that are the most practical, convenient, and most of all, allow you to recapture your childhood feelings. The whole idea is to get out there and play!

After you've allowed yourself to play, write about your experience or dictate your thoughts into a recorder. You can even consider which of these activities you want to introduce back into your life today in some way and start doing them!

Index

A

accidental creations, 48
accomplishments, 268-269
action plans stage, 41-42
active listening, 208
adrenaline, 18
adventurous, 55
affiliations, 6-7
affirming creativity, 99-100
Amabile, Teresa, 31
ambiguity, 237
ambitions, 57
analysis stage, 41-42
Andrade, Jackie, 142
anxiety, 75
aptitude, 10-11
artistic expression, 227-228
The Artist's Way (Cameron), 118
Art of Possibility (Zander), 89
assessment, 246
assumptions, 130
Astaire, Fred, 159
attention, 219
authentic expression, 283-284
awareness, 280-284

B

balance
　daily applications, 260-261
　life, 30
beach climate ideas, 230
beginners, 88

believing in yourself, 96-98
benchmarking, 216
benefits
　business, 14-15
　personal, 17
　　energy level increases, 18
　　lowering stress levels, 19
　　meaningful lives, 20
　　self-empowerment, 19
　relationships, 16-17
blocks, 68
　deep-rooted versus temporary, 79
　fears, 72
　　anxiety, 75
　　comparison game, 75-76
　　criticism, 77
　　failures, 72-73
　　past discouraging/ derogatory comments, 76
　　rejection, 74
　　success, 73-74
　　uncertainty, 74
　finances, 70
　"I'm too" excuses, 71
　lacking confidence, 71
　negative thoughts, 79
　overcoming, 86
　　affirmation, 99-100
　　being a beginner, 88
　　believing in yourself, 96-98
　　getting help, 94
　　giving yourself permission, 96
　　handling mistakes, 88
　　not trying, 95

　　passions, 147
　　practicing gratitude, 98-99
　　prioritizing, 86-87
　　reasonable expectations, 92
　　redefining life, 101
　　risk-taking, 92-93
　　self-empowerment, 90
　　vulnerability, 89
　perfectionism, 70-71
　time, 68-69
　trusting yourself, 80
bonding opportunities, 202
boosting creativity. *See* stimulating creativity
bottom lines and creativity, 172
brainpickings.org website, 269
brainstorming, 137-138
brainwriting, 189-190
Brown, Sunni, 142-143
burnout
　causes, 216-218
　fighting, 263
　remedies, 218-220
businesses
　accepting failure, 196
　associations, 7
　benefits, 14-15
　burnout
　　causes, 216-218
　　remedies, 218-220
　collaboration, 207-208
　creating something out of nothing, 214-215
　creativity and the bottom line, 172